Rethinking imagination

The essay
the notion
part of the
more it th
but from
backgroun
apocalyps
last decad
confirmati
interprets
be addres
stance of
denotes a
ommende
provides
sublime. Y
claim to th
legacy of
imaginatio
explores f
seen as a s
that of ar
Against li
iadis and
the imagi
the ontol
(Arnason)
open to c
also uses
observer is the inescapable condition of all possible cognition.

Gillian Robinson lectures in Politics at Deakin University; **John Rundell** is
Ashworth Lecturer in Social Theory at the University of Melbourne.

Rethinking imagination

Culture and creativity

Edited by Gillian Robinson
and John Rundell

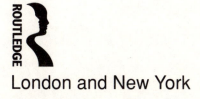

ROUTLEDGE

London and New York

First published in 1994
by Routledge
11 New Fetter Lane, London EC4P 4EE

Simultaneously published in the USA and Canada
by Routledge
29 West 35th Street, New York, NY 10001

Typeset in 10/12pt Times by
Ponting–Green Publishing Services, Chesham, Bucks
Printed and bound in Great Britain by
T.J. Press (Padstow) Ltd, Padstow, Cornwall

British Library Cataloguing in Publication Data
A catalogue record for this book is available from the British Library

Library of Congress Cataloging in Publication Data
Rethinking imagination: culture and creativity / edited by Gillian Robinson and John
Rundell.
        p.   cm.
Chiefly papers presented at a conference, held in Melbourne, Australia,
Aug. 4–8, 1991
      Includes bibliographical references and index.
      1. Imagination (Philosophy) – Congresses.
      2. Imagination–Social aspects–Congresses.
      3. Creative thinking–Congresses.   4. Modernism–Congresses.
I. Robinson, Gillian.   II. Rundell, John.
B105.I49R47   1993
128'.3–dc20   93-17209

      ISBN 0–415–09192–6
      ISBN 0–415–09193–4 (pbk)

Contents

Contributors

Johann P. Arnason is Reader in Sociology at La Trobe University, Melbourne. His main publications are *Praxis und Interpretation: Sozialphilosophische Studien* (1988) and *The Future That Failed: Origins and Destinies of the Soviet Model* (1993).

Cornelius Castoriadis founded *Socialisme au Barbarie* (1945–65). He was until recently Director of Studies at the Ecole des Hautes Etudes en Sciences Sociales, Paris, where he is now a practising psychoanalyst. His main writings in English are *Crossroads in the Labyrinth* (1984), *The Imaginary Institution of Society* (1987), and *Philosophy, Politics, Autonomy* (1992).

Agnes Heller is Hannah Arendt Professor of Philosophy at the New School for Social Research, New York. Among her many works are *Beyond Justice* (1987), *General Ethics* (1987), *A Philosophy of Morals* (1990), *The Grandeur and the Twilight of Radical Universalism* with Ferenc Feher (1991), and *A Philosophy of History in Fragments* (1993).

Martin Jay is Professor of History of Ideas at the University of California, Berkeley. He is noted for his works on critical theory and western marxism, especially *The Dialectical Imagination* (1973), *Marxism and Totality* (1984), and *Fin-de-Siècle Socialism* (1984). Recently he has turned his attention to post-structuralist thought and the interrogation between vision and visuality in *Force Fields Between Intellectual History and Cultural Critique* (1993).

Niklas Luhmann is Professor of Sociology at the University of Bielefeld, Germany. He is the author of many books on social theory amongst which are *Differentiation of Society* (1982), *Soziale Systeme* (1982), and *Love as Passion* (1986).

Gyorgy Markus is Reader in Philosophy at the University of Sydney, Australia. His main publications are *Marxism and Anthopology* (1978) and *Language and Production* (1986).

Paul Ricoeur was Director of the Centre d'Etudes Phenomenologiques et Hermeneutiques, Paris, as well as Professor of Philosophy at the University of Nanterre and the University of Chicago until his retirement. Among his many works on the inter-related problems of hermeneutics, language and meaning are *Freud and Philosophy: An Essay on Interpretation* (1965), *The Rule of Metaphor* (1975), and *Interpretation Theory: Discourse and the Surplus of Meaning* (1976).

David Roberts is Professor of German at Monash University, Melbourne. He has written extensively in the area of critical theory and German aesthetics. His major publications are *The Inclinations of Desire* (1980) and *Art and Enlightenment: Aesthetic Theory After Adorno* (1991).

Gillian Robinson is a lecturer in Politics at Deakin University, Melbourne. She is co-editor with Peter Beilharz and John Rundell of *Between Totalitarianism and Postmodernity* (1992), and is currently writing a book on the political philosophy of Hannah Arendt.

John Rundell is Ashworth Lecturer in Social Theory at the University of Melbourne, Australia. He is author of *Origins of Modernity: The Origins of Social Theory from Kant to Hegel to Marx* (1987), and is co-editor with Peter Beilharz and Gillian Robinson of *Between Totalitarianism and Postmodernity* (1992).

Preface

Rethinking Imagination: Culture and Creativity grew out of a conference on 'Reason and Imagination in Modern Culture' held in Melbourne, Australia, between the 4th and 8th August 1991 and organized by the journal *Thesis Eleven*. Except for the seminal paper by Paul Ricoeur, all the essays published in *Rethinking Imagination* were written in the light of this conference. Ricoeur's paper was published previously in *Analecta Husserliana* (vol. VII, 1978, pp. 3–22), (all rights reserved; this translation copyright © 1978 by D. Reidel Publishing Company, Dordrecht, Holland). We reprint it because it problematizes the imagination outside the categories in which the imagination has been usually thought. In this way, it also provides an insightful point of contact with some of the other essays in this volume.

The editors would like to thank the Vice-Chancellor of Montash University, Mal Logan, and the Vice-Chancellor of La Trobe University, John Osbourne, for their generous support which made the conference possible.

The editors would like to thank all those who participated at this conference, and especially Johann P. Arnason and David Roberts for their assistance and comments at all stages while preparing the papers and the Introduction for publication. We would also like to thank Sue Stevenson for wordprocessing.

Introduction

John Rundell

Contemporary debates oscillate between competing sets of ideas which are often used as counterpoints, and yet are in ever present danger of collapsing into each other: modern and postmodern, creativity and sublimity, progress and apocalypse, democracy and redemption, Enlightenment and Romanticism, reason and imagination.

The essays collected together in *Rethinking Imagination: Culture and Creativity* aim to thematize these debates from the perspective of the imagination. They can be further brought into focus from two directions. The first direction concerns a socio-cultural interpretation in which the distinguishing features of modernity can be viewed as a continuing differentiation and autonomization of spheres or systems that goes well beyond the functional division of labour, and, concomitantly, a continuing decentring and fragmentation of subjectivity. This very process of pluralization is, moreover, also the precondition for a culture of critique.

These concerns are not disconnected from another set of reflections that become visible from a second direction – an ongoing philosophical discourse about the imagination and its relation to reason which has been present since the Enlightenment.

The structure of the book and its division into two separate yet interconnected parts – 'Decentring Society, Recentring the Subject' and 'Creating Imagination' – is indicative of these two directions and the motifs of culture and creativity which inform them. In the light of this division, the following discussion of the essays, which locates them in terms of those wider points of reference will also clarify the aims and issues of *Rethinking Imagination: Culture and Creativity*.

DECENTRING SOCIETY, RECENTRING THE SUBJECT

Gyorgy Markus argues, in his paper, 'A Society of Culture: The Constitution of Modernity', that modernity is *the* culture that stands between creativity and critique. It is the tension that is generated between them that has fuelled modernity's development and self-understanding. Markus states that 'the broad or anthropological notion of culture originated in Enlightenment as *critique* . . . [A] conception of culture emerged of inherited and inheritable human objectivations constituting both a *determining force* upon, but also a *determinable resource* for, our activities'. Culture thus became a storehouse of possibilities which could only be unlocked if a critical and distancing attitude was taken to what was available from both the past and the present. The hallmark of this 'critical consciousness' (Ricoeur), the thing that sets the past and the old apart from the new, was a notion of creativity which emerged in two senses. On the one hand, what is produced must be seen as novel, and on the other there was a semantic shift in the meaning of creativity from that denoting a unity of art and life to one in which 'definite types of personal dispositions or abilities [signified] particular activities of objectivation'. In an argument similar to Ricoeur's in 'Imagination in Discourse and in Action', and Richard Kearney's in *The Wake of Imagination*, Markus points out that the notion of art moved from a mimetic relation between object and meaning to one in which they became separate. The physical reality of the object became merely a vehicle constituting and conveying an interior, essential presence.

This process of referring to the inner authenticity of the work of art (what Markus terms 'idealization') also meant the development of the autonomy of culture. This occurs not only in a structural process of culture's external differentiation from and conflict between the spheres and values of politics, economy and religion – a point that is made also in Agnes Heller's 'The Elementary Ethics of Everyday Life' and taken for granted by Niklas Luhmann in 'European Rationality' – but also as an internal differentiation between high and low culture. In a richly contextualized reconstruction which has some historiographical, if not value affinities with Alistair MacIntyre's *After Virtue*, Markus argues that this double differentiation also entailed the collapse of the autotelic conception of culture: in the pre-modern world, cultural practices were not separated from the virtues of seeking to fulfil a good life and satisfy noble human desires. Cultural autonomy and differentiation thus entailed the development of what Markus terms *autochthony*, the determination of the activities in question solely in terms of their own requirements and logics. These revolve around the unleashed dynamics of innovation and creativity which were to be harnessed to 'universally valid ends'.

The postmodern critique has undermined the conditions and criteria through which culture could be articulated in modernity. 'The shock of the new', so vividly portrayed by Robert Hughes in 1980, is not so much the loss of stability of tradition, but rather the violent discord produced between culture and creativity when culture is permanently celebrated and institutionalized as only fashion and manipulation. The cultural constellation of (post)modernity appears to swing between the experience of open-ended creativity and the parade of manufactured images consumed by a voyeuristic, privatized public. Each appears to loosen subjectivity from its moorings.

It is this cultural constellation that Martin Jay and Agnes Heller address directly.

According to Jay, in his 'The Apocalyptic Imagination and the Inability to Mourn', the postmodern imagination works with one side of an apocalyptic tradition that has accompanied the onto-theology of Western metaphysics (Heidegger, Derrida): the malign face of obliteration, not the benign face of revelation. For the postmodern image of the Apocalypse, the Fall is still present – but it is de-dramatized and de-moralized. The Fall takes place in a world beyond good and evil, of agonistics and power-saturated players, where the postmodern apocalyptic imagination focuses on 'the permanence of destruction'. Far from releasing itself from the redemptive paradigm, postmodernism according to Jay has tended to relive it in its phantasies of termination without end and its celebration of excess as exemplified by 'Lyotard's fascination with libidinal intensities, Derrida's valorization of infinite unconstrained linguistic play, and Baudrillard's celebration of the hyperreal world of simulacral overload'.

What is left, according to Jay's reading of the postmodern apocalyptic imagination, prompted but not constituted by another *fin de siècle*, is not celebration but melancholy, bereavement and hysteria – the distinctive symptoms of decentredness. For this reason, Jay argues that the apocalyptic imagination can be better elucidated psychoanalytically, rather than remaining at the level of cultural analysis.

Drawing on Freud's 'Mourning and Melancholia' and Kristeva's *Black Sun*, Jay argues that melancholia heightens the normal sense of grief by prolonging the 'profound dejection and loss of interest in the world', but unlike grief engages in punitive self-reproach and self-hatred. This results in a regression to narcissism in which the melancholic subject cannot separate himself or herself from the lost object and consequently cannot give it up. Behind this frightful feeling and expression/experience of loss (real or imagined) stands not just any love-object – but the primary love-object – the mother. And it is here that Jay turns to the work of Kristeva, where the mother is central. She is the source of all needs in the pre-linguistic and pre-symbolic world of the infant who responds to her disappearance with both fury and despair. For Jay, it is this complex construction of melancholy and mania growing out of a world without rationality, a world without a centre, a nothingness, which is projected by the apocalyptic imagination onto the world as a whole. In Kristeva's terms 'melancholia is [ ] less an illness to be overcome than a permanent dimension of the human condition', which raises decentredness to an ontological condition.

Yet Jay himself can advocate the permanent condition of neither grief and melancholia nor decentredness. Mourning in a postmodern sensibility is not dialectical sublation, but 'rather a willingness to tolerate impossibility', that is, the impossibility of regaining the lost object, and thus a full reconciliation with it. Once this willingness is raised to the level of consciousness, rather than remain unconscious and hysterical, we have moved to the side of the Enlightenment, not necessarily guided by a strong idea of reason, but at least committed to the liberty of reflection.

More than any other of the essays in *Rethinking Imagination: Culture and Creativity*, Agnes Heller's 'The Elementary Ethics of Everyday Life' is an explicit counterargument against the apocalyptic imagination with its redemptive-totalizing undertone and onto-anthropology of the decentred subject which has emerged from the so-called humanist controversy along two broad fronts: Nietzsche–Heidegger–Derrida–Foucault and Saussure–Althusser/Lacan.

Heller accepts the other image of late twentieth-century society with which postmodern thought works – a pluralist world in which people chose their own gods and demons (Weber), and a differentiated world in which systems generate their own values, normative patterns and expectations. As Heller recognizes, this pluralization and differentiation has also resulted in a pluralization and decentring of ethics and morals, and the patterns of action and types of 'truth' they refer to. If ethics and morals are pluralized, then there is no centre to which they can refer their truths. However, in her view what appears as decentredness is actually 'modernity's dynamic that requires that men and women constantly query and test the contents of most traditional moral customs and virtues'. In other words, modernity destabilizes rather than decentres morals.

In this context, Habermas's attempt to remake a centre by way of a communicatively grounded discourse theory of ethics can reconstruct ethics only in procedural terms through argumentation. Yet this leaves the issue of morals untouched. In Heller's view, morality cannot be discursively re-deemed; one cannot *give reasons* for being or becoming good. As she says, 'the source(s) of morality is (are) not, and cannot become, subject-matter(s) of discourse; they are *prior to discourse*' (emphasis added). Morals is not a topic for either epistemology or genealogy. It is not a form of knowledge. Heller can thus suggest that the postmodern image of the decentred subject has prematurely dissolved and jettisoned the connection between the subject and everyday life and morals which themselves constitute the home of identity formation.[1] There is, though, a foundation to morals – it is derived neither from reason nor from discourse, but rather from a *gesture* which itself is transcendent. In modernity the first foundational gesture for Heller, following Kierkegaard, is an existential choice of 'taking responsibility'. In so doing, one already faces others. For her, intersubjectivity is the precondition both for reflective subjectivity and a capacity for moral questioning. As she has stated elsewhere, 'my concept of the subject eschews linguistic (not language) games, and it places the emphasis on relation, not on sub-jection'.[2]

This does not mean, though, that there ought to be an expectation of reciprocity in moral behaviour. In an effort to subvert or sublate power-saturated discourses in which strategic relations between social actors predominate, Heller emphasizes the 'monological' gesture and attitude of taking responsibility. Reciprocity points to something *beyond* reciprocity – to an imaginary horizon which is capable of being universalized and generalized. For Heller, care is the universal orientative principle of morals. It is orientative rather than foundational because it leaves the content open. It is substantive, discretionary and interpretive, that is, open to plural inter-pretations and dimensions. In this sense only is it postmodern.

If Heller's paper indicates a position in which reason is not a referent or a 'beyond' which underpins relations in the world, but is itself dependent on a pre-rational and, by implication, imaginary background, then Luhmann's paper, 'European Rationality', is the more extreme articulation of such a position. To be sure, Luhmann eschews any reference to phenomenological or existential motifs which are present in Heller's interpretation. Rather, his reference point is the system/environment distinction, more precisely it is a reflection within the framework of his systems-theoretic perspective. In a paper that provides a bridge between Parts I and II, Luhmann argues that European rationality has been shaped by the tension of two opposing forces; on the one side a quest for unity and integration, and on the other side the use and recognition of distinctions, difference, otherness. Luhmann's approach is not only anti-Hegelian; unlike post-structuralism, it is *also* anti-Heideggerian. For Luhmann, the issue is not, strictly speaking, a post-ontological re-articulation of the question of Being but the delimitation, 'in a conceptually more exact fashion', of a rationality orientated to distinction rather than unity.

In Luhmann's view, and not wishing to oversimplify a complex argument, to thematize the issue of distinction is to thematize the issue of observation and the observer, and by so doing move from ontology to what he terms *autology* in which the observer becomes the reference point for both the generation of distinctions and the re-entry of them into more elaborate conceptual schemes. He terms this second-order observation. What Luhmann calls first-order observation is a way of characterizing the pre- and early modern tradition and its belief in an accessible and objectively determinate world. We all observe. In the process of observation a distinction, i.e. selection, is made usually between what is *included* (usually in forms of factual 'data') and what is *excluded* and may, but need not, also be devalued as false, chaotic, irrational, or imaginary. In all this, the observer remains an excluded third, occupying a privileged position even though he or she may be either unrecognized, marginalized or located *outside* the process of observa-tion as Subject, History, God, Worker, Man, Woman. Once the privileged position of the observer is questioned and the observer re-enters, a new rule emerges: 'observe the observer'. Moreover, observation of the observer takes place on the one side of form, that is, only on the side of that which can be *known*, not as a unity, but as a distinction. David Roberts notes in his Epilogue that 'the re-entry of form constitutes, for Luhmann, the key to the problem of European rationality. It transfers our attention from what is distinguished to how it is distinguished and by whom'.

Implicit within Luhmann's argument is that differentiation is the *modus operandi* of modernity – the greater degree of differentiation, the more interstices and gaps, the greater the capacity for non-observation, for not knowing. Knowledge is partial, never total. For Luhmann, the interstice is a distinction, but the interstice could also be viewed as chiasm in which the work of the imagination becomes visible (Merleau-Ponty). Or, to put it another way, in the collapse of totalizing projects of society with their images of a totalizing metaphysics, the gaps emerge into which the imagination breaks through. Luhmann's conclusion that the unity of Being is accessible only in terms of the unity between the rationally delimited and its imaginary other provides a bridge from Part I to Part II.

CREATING IMAGINATION

The second part of the book focuses more explicitly on rethinking imagination and its relationship with reason. The approach common to the papers, notwithstanding the differences between them, differs from the two most representative adversaries in the contemporary debate around the idea of reason: Derrida's reworking of the Heideggerian legacy within a post-structuralist register and Habermas's linguistic turn towards a theory of communicative reason. Derrida has attempted to overturn what he sees as the onto-theological privileging of speech over writing in the Western metaphysical tradition. Writing is seen within this tradition as simply representation, and this interpretation is in turn grounded in the assumption that that which is spoken coincides with, or by nature is closer to, truth as full presence. The project of *différance* explodes this set of assumptions. Inasmuch as it involves the release of signifying play from metaphysical constraints, it could be construed as a covert appeal to the imagination, but the latter is not theorized as such, nor is there questioning of its traditional linkage with the aesthetic sphere. Habermas, by contrast, constructs a comprehensive model of reason and strives to incorporate the 'expressive sphere' into it. The latter, which is the source of permanent conceptual problems within his theory, is the territory reserved for the imagination. Habermas's project can therefore be understood as a particularly determined effort to assimilate imagination to reason and at the same time confine it within the narrower borders of aesthetics. This assumption is contested in one way or another by the contributors to Part II.

They insist, first, that aesthetic creation is the only one aspect of the multifaceted activity of the imagination. In this sense, Castoriadis's concept of the radical imagination captures something that the other authors are also concerned with: the need to uncover a deeper and generative layer neglected by traditional theories of the imagination. This leads to a second point. To rethink the imagination is to question not only the way in which it has been viewed, but also its status and location with regard to reason and some other central categories of the philosophical tradition.[3] Thirdly, as the preceding discussion of the papers has indicated, this is also linked to theoretical reflections concerning the trajectory of modern culture and the contemporary preoccupation with 'postmodern' themes and issues.

In this context, Kant, rather than the more distinctively romantic thinkers such as Fichte and Schelling, emerges as the figure standing at the crossroads between imagination, creativity, and cultures of critique. John Rundell's 'Creativity and Judgement: Kant on Reason and Imagination' argues that Kant, in his attempt to construct a transcendental notion of reason, cannot avoid the power of the imagination. As Kant discovers, the imagination is neither simply an aid nor a conduit to the understanding and reason, but rather 'an indispensable dimension of the human soul', what can be termed the transcendental imagination. Reason without imagination is dead reason. This is the mystery of Kant's 'X'. For Kant, in the *Critique of Pure Reason*, the imagination becomes paradoxically the concealed, yet 'real', condition of all knowledge. It is the imagination rather than reason which is truly transcendental, for it loosens humankind's relation to and reliance on wholly empirical conditions. His major insight, that the 'imagination is the faculty of representing in intuition an object that is *not itself* present', means that, in a reading of Kant which emphasizes the centrality of the transcendental imagination, the categories of pure reason are creations and representations of an imagination which is only partially *presented*, yet ever *present*. In the space between presence and presentation, rather than absence and presence, humankind invents the conditions of its own existence. For Rundell this motif means that Kant's second encounter with the power of the imagination in the *Critique of Judgement* is not only an encounter within an aesthetic register but is also an ethico-political one concerning humankind's permanent unsociable sociability.

However, as Rundell, Arnason, Markus and Castoriadis all note, Kant retreats from his insight concerning the creative and formative power of the imagination and restates a conventional division between critique, or what Ricoeur has termed critical consciousness, and creativity, reason and imagination, science and art, especially in the second edition of the *Critique of Pure Reason* where it is relegated to 'a more subaltern and intermediary role between intellect and intuition' (Arnason). Critique collapses into cognitivism, and the imagination is treated either mediately or aesthetically.

As Kant's work demonstrates, the issues of creativity and imagination are the hardest to capture and to maintain. Against linguistic and deconstructive strategies, the papers by Ricoeur, Castoriadis and Arnason represent theoretical proposals for a positive interpretation of the imagination, whether it is constructed as the semantic imagination (Ricoeur), the ontological imagination (Castoriadis), or the interpretative imagination (Arnason).

Ricoeur approaches the problem of the imagination from the vantage point of a theory of metaphor, which disconnects the problem of the imagination from the way that it has been traditionally conceptualized. Rather, he argues the imagination is 'an aspect of *semantic innovation* characteristic of the metaphorical uses of language'. Taking as his starting point the poetic image, but not in the romantic vein in which it is seen as expressive of an inner force, Ricoeur argues that poems reverberate, not from what is seen but from what is heard. In other words, images are 'spoken' or uttered before they are seen. In this context poetic metaphors are deviant uses of predicates which produce 'a sort of shock between different semantic fields'. Imagining is, then, a restructuring of semantic fields in which the imagination gives an image to meaning which emerges from reverberations and echoes of the shocks generated from the use of unusual predicates.

Thus, in Ricoeur's formulation, the imagination is creative rather than associative, but creative as a referential dimension which *redescribes* reality, beyond that to which ordinary language and the reproductive imagination refer. Furthermore, for Ricoeur, the capacity for redescription also indicates that there is 'no action without imagination', from the vantage point of both projects and the capacity to act. In this way, and borrowing from Mannheim's earlier work the constitution of 'forms of life' (Wittgenstein) is inseparable from a more or less permanent redescriptive dimension, which Ricoeur terms utopias, or the capacity to 'radically rethink'. The important and challenging aspect of Ricoeur's essay is that it provides a counterpoint and counterargument to those post-traditional perspectives on the imagination which view it as either a romantic or psychoanalytically derived trope for the work of a hidden power, often repressed and distorting *or* revealing, which makes its work known only through images. In Ricoeur's view, the creative imagination comes alive in the intervocality, in the field, between 'speaker' and 'listener'.

In contrast to Ricoeur and from a perspective which shares with Heidegger the sensitivity to the question of being, but answers it in a diametrically opposed way, that is with an emphasis on the plurality of meanings of being, Castoriadis argues that the imagination should be viewed *ontologically*. He radicalizes Kant's construction of the imagination in the *Critique of Pure Reason* and emerges with a double-sided ontology of the autonomous and creative imagination. They are the two inseparable dimensions which indicate the *differentia specifica* of the human animal. The imagination is autonomous, first in the sense that its activity goes beyond any external and somatic determination. But it is also creative in the more far-reaching sense that it can create its own level of reality. Autonomy, however, re-emerges at a higher level: as the capacity of the imagination to disengage itself from and to question its own creations. Even in this context, however, it remains linked to creativity: autonomy without creative manifestation lacks meaning.

What appears at first sight to be a theory deeply indebted to psychoanalysis can be read from a different perspective. As has been noted elsewhere, Castoriadis's major contribution has been to link a radicalized idea of the imagination to the problematic of meaning.[4] While a sign system may well be constituted by an arbitrary relation between signifier and signified, the issue for Castoriadis is not that of *otherness*, but *openness*. Linguistic meaning draws on non-linguistic sources, but these sources are not, for Castoriadis, located in the liminal (Levinas) and marginal regions which contribute an 'other' of a text. Rather, meaning itself is a referent which relies on a creative–imaginary dimension beyond it which ensures it remains both indeterminate and infinitely determinable.

The title of his paper – 'Radical Imagination and the Social Instituting Imaginary' – is indicative of a strategy which emphasizes the two irreducible dimensions through which meaning is constituted. One pertains to subjects, the other to societies. The radical imagination is, for Castoriadis, the flux of emergent representations, a 'magma' within the psychic monad which while socialized into a social individual, permanently resists this imposition of sociation. (The term 'subject' is in fact a misnomer – Castoriadis prefers the term psyche.) The social instituting imaginary by contrast is the pattern of collectively, that is, socially, created meanings which are institutionalized and become a society's point of reference. (Likewise, the term 'society' with its sociological reference to structure and function is called into question.) It is the incommensurability, and often the clash, between psyche and society which enables meaning to remain *in principle* open, or if in danger of closing upon itself, to be reopened through questioning, or – in Castoriadis's terms – interrogation. In contrast to Ricoeur, who links the creative dimension of the semantic imagination to the capacity to fictionalize, Castoriadis most emphatically links it to the capacity to question the existing, the given.

Castoriadis's recasting of the problem of meaning in terms of the creative formation of imaginary significations, and thus of human creativity, as well as Ricoeur's conception of the semantic imagination, is the point of departure for Arnason's reflections in 'Reason, Imagination, Interpretation'. The efforts of these two authors to thematize and categorize the imagination have thrown light on its central but elusive role in the development and self-understanding of modern culture. As Arnason argues, it is the confrontation between Enlightenment and Romanticism, rather than an exclusive project or dialectic of the former, that constitutes the cultural horizon of modernity, and the principle of reason is as central to the Enlightenment as the power of the imagination is to Romanticism. Both currents are, however, articulated in terms of key distinctions and conflicting interpretations, rather than definitive paradigms. Alternative models of reason have been formulated more explicitly and discussed more extensively than those of the imagination, but the classification proposed by Ricoeur suggests some basic parallels between the modern trajectories of both notions. However, the linking of reason and imagination to the distinctive bipolarity of modern culture is only the first step towards a hermeneutical transformation of the problematics that have crystallized around these two concepts. The next and decisive step, according to Arnason, would be the incorporation of the cultural context, that is, an explicitly culturalist redefinition of both reason and imagination. This begins with the shift from reason to rationality and from the imagination to the imaginary.

It is widely accepted that a theory of rationality should replace the philosophy of reason, but there is no agreement on the meaning of the change: for some authors, it represents a radical break with tradition, whereas others see it as a translation of traditional concerns into modern language. By contrast, the tendency to focus on the imaginary, rather than on the imagination, is a more recent and limited development, and the various lines of argument which it opens up have yet to be explored in detail. Moreover, there has been no attempt to incorporate both shifts into a more comprehensive interpretation of culture. Arnason's paper concludes with the suggestion that the later work of Maurice Merleau-Ponty could be taken as a starting point for such a project.

Agnes Heller's and Martin Jay's essays can be read, in their own way, as warnings concerning the overextension of the notion of creativity, and the idea of creativity without limits, or what has been termed sublime creativity – which constructs redemptive relations with the world. This theme is taken up, in part, by David Roberts in his Epilogue entitled 'Sublime Theories: Reason and Imagination in Modernity'. As Roberts points out, Romanticism, which made the category of the sublime its own through a move from the transcendental to the protean imagination, married an image of unlimited and irrational creativity with an often redemptive critique of modernity. As Gyorgy Markus also indicates Romanticism appealed for the integration of the differentiated spheres and their autonomy, especially the one of high culture, into the totality of life which would result in its resacralization and its return on a higher level to a condition of immediacy.

Yet Roberts's Epilogue is more than a genealogy and discussion of Romanticism's central motif of the sublime, drawing as it does on Kant's discussion of it in the third *Critique*. He uses the category of the sublime as a way of drawing parallels and pinpointing affinities between what appear at first sight to be the two most contrasting papers in the volume – Luhmann's 'European Rationality' and Castoriadis's 'Radical Imagination and the Social Instituting Imaginary'. Both are, in Roberts's view, sublime theories. By this he means that both Castoriadis and Luhmann build into their theories the condition of sublimity in which the imagination pursues infinity and exposes the limits of representable reality to the point at which an abyss beyond representation opens up. However, neither are theories of the sublime, but rather sublime theories about the interplay between limitlessness and limits. In Castoriadis's case it is the interplay between the *natura naturans* of the creative, instituting imaginary, and the *natura naturata* of the instituted social imaginary. In the case of Luhmann's systems theory the interplay is present in 'the operation of distinction *itself*'. In each case the outcome is a self-limiting theory 'which is aware that it cannot encompass and exhaust the transcendence of the world and know the limits of conceptualization and systematization'.

It is in this context of the relation between limits and limitlessness that the dialectic between Enlightenment and Romanticism plays itself out. This unresolvable dialectic provides a point of reference for the volume as a whole after the critiques of totalistic and representational philosophy. If the imagination is a metaphor or a condition for creativity, it is also a metaphor or condition for the utopic and dystopic forms it takes. Because creations are often dystopic, they confront the limits of the sublime, of what is *im*possible. This confrontation may force us back near the ground of the beautiful as a politics which accepts coporeality and finitude. This form of the political is, thus, a form of the imagination not as redemption nor reconciliation, but as a possibility to imagine differences, plurality and the autonomy of others. Rethinking the imagination is an indication of philosophy's possible renaissance, of its capacity to raise questions and do this, if not on transcendental grounds, at least from a stance of a minimal universalizable horizon of symmetrical reciprocity.

NOTES

1   On this point see her 'Death of the Subject', *Thesis Eleven* 25 (1990), pp. 22–38, and 'World, Things, Life and Home', *Thesis Eleven* 33 (1992).
2   'Are We Living in a World of Emotional Impoverishment', *Thesis Eleven* 22 (1989), p. 59. Reprinted in Peter Beilharz, Gillian Robinson and John Rundell (eds), *Between Totalitarianism and Postmodernity* (Cambridge, Mass., MIT Press, 1992).
3   In many respects the dispute about of the imagination concerns its separation into two aspects, which has been stylized historically and culturally: the reproductive imagination and the productive imagination. Richard Kearney in his *The Wake of Imagination* makes a useful threefold distinction between the classical/medieval imagination with its theocentric paradigm of iconography in which mimesis or reproduction is its central motif, the modern imagination with its anthropological paradigm of self-portraiture which emphasizes creativity or production, and the postmodern imagination with its excentric paradigm of parody in which the 'labyrinth of looking glasses is its central motif' (Richard Kearney, *The Wake of Imagination* (London, Hutchinson, 1988)). See also James Engell, *The Creative Imagination* (Cambridge, Mass., Harvard University Press, 1981), which is a particularly detailed reconstruction of the emergence of the idea of the creative imagination from the Enlightenment to Romanticism.
4   See Johann P. Arnason, 'Culture and Imaginary Significations', *Thesis Eleven* 22 (1989), pp. 251–255.

Part I

Decentring society, recentring the subject

Chapter 1

A society of culture: the constitution of modernity

Gyorgy Markus

The connection between reason and imagination, on the one hand, and modernity as culture, on the other, may be too intimate to be captured solely in the causal terms of impact and influence. The opposition between reason and imagination is itself the product of cultural modernity, and, at the same time, it is what confers upon this culture (at least in one of the constitutive meanings of this term) the character making it modern. The notions of 'reason' and 'imagination' have, of course, a genealogy quite independent of, and reaching far back beyond, such a relative newcomer to our conceptual equipment as the idea of 'culture'. But it is only as cultural powers, that is, as culture-creating, that reason and imagination appear in an antithetic unity, replacing the old antinomies between reason and the passions, the senses, or revelation. Only conceived in this way does *phantasia*, originally understood as the intermediary between perceiving and thinking,[1] or even as an inferior component of rational knowledge itself providing the primary material for the *katalepsis* of the intellect,[2] acquire the dignity to be the excluding supplementary to reason, as equally original and fundamental to our capacity of being human. In a Hegelizing language the concept of culture is the *ground* upon which the opposition between reason and imagination can become erected, and the space that is filled by them, and thus transformed into an articulated field endowed with a force of its own. So to be *gründlich*, to grasp this opposition at its originating ground, it is perhaps advisable to enquire into the constitutive connection linking it with the concept of 'culture'.

Heidegger once listed [3] – alongside such rather self-evident features as machine technology, modern science or secularization – the conception of culture, the comprehension and performance of human activities as culture, among the most fundamental phenomena of modernity. Let us make, at least for the time being, a somewhat more modest claim: it is only under conditions of modernity that the ways people live and act in the world, and also the manner they understand this world, are conceived by them as constituting a form of culture, that is, as not being simply natural, or God-ordained, but as something man-made and re-makable which conforms with equally humanly created and changeable standards and ends. Cultural modernity is a culture which knows itself as culture and as *one* among many. And precisely because this self-reflexive consciousness belongs specifically and particularly to modernity, its positing of itself as a society of culture makes it *the* society of culture, or, as Hegel would say, defines it as the world-epoch of *Bildung*.[4]

This consciousness of culture is, however, a deeply ambiguous, if not split, one, for the designation 'culture' interrelates and unites two concepts that seem to be utterly different. On the one hand, 'culture' means some pervasive aspect of all non-biologically fixed human behaviour in its dominant and contemporary understanding: the meaning-bearing and meaning-transmitting aspect of human practices and their results, 'the symbolic dimension of social events' (Geertz) that allows individuals to live in a life-world, the interpretation of which they essentially share, and to act in it in ways that are mutually understandable to them.

This broad or anthropological use of the word 'culture' is, however, accompanied by another, seemingly quite unrelated one which could be called the 'high' or value-marked meaning of the same term. In this latter sense it designates a circumscribed and very specific set of human practices – first of all the arts and the sciences – which, under the conditions of Western modernity, are regarded as autonomous, that is, as having a value in themselves. In spite of the efforts frequently undertaken to construct either an immanent meaning-connection between these two ideas of culture, or to dissociate them completely, they also remain in contemporary discursive practices in this paradoxical relation of close association of incomparables. The force which keeps them together is not that of logic, but of their historical origin. Culture as we understand it is the invention of the Enlightenment, or perhaps more exactly, the outcome of the way the Enlightenment invented and defined itself, both negatively as critical, and positively as a constructive historical power. The perplexing unity of the two meanings of culture is the unity of these two aspects in the project of Enlightenment.

The broad or anthropological notion of culture originated in the Enlightenment as *critique* in its effort 'to raise the edifice of reason upon the ruin of opinions'. In the attempt to destroy the irrational 'superstitions' of the age, seen as the cause of all its ills, the Enlightenment mobilized the hitherto neglected regions of human time and space. It endeavoured to demonstrate that people living beyond the pale of our traditions, following other precepts of conduct and possessing a different set of beliefs, had nevertheless led a satisfactory and/or civilized way of existence. And as it became increasingly obvious that the 'prejudices' distorting reason have an 'external' social-institutional support, this critique also became more and more radical, finding ever new targets, spreading over new spheres and arenas of life; initially, the theological and metaphysical systems of the past; then the canons of classical literature; followed by the ascetic morality and the overall authority of the Church; 'heroic' historiography and its myths; the artificial manners of the court and the parasitism of the aristocracy; together with the institutions of feudalism and the antiquated system of economy supporting them; and lastly the arena of politics itself and the institution of the absolutist state. In this steady expansion of the scope of critique not only has the subject-matter of history been enormously extended, but also a new way of comprehending the present has arisen. Contemporaneity was no longer seen in terms of the hallowed tradition of our ancestors which conferred legitimacy upon its institutions and provides us with exemplary models of action. Generally speaking, the legacy of the past lost the meaning of tradition: something which has a normatively valid, internally binding claim upon the living. It now acquired the sense of all those accumulated and enduring 'works' and accomplishments of earlier generations – be they the most humble and ordinary – which transmit definite forms of conduct and ways of thinking, embody acquired abilities and tastes that can either contribute to *or* hinder the perfectioning of human spirit and the amelioration of life. Thus a conception of culture emerged as inherited and inheritable human objectivations constituting both a *determining force* upon, but also a *determinable resource* for our activities. They are the power the past exercises upon us, conditioning the way we live. But they are also the material, the storehouse of possibilities which we can – if we do not fall under the spell of blind habit and uncritically accepted 'opinion' – selectively use to create something *new*, to make novel acquisitions and discoveries satisfying the demands of reason under the changing conditions of existence. Enlightenment thus proclaimed a new age and type of society – a society of culture as opposed to societies of tradition, to 'traditional' societies.[5] And it was precisely for this reason that the new . age could acquire its self-consciousness under the nonsensical name of 'modernity'.

'Modernus', 'modern', means simply what is just now, the contemporary, as opposed to the 'antiquus', to the by-gone, the passed away. To obtain a non-relativized sense which can designate a whole new epoch of world history, the 'modern' had to acquire a new antonym so it could be opposed not to the 'ancient', but to the 'traditional', to that which cannot keep up with the relentless force of historically progressing time. By announcing itself to be modern, the age located its essence in its ability to be always up-to-date, to be abreast of the times, where time is conceived of not as the inertial power of erosion, but as the creative force of change, which can be missed or harnessed for human ends.

However, this creativity of time needs harnessing. And at this point the Enlightenment inextricably fused the broad, anthropological notion of culture with another one as its necessary supplement in one and the same practical project. Replacing the principle of imitation with that of rational innovation, the new age inaugurated by the Enlightenment proclaimed itself as an unprecedented expansion and the steady perfectioning of human potentials. This opening up of the horizon of historical expectations, however, did not mean the affirmation of an unforeseeable and uncontrollable dynamism of change. The coming epoch of the reign of reason was at the same time envisaged as that of a never before encountered social cohesion, security and stability. The Enlightenment hoped to create circumstances in which change would no longer signify the breakdown of the normative order and a loss of social identity and continuity, due to either accidents or to the play of passions and naked interests. The positive programme of the Enlightenment was to impose a unique direction charted out by reason upon the processes of change for which the path had been cleared by the destructive force of critique. This demanded, as guarantees, appropriate powers stemming from and directly expressing the very font of human specificity and superiority: man's ability to create an order of meanings and values and to superimpose it upon the senseless causal sequence of events. Only if activities embodying and directly realizing human spirit, *esprit humain, Geist,* can be set free from all restrictions, can social and cultural change – cultural in the broad sense of the word – be submitted to the *universally valid ends* which culture, in its highest and most authentic sense of 'high culture', provides. And only then can innovative progress, on the one hand, and social integrity and stability, on the other, be reconciled, for culture then will no longer be merely conventions and opinions, but rather will be based on the progressive realization of the conscious values that are dictated by a rational and free spirit as the genuine 'nature' of man.

Socially stratified societies usually possess some hierarchical classification of various types of activities and interpret some of them as 'higher' or 'elevated' in the sense of befitting persons of distinction, power or prestige. Without doubt, the way 'high culture' of modernity became concretely constituted and conceived depended, to a significant extent, upon such a pre-given, inherited evaluation of the social practices in question, which, as the conjunctural outcome of a particular historical development, represented both the precondition and the unreflexively accepted tradition of the Enlightenment itself. But it did not simply codify these activities by conferring upon them a new legitimation and label: the transformation from what belongs to *politesse* and cultivation into what is cultural (in the narrow/'high' sense of the word) involved the imposition of an interpretive grid which also served as a latent principle of selectivity. The very notion of culture implied criteria by which practices, accepted as *cultural sui generis,* were thought of as being able to satisfy. In this way the Enlightenment conferred a degree of systematic and conceptual organization upon the emerging sphere of high culture, both reinforcing processes under way and endowing them with new direction and meaning. The most important criteria and requirements in question perhaps can be signalled by the catchwords of *objectivation, innovativeness, dematerialization,* and *autonomy.*

To qualify as belonging to the realm of high culture, a practice, first of all, had to meet the requirement of *creativity,* and in two senses. On the one hand, it had to be interpretable as being *productive*, that is, as bringing forth something detachable from the comportment and person of the practitioner, something which in the continuity of its subsistence can intersubjectively transmit accumulated experiences, insights or abilities. During the eighteenth and early nineteenth centuries all the terms we now use for the designation of various branches and kinds of high cultural activity ('science', 'philosophy', 'art', 'literature') underwent, by and large simultaneously, a fundamental semantic shift from connoting definite types of personal dispositions (habituses of mind) or abilities to signifying particular activities of *objectivation* and/or the totality of their products.

High-cultural activities, however, must also be thought of as creative in another, stricter sense of this word: what they produce must be novel, not in simply transmitting but enlarging the scope of human possibilities. The historical transition to a society of culture meant the replacement of the authority of the *origin* as the standard to be followed, with the demand of *originality*, which any 'work', *objectivation*, must satisfy to be regarded as belonging to the sphere of culture in the strict sense. Novelty became both a constitutive condition and one of the criteria of evaluation for all that claims a *sui generis* cultural significance.

The creation of something new, however, only has such a significance when it is a work, an embodiment of 'spirit', that is, when the resulting objectivation can be thought of as fulfilling its function solely in the character of an *ideal* object, that is, as a complex of meanings. In their social interpretation, practices qualifying as high-cultural ones have undergone a process of 'dematerialization': the physical reality of their product became regarded as the transparent, diaphanous vehicle of significations constituting their essential reality. Works of culture are objects that are appropriated solely through being understood. This process of 'idealization', which certainly began much earlier than the Enlightenment, found its most dramatic manifestation in the dominant conception of the fine arts – from the late Renaissance theories of *disegno* and *concetto*, through to the classical conception of the ontological status of the art-work as *Schein*, as sensuous presence 'liberated from the scaffolding of its purely material nature',[6] to the expressivist theories of art like that of Croce and Collingwood, or to the Sartrean characterization of the being of the work of art as irreal. Less spectacular, but essentially parallel processes, can also be observed in the case of discursive and literary textual practices. Here one also meets a tendency to divorce what a work of science, philosophy, or literature (up to the great turn of modernism) really *is* from the linguistic medium of its expression and its direct inscription. This is unreflexively entailed not only in the customary use of such notions as 'scientific theory' or 'philosophical system', but underlies many of our elementary cultural practices, such as those of 'translation' or 'quotation' in their modern sense.

I cannot attempt here to give even a cursory characterization of these constitutive criteria of the 'cultural'. I wish merely to underline their effectivity, perhaps most clearly exemplified by the case of *religion*. In most 'traditional' societies religious representations and practices provided the fundamental and ultimate framework of interpretation through the sense which they gave to existential experiences. The majority of the representatives of the Enlightenment regarded such a function as indispensable. Nevertheless, religion, the validity of which was directly linked to the sanctity of its transcendent source and origin to be preserved in unchanged purity, did not enter the realm of high culture. One important facet of the process of secularization consists precisely in this loss of the function of a central *cultural* power to be distinguished from the actual spread of belief and disbelief as a sociological fact.

I would like, however, to make at least some very schematic remarks concerning the concept of *autonomy*, usually associated, as its distinguishing mark, with the culture of modernity. First of all, autonomy should not be simply identified with the social evaluation of some activities as being *autotelic*, that is, valuable in and for themselves. Such an understanding is much more widespread and is well illustrated by the classic conception of *philosophia* as the highest and purest form of *praxis*. But in pre-modern societies activities are usually regarded as autotelic because they are seen as satisfying the noblest human desires, so that their exercise coincides with living the best, the most fulfilling, human life. The modern conception of autonomy represents, in a sense, the direct negation of this idea, since it implies that the objectified results of definite kinds of practices are valuable in themselves according to criteria wholly immanent to them and completely independent from their direct impact upon the life-activity of their producers and/or recipients. The idea of the autonomy of culture, in this (its negative) sense, expresses and reinforces processes through which definite types of practices became *socially disembedded* (through the dissociation of patronage-relations, commodification, professionalization, etc.), that is, ceased to be, on the one hand, subordinate to pre-given, externally fixed social tasks, and on the other, to be internally organized around determinate social occasions and situations and addressed to some particular, restricted circle of recipients.

But it essentially belonged to the Enlightenment's idea of culture that this process of social dissociation was conceived by it as emancipation, as guaranteeing that freedom which alone is appropriate to the activities of the 'spirit', *geistige Tätigkeiten*. Cultural autonomy also meant *autochthony*, the determination of the activities in question solely by internal-immanent factors, their ability to follow in their change and development no other requirements and logic but that of their own. Cultural practices in this understanding constitute a sphere in which no other authority counts but that of talent and no other force is applied but that of the better argument. They can be archonic, directing and guiding processes of social change towards the realization of genuinely valid ends, because in their internal organization they embody what is the, perhaps never completely realizable, *telos* of social development: the reconciliation of the self-conscious autonomy of each individual with the harmonious integration of all, made possible when everyone follows the dictates of the 'universal voice'. As embodiments of the end of social evolution and as creators of binding ends for social evolution, 'high-cultural' activities, freed from being subordinated to externally imposed and particularistic social tasks, do not become afunctional – only in this way do they acquire the *universal* function of general social orientation and integration which in the past was usually performed by sacralized, and therefore, ossified systems of historically conditioned religious belief.

It was Kant who first consistently and comprehensively charted out the internal constitution of such a sphere of high culture and, by conceptually articulating it, also uncovered its deep internal strains. As distinguished from the *culture of skill* – a cultivation consisting in the development of our capacity to realize purposes in general, any kind of purposes, be they right or wrong – the *culture of discipline* (*Kultur der Zucht*) means the cultivation of our capacity to freely posit meaningful and valid ends for our activities: it consists in the 'liberation of the will from the despotism of desires which . . . renders us incapable of making our own choices'.[7] This sphere of a 'higher culture' which 'prepares man for a sovereignty in which reason alone is to dominate'[8] consists of the sciences, on the one hand, and the fine arts, *schöne Künste*, on the other: it is constituted through their strict antithesis (even if, though on a single occasion,[9] Kant mentions the *humanioria* as a mediating link between the two).

The sciences are based upon the legislative power of *understanding (Verstand)*, as it progressively emancipates itself from the empirical limitations of the human senses and from the pragmatic restraints natural needs impose upon cognitive interests. Artistic creativity, on the other hand, is rooted in the emancipation of *productive imagination* precisely from the constraints of understanding and its pre-given concepts. Both articulate and objectify attitudes and viewpoints towards the world as empirical-phenomenal reality which are communicable, capable of being shared, and inter-subjectively binding, but these attitudes are diametrically opposed to each other. They are opposed as the objectivity of knowledge is opposed to the subjectivity of feeling; as the unity of scientific truth, ideally constituting a single, coherent system, is opposed to the irreducible plurality of objects of beauty, each strictly individual and irreplaceable; as the unambiguous and univocal meaning of concepts is opposed to the plurivocal and inexhaustible meaning of the aesthetic ideal ('a presentation of imagination which prompts much thought, but to which no determinate thought whatsoever, i.e. no *concept*, can be adequate, so that no language can express it completely'[10]); as the strict, universal and exactly reproducible rules of scientific method are opposed to a free creativity which no determinate rule can encompass and the unity of which is manifested only in an inimitable 'manner' as the expression of a unique personality. Science represents a collective endeavour in which even the most significant individual achievements become surpassed in the cumulative process of cognition, so that even the greatest scientific minds are only artisans, technicians of reason, *Vernunftkünstler*,[11] since the tasks they solve must be impersonal, their solution exactly replicable by others for their achievements to count as scientific at all. Fine art, on the other hand, 'is the art of the genius',[12] a favourite of nature, possessing skills that 'cannot be communicated',[13] the work of which can only serve as an exemplary model to be followed, but not reproduced or imitated. And, most importantly, in science we encounter nature as the sum total of all objects of possible experience insofar as they stand in a thoroughgoing interconnection according to empirical laws, the meaning and necessity of which is unfathomable to human insight. In the arts, on the other hand, we imaginatively create a 'second nature', a nature which 'has held us in favour',[14] *Gunst*, and which is in harmony with the free play of the constitutive powers of our consciousness and thus satisfies our deepest, specifically human, needs. The dichotomy between the rational-intellectual and the imaginary thus receives here a clear articulation and in their polarity they demarcate the legitimate realm of the cultural – but with an important proviso.

For this great reconstruction which confers a conceptual grounding upon the *de facto* articulation of high culture, simultaneously 'deconstructs' its conception in the Enlightenment. How can the idea of a unity of culture – without which its guiding role is inconceivable – be upheld if it is organized around the direct opposition between intellect (understanding) and imagina-tion (and the power of judgement associated with it)? In Kant's formulation, the autonomy of the aesthetic experience should have provided the transition and the mediating middle between theoretical and practical reason attesting to their unity – in fact its introduction resulted only in a new dualism. Kant conceives the relationship between the sciences and the arts as one of complementarity, but he never indicates how to demarcate the legitimate scope of those opposed attitudes towards the world which they objectify and make autonomous. The premises of the Weberian conclusion concerning the irreconcilable conflict between the great cultural value-spheres were already, even if unintentionally, laid down by Kant.

This unintended outcome partly follows from a seemingly strange archi-tectonic imbalance in Kant's transcendental constitution of the realm of a 'culture of discipline'. Of the three superior cognitive powers, *Erkennt-nisvermögen*, which in their interplay constitute the specific structure of human consciousness and in their diverse relations ground the possible human attitudes to the world, only two have a cultural 'representation': reason, fulfilling the highest function of the unification and alone legislating in the realm of morality, does not ground any independent sphere of cultural activity. Or does it? For what are, on Kant's own account, the historical forms of positive religion (what he calls *Kirchenglaube*) if not cultural embodiments of practical reason? Nevertheless, Kant does not admit them to the realm of a higher culture. For, in contradistinction to science and art, religion in the form of some 'ecclesiastic faith' does not emancipate its underlying transcendental principle, but acts in just the opposite way: that is, it introduces heteronomous incentives into the realm of moral action which, to be deserving of its name, must always already be thought of as autonomous. Precisely therefore, and again in opposition to genuine cultural forms, a form of positive religion 'is incapable of being universally communicated with convincing force'.[15] Its necessity is based solely on 'a peculiar weakness of human nature'[16] as an empirical fact, giving rise to a need for props to ensure even the external compliance *en masse* with the imperatives of morality.

However, by this Kant seems to undermine the very meaning the Enlightenment ascribed to a 'higher culture'. For not only is it the case that, given 'human weakness', the question of possible social effectivity necessarily also arises in respect of those spheres (of truth and beauty) which can acquire their autonomy only through cultural development: as is well known, from the mid-1880s on, Kant is increasingly preoccupied and pessimistic about the problem of the spread of the Enlightenment. Much more importantly, his conception inevitably raises the question: How can culture provide us at all with the guiding ends of social development, if the sole ends and values in themselves, those of morality, cannot be transformed into direct cultural powers? Up to the end of his life Kant gave contradictory answers to this problem of the possibility of a 'moral cultivation' through history. But the sole answer which is reconcilable with the logic of his system (and the only one to be found in his systematic writings) is *negative*: cultivation through high culture merely provides the negative condition for, but in no way guarantees, the ability to follow genuinely valid ends, befitting our humanity. It merely weakens or eliminates the despotism of natural desires to do good *or* evil by our own choice. Culture is the ultimate purpose *(letzter Zweck)* of nature with man, but it does not endow us with a directive with which to approximate the final purpose (*Endzweck*) of human existence. In all, its autonomy must rely on something else.

Thus the first, and paradigmatic, attempt at the philosophical articulation and legitimation of the Enlightenment's conception of culture actually ended with the revocation of the basic idea of its project. Not surprisingly it was then almost immediately followed by the cultural utopias of an anti-Enlightenment, which were motivated by the intention to realize the failed promises of the Enlightenment. Before the turn of the century this had received an exemplary formulation in the enigmatic document referred to as the *Earliest System-Program of German Idealism*. It proclaims the idea of the unification of the 'monotheism of reason and heart' with the 'polytheism of imagination and art' in a 'new mythology', but a mythology which 'must be in the service of Ideas, must be a mythology of Reason'.[17] Instead of the differentiation and autonomy of the cultural spheres, this programme announces the need for their reintegration into the totality of life; instead of the replacement of religion and sacralized tradition by the free activities of value-creating spirit, it proposes a re-sacralization of the latter. Instead of a culturally produced 'second nature' which, by its very character, demands and evokes a critically distanced and reflective attitude, it aims at the synthetic creation of a 'second naturalness' as a higher level return to immediacy. But making philosophy mythological still only intends 'to make people rational', to 'create a higher unity' in which 'enlightened and unenlightened clasp hands', so that there will never again be a 'blind trembling of people before its wise men and priests' but 'universal freedom and equality of spirit will reign'.[18]

This anti-Enlightenment, which still retains at least some goals of the Enlightenment, is, from early Romanticism on, a regularly recurring feature of the history of cultural modernity. Some of its ideas even resound in theories of post-modernity: a programmatic syncretism, a tendency towards the aestheticization not only of theory but of ethics and politics as well. In general, one could see in the narrativization of all discourses merely a diluted version of their mythologization. However, this mythologization is not presented today in the name of the utopia of a future all-encompassing unity. Even if the often celebratory tone in which some representatives of post-modernism talk about difference, dissence, and dispersal evokes some associations with the anarchist project (itself one of the heirs of the Enlightenment), the overall thrust and sense of these theories is deeply anti-utopian. While many elements in the proposed diagnoses of a post-modernity – let us say, the dissolution of all *grand narratives* in Lyotard, or the reign of *simulacra* in Baudrillard – show far-reaching similarities of content with some of the most despairing criticisms of cultural modernity (in Heidegger or Adorno), these phenomena are now accepted with an air of aestheticizing self-satisfaction or resigned disillusionment.

Historical experiences have certainly much to do with the fact that anti-Enlightenment – or should one say, less contentiously, a fundamental critique of Enlightenment – no longer takes on the form of the utopia of a remythologization. But it also no longer needs to appear in such a form. For, in the meantime, not only the promises of the Enlightenment – which degenerated into the myth of engineering a society of universal happiness on the basis of the sole 'scientific worldview' – but also the basic concepts in terms of which the original project could only be formulated, have lost believability and attractivity; not least, the idea of a 'higher culture' itself has seemingly been divested of empirical support. Their critique no longer needs to invoke other alternatives to attack the way they have been legitimated. It can rest satisfied by the demonstration that these ideas have no hold upon, or relevance to, contemporary reality.

Modernism and postmodernism have brought forth cultural processes which seem to undermine the very conditions and criteria through which the conception of a 'high culture' could and had been articulated in modernity.

Loosely, one can speak of processes of *desobjectivization, rematerialization, divorce of novelty from creativity*, and *heterochthony* as tendencies indicating the direction of changes in the character of appropriate practices and/or their dominant interpretations.

By *desobjectivization* I mean a trend towards the unmaking of the idea of a 'work' of culture as a self-subsisting (ideal) object – either, in the hard sciences, in favour of an uninterrupted *process* of decentred communication mediated perhaps only by signals of interlinked electronic apparatuses, or, in the case of the arts, in favour of the discontinuous and disruptive *event*, an occurrence without clear boundaries. (And one should also include here interpretations according to which even traditional 'works of art' acquire an aesthetic significance only in the fleeting and unreplicable acts of appropriate reception alone.) *Rematerialization* refers to a process of the *evaporation of the sense*, either (in the sciences) its reduction to a complex of formulae, the non-operative constituents of which seem only to fulfil a referential function in, and in relation to, highly specific and particular experimental situations, but do not constitute a universe of comprehensible meanings, a systematically intelligible interpretation of their alleged referents; or (in the arts) an intentional blockage of relations of signification, in order to self-referentially foreground the signifier, the material medium of communication itself, and for setting free its 'energies of semiosis'. *Novelty*, of course, retains its role of the constitutive criterion of cultural significance. However, its ever more radicalized demand becomes dissociated from the idea of a *creative subject* as the intentional source of a consciously willed originality. This is expressed not only in such interpretative-theoretical ideas as 'the death of the author', but also, to some degree, in the changes in the character of the respective practices themselves, seen, for example, in the predominance of multiple authorship in the 'hard' sciences, often comprising scientists of different specialities, none of whom possess (at least formally recognized) competence in respect of the whole content and subject-matter of the paper. In some theories of intertextuality cultural activities in general come to resemble the image of Novalis's 'monstrous mill' which, without a builder and a miller, only grinds itself.

Lastly, the problem of *autonomy*. High-cultural practices are certainly autonomous and not only in the sociological sense of taking place as specialized-professional activities within the framework of some functionally differentiated network of institutions. They are also autonomous in the sense that their results are socially posited as valuable in themselves; that is, evaluable only according to standards and criteria internal and immanent to the particular sphere in question, without taking into account their potential and 'external' socio-practical effects. However, this normative autonomy of cultural practices does not ensure their *autochthony*, that is, both the internal and independent determination and direction of their development. This can best be illustrated by the example of the *empirical natural sciences* which represent the most convincing candidate for the role of a practice, the dynamic of which is conditioned by its own logic – the logic of a problem-generating problem-solving paradigm – and where the appropriate internal criteria of evaluation are the most unambiguously articulated and consensually accepted.

The rationality of modern science is fundamentally tied to the intersubjective empirical (experimental) verifiability/falsifiability of its theoretical results. To fulfil such a role, scientific experiments themselves must be interpreted according to the discursive norms which pertain to the genre of the 'experimental report'. Roughly speaking, these demand a completely depersonalized description of the complex of intentional action and interactions situationally contingent upon the local conditions of a laboratory, that is, a stylization which transforms them into a coherent sequence of events taking place under standardized conditions, in the occurrence of which the experimenter-'author' (usually a number of persons within a complex, hierarchical organization) plays only the role of the anonymous executor and distanced observer of methodologically codified operations. To be able to fulfil a verificatory/falsificatory function the experimental report ought to mention, as a cognitive norm, only those, but then *all* those, so described physical conditions and processes which could influence the outcome of the experiment. Only the satisfaction of this condition ensures its replicability, and thereby makes the claim to intersubjective validity rationally legitimate.

It is clear, however, that in this generality the norm is in principle unfulfillable: in a fallibistic science the range of potentially relevant conditions is open. Any description of an experiment is to be actually understood as claiming validity under an unspecified and unspecifiable *ceteris paribus* clause. Therefore, any experimental report is open to the objection of not having taken into account all the possible relevant factors and considerations. Since such criticism can always be made, it also has no force whatsoever. It only acquires significance if one can present substantive considerations as to the concrete nature and character of some unaccounted intervening factor. And while this is often possible on the basis of theoretical argumentation alone, this latter becomes a *tentative falsification* of the original interpretation of the experiment (and the theory which supported it) only if it can be corroborated by experimental data incompatible under the given interpretation with the outcomes of the original experiment. This, however, demands its 'replication'. But whether or not such a replication is *practically worth while and feasible* depends, in the situation of highly specialized and extremely costly contemporary research, on conditions in which 'external' viewpoints and criteria play a significant, if not decisive, role. In fact, the possibility of such replication will, as a rule, ultimately depend upon financial and administrative decisions of bodies and organizations who, from the viewpoint of science, are not competent to make such decisions rationally, since usually the majority of their members are not expert specialists working in the particular area of research. In general this means that the actual direction of scientific development is in fact underdetermined by the internal cognitive criteria of scientific rationality. This does not make these latter ineffective – they constitute a normative framework which makes possible the intersubjective evaluation and re-evaluation of the results of research. However, the character of these very norms (their counterfactuality) is such that their effectuation *requires* the intervention of 'external', from the viewpoint of the cognitive structure of science, conjunctural factors which are dependent both upon its own social organization (e.g. the presence/absence of monopolies of research) and upon its linkage with the overall power structure of society. The connection between science and power is immanent to the *functioning* of science itself. The 'rationality' of scientific development has no internal guarantees. Its standards and criteria, which make operational the idea of 'objective truth' (in the Kantian sense of the word), ensure, in principle, the revisability of the results of earlier, 'externally' influenced, choices between competing theories and interpretations, but they ensure it only under the condition that there is, again, 'external', social space and motivation for their effectuation.

All these considerations, which refer to diverse processes of change in the character of 'high-cultural' practices, are – and in various degrees – one-sided, and do not provide a balanced picture of the complex metamorphosis they are undergoing today. However, in their ensemble they have sufficient empirical relevance and force to make the 'classical' conception of a 'higher culture', inherited from the Enlightenment, inapplicable as an interpretive description of what these practices are, and untenable as an ideal of what they can and should become. The sciences of today no longer offer, or promise to offer, a 'worldview'; they have become completely monofunctional: the intellectual component of a (potential) technique, a matter of mere expertise. 'Free' arts became genuinely free of all function; they are no longer the harmonious play of imagination and understanding, but complex games, no doubt amusing in the incessant and unforeseeable change of their rules which also endow their players with a social badge of distinction. And the connection between these autonomous realms and the signifying-interpretative systems that orient our everyday activities, that is, culture in the very wide sense, appears to be constituted merely by the visible and invisible mechanisms of power that permeate them both.

Nevertheless, the inherited idea of a 'high culture' which was forged by the Enlightenment, is still with us, untenable and indispensable at the same time. It acts as a countervailing corrective precisely against the tendencies just described. It still exercises a weak, and certainly non-messianistic, power from which eccentric impulses originate keeping the direction of cultural development open. And this idea is still present not only in the critical questionings of the function of these practices and their relations to power, but also in those forms of concrete-practical self-reflexivity, the emergence of which Foucault regarded as the sign that what remains from the task of the Enlightenment is today shouldered by 'specific intellectuals';[19] it is equally present as embedded in the very practices themselves.

It is not only a naive and misguided public which still from science expects the disclosure of what the world really 'is' to make our place in it understandable and allow us to judge not only the conditions of successfulness but also the sense of our ends. Anticipations of an 'ultimate ontology' are also operative within the practice of science itself. For, to correct an earlier one-sidedness, the theory-choice is externally conditioned not only by the outcome of quasi-political negotiations and decisions between persons of authority, within and outside science, it is also often influenced by the diverse beliefs of the members of the scientific community in some final shape of truth. God does not 'play dice', the unified field theory is just not crazy enough – such intimations and sentiments, even gut feelings, are, from the viewpoint of the existing standards of scientific rationality, not merely external, but 'irrational', and not because they are radically conjunctural, but because they presume a notion of truth not reducible to warranted assertability. They played, and play, however, an important role especially in the critical re-examination of the dominant paradigms of research which direct its general development.

Whatever concerns the art of our time, it is – in spite of its ironic self-reflexivity – not ruled by the consciousness of art-history alone. The effort, both creative and interpretive, and the demand to express 'ideas' which refer to what is beyond art and what would otherwise remain ineffable, returns again and again, interrupting or derouteing the would-be logic of a filiation of forms as dictated by the ever more radical requirement of innovation or problematization of the concept of art itself. If postmodernist works of art, a most heterogenous multitude, no longer present us with closed meaning-totality as the aesthetic prefiguration of a utopian reconciliation and harmony, they nevertheless often retain the intention and impulse to challenge our habitual sensibility, to make us experience the joy or, more frequently, the pain of the Other and the others – and sometimes they even succeed in it. The ambition to be the universal language, the 'bridge from soul to soul' is still at work in art – and who today can give credence to such claims?

To cling to ideas and beliefs that are known to lack legitimacy seems to be the classical case of 'bad faith'. We are the inheritors of the Enlightenment; it is the 'bad faith' of our culture, a culture still haunted – by Spirit. The effort to exorcise and extirpate it is certainly understandable. Yet, I am convinced that its success would deprive our culture of the basic impulses of its critical vitality. This is our perplexity.

NOTES
1 Cf. Aristotle, *De Anima*, III, 427b–429a.
2 Cf. Cicero, *Academics II*, I, 40–42.

3 Heidegger, 'Die Zeit des Weltbildes' in *Holzwege* (Frankfurt, Klostermann, 1972), pp. 69–70.
4 Cf. Hegel, *Phänomenologie des Geistes*, chapter VI, B.I.
5 Or, as the young, still 'Graecoman' Friedrich Schlegel, perhaps for the first time giving a genuinely historiosophical formulation to this idea, stated this contrast: modern times represent a society of 'artificial culture' characterized by the *System der unendlichen Fortschreitung* as opposed to societies of a 'natural culture' developing according to the *System des Kreislaufes*. cf. 'Vom Wert des Studiums der Griechen und Römer' in *Kritische Ausgabe* (Padeborn, Schöningh, 1969), Abt. I, Bd I, pp. 631ff.
6 Hegel, *Aesthetics*, vol. 1 (Oxford, Oxford University Press, 1975), p. 38.
7 Kant, *Kritik der Urteilskraft*, section 83 (*Werke*, Cassirer edn, Bd 5 (Berlin, Cassirer-V, 1914), p. 512).
8 Ibid., p. 513.
9 Ibid., p 432.
10 Ibid., p. 389.
11 Kant, *Kritik der reinen Vernunft*, B867.
12 Kant, *Kritik der Urteilskraft*, p. 382.
13 Ibid., p. 384.
14 Ibid., pp. 458–459.
15 Kant, *Die Religion innerhalb der Grenzen der blossen Vernunft*, *Werke*, Bd 6, p. 255.
16 Ibid., p. 248.
17 Hegel (?), 'Das älteste Systemprogram des deutschen Idealismus' in C. Jamme and H. Schneider (eds), *Mythologie der Vernunft* (Frankfurt, Suhrkamp, 1984), p. 13.
18 Ibid., p. 14.
19 Cf. Foucault, 'Truth and Power' in P. Rabinow (ed.), *The Foucault Reader* (New York, 1984), pp. 67–73.

Chapter 2

The Apocalyptic imagination and the inability to mourn

Martin Jay

> Let us remember. Repetition: nonreligious repetition, neither mournful nor nostalgic, the undesired return. Repetition: the ultimate over and over, general collapse, destruction of the present.
>
> (Maurice Blanchot[1])

There can be no doubt; it is happening again. Another century is approaching its end; another century is about to begin. Indeed, we are at the hinge of a millennial shift, the like of which has not been experienced, it can be safely assumed, for a thousand years. And with the inevitable countdown to the new millennium has come a flood, even more copious than usual, of all of those overheated fantasies of destruction and rebirth that somehow seem to attach themselves to decisive turns of the calendar page.

These fantasies derive a great deal of their energy, imagery and rhetoric from another, even more powerful, tradition with which they have often been associated.[2] Known since the second century BC Book of Daniel as apocalypse, from the Greek translation of the Hebrew *gala* or unveiling, it was given an especially ominous twist by the lurid imagination of John of Patmos.[3] Here, too, an explosive mixture of anxiety and expectation is expressed in prophetic images of violent ends and new beginnings. Here, too, what Hillel Schwartz, the author of a recent cultural history of *fin de siècles*, has called a 'janiform'[4] logic – 'janiform' from the two faces of Janus – has yoked together benign images of revelation and malign ones of obliteration.

Even before the palpable *fin* of our *siècle* is upon us, apocalyptic thinking has returned with a vengeance. Indeed, it may well seem that all manner of rough beasts have been slouching unimpeded in every direction throughout the entire twentieth century. Only now, with the added impetus of centurial – or better, millennial – mysticism, they seem to have picked up added speed.[5] As Schwartz puts it, our century's end 'has become – as it was fated to be – a Now or Never time. Living through it, we will feel all middle ground slipping away toward one or another pole of apocalypse, toward a glory revealed or a globe laid waste.'[6]

Prognosticating whether or not the centre will indeed still be holding in a decade's time, and these drastic alternatives remain unrealized, is not my concern now. Nor do I wish to provide yet another learned survey of the past expressions of the apocalyptic imagination; of these enough are already in print.[7] I want to focus instead on one of the most curious aspects of the apocalyptic tradition, which is especially evident when it is mixed with centurial or millennial fantasies. That is, I want to try to make some sense of the paradoxical fact that a body of thought so obsessed with radical ends and new beginnings somehow seems to recur with tiresome regularity.[8] Why, I want to ask, is the only sure thing we can reasonably predict in connection with the apocalypse the fact that its four horsemen will continue to come around the track again and again? Why, to put it another way, does the apocalyptic 'marriage', which M.H. Abrams has identified as its culminating image, inevitably end in divorce and renewed courtship?[9]

To begin to answer so speculative a question will require taking seriously the multiple levels of apocalyptic thought that are discernible in our own time. For if we can see similarities amidst their differences, then perhaps a pattern will emerge that will suggest a common source. In an essay of 1983, the political scientist Michael Barkun wrote of 'divided apocalypse' in contemporary America, by which he meant the existence of two separate traditions of religious and scientific thinking that believed history might well be near its end.[10] The former could be traced back to biblical times and the later chiliastic sects of the type Norman Cohn famously described in *The Pursuit of the Millennium*.[11] Based on the assumption that the world is a moral order providentially designed, it read historical and/or natural disasters as portentous signs of God's wrath for mankind's sins. Only a remnant of the saved would survive the final holocaust.

Reinvigorated by the creation of the state of Israel in 1948, which emerged from the ashes of a penultimate holocaust, strengthened by the spread of Christian fundamentalism from the Bible Belt to new, often urban, settings, emboldened by its successful entry into the political mainstream with the rise of the New Right, religious apocalypticism has continued to grow in importance. Ronald Reagan's notorious evocation of Armageddon in one of his debates with Walter Mondale struck a chord among millions of Americans, who apparently took it as more than a mere metaphor.[12] Significantly, the most successful non-fiction, English-language best-seller of the 1970s was the millenarian evangelist Hal Lindsey's *The Late Great Planet Earth*, which sold over 7,500,000 copies.[13] In the wake of the Gulf War, comparable books like Charles H. Dyer's *The Rise of Babylon* are bidding fair to be its 1990s successor.[14]

Although few intellectuals are likely to be among the purchasers of such works – Barkun claims that as a group they never recovered from the so-called 'Great Disappointment' following William Miller's notorious failed prediction of the Second Coming back in 1843–1844 – they too have had their own apocalyptic tradition to support. We often associate the scientific spirit with a certain optimism about the progressive amelioration of the human condition, but there has always been an undercurrent of anxiety about the unintended consequences of dominating nature and brutally revealing her secrets. In the 1960s and 1970s, these gained a new hearing with the rise of environmental concerns, renewed Malthusian alarm about overpopulation, feminist critiques of the gendered underpinnings of science, and the heightened awareness of the implications of nuclear war. Such writers as Barry Commoner, Robert Heilbronner and Jonathan Schell made scenarios of global destruction and the termination of life, perhaps only cockroaches aside, plausible to an educated audience often contemptuous of explicitly religious fantasies of the last days.[15]

Ironically, as religious prophets turned more and more to political signs of the coming end and disregarded natural portents, their secular counterparts began to read the natural world for indications of impending disaster. Scientific apocalypticism also differed from its religious *Doppelgänger* in its preference for statistical extrapolations over symbolic signs of God's wrath. And it spoke the language of identifiable causality rather than one trusting in the mysterious workings of an ineffable deity.

But the two apocalyptic discourses have often shared a strong moral tone. For the scientific doom-sayers, humans were still in large measure responsible for the ills that might befall them, even if it were now possible for those same humans to hold off doomsday by acting in time. Similarities between the two variants of apocalypticism have been especially manifest in the confused reaction to the onset of AIDS, which easily evoked fantasies of punishment by plague for excessive sexual licence. As Elaine Showalter has noted in her recent study of gender and culture at the *fin de siècle*, 'sexual epidemics are the apocalyptic form of sexual anarchy, and syphilis and AIDS have occupied similar positions at the ends of the nineteenth and twentieth centuries as diseases that seem to be the result of moral transgression and that have generated moral panic'.[16] Although such panic has perhaps been most explicit among religious apocalyptic believers, it has not been entirely absent in the ranks of their secular counterparts, who often seem unable to overcome anxieties about the costs of the so-called sexual revolution.

Although Barkun reassures his readers that the two traditions are not likely to come together, he nonetheless acknowledges that 'the disquieting possibility remains . . . that if both strands of apocalyptic thought should agree on the reading of events, then the potential for one grand self-fulfilling prophecy is greatly increased, and panic may produce the effects once assigned to supernatural agents'.[17] This dark prophecy is perhaps given even more weight if we acknowledge the existence of yet a third strain in contemporary apocalyptic thinking, unmentioned by Barkun, which we might call its postmodernist version.

For in the cultural ruminations of such figures as Jean Baudrillard, Jacques Derrida and Jean-François Lyotard, explicit evocations of apocalyptic imagery and ideas can also be found.[18] These are often linked, and not for the first time,[19] with an aesthetics of the sublime, in which terror is mingled with intimations of unrepresentable glory. A common source for many of their ideas can be found in Heidegger's dark prophecies of the tragic fate of the West, destroyed by its fetish of technology and humanist hyper-subjectivism. As a result, theirs often seems, to borrow the title of one of Maurice Blanchot's works, 'the writing of the disaster'.

In the tradition of aesthetic modernism, to be sure, similar preoccupations abounded, as Frank Kermode has shown in the cases of figures like Lawrence, Yeats and Conrad.[20] In the visual arts, Yve-Alain Bois has also noted, 'the whole enterprise of modernism, especially of abstract painting, which can be taken as its emblem, could not have functioned without an apocalyptic myth'.[21] What makes the postmodern version somewhat different is its suppression of one of the traditional faces of the janiform visage of apocalypse. That is, whereas modernism still held out hope for the redemptive epilogue after the millennial last days – Yeats's 'second coming' or Lawrence's 'epoch of the Comforter' – postmodernism has focused only on the permanence of the destruction.

In the terms of the German critic Klaus Scherpe, postmodern versions of the apocalypse have thus 'de-dramatized' the tradition, leaving behind any hope of rebirth or renewal. 'By dismissing apocalyptic metaphysics and insisting on a pure and self-sufficient logic of catastrophe', Scherpe writes, 'postmodern thought frees itself from the necessity of expecting an event that will alter or end history.'[22] Instead, it promotes an emotionally distant attitude of aesthetic indifference, which abandons traditional notions of dramatic or narrative resolution in favour of an unquenchable fascination with being on the verge of an end that never comes. As Lyotard has repeatedly stressed, the 'post' in postmodernism does not mean 'after' in any chronological sense; it is always already present in the interstices of modernity. The postmodernist rejection of redemptive hope, which reflects its often proclaimed belief that we live in an age of *posthistoire*,[23] produces a result which, Scherpe suggests, is not simply apocalypse now, but apocalypse forever.

A salient example of this attitude can be found in one of the most direct expressions of the postmodern concern for the problem, Derrida's contribution to the 1980 Cerisy-la-Salle conference on his early essay 'The Ends of Man', entitled 'Of an Apocalyptic Tone Recently Adopted in Philosophy'.[24] Derrida's stress is not so much on the content of apocalyptic fantasies as on the prophetic tone of dread and hysteria accompanying them. He takes his cue from Kant's 1796 essay 'Of a Condescending Tone Recently Adopted in Philosophy',[25] in which the great champion of the *Aufklärung* warns against the danger an exalted, visionary tone presents to the sober work of genuine philosophical inquiry. Kant, Derrida points out, anxiously worries that nothing less than the life or death of philosophy is at issue when mystagogues pretend to have revelatory powers, able to *know* what is only *thinkable*.[26] The remedy for Kant is a kind of thought police comparable to the universal tribunal he had suggested in his *Conflict of the Faculties* to arbitrate disputes between disciplines.

But for Derrida, Kant himself unwittingly unleashed a certain kind of apocalyptic thinking when he claimed that he was putting an end to outmoded metaphysics. For in so doing he was adopting the very model of eschatological prediction that characterizes such thinking. 'If Kant denounces those who proclaim that philosophy is at an end for two thousand years, he has himself, in marking a limit, indeed the end of a certain type of metaphysics, freed another wave of eschatological discourses about philosophy.'[27] That is, all subsequent proclamations of the end of something or other echo Kant's unintended apocalypticism. All of the one-up-manship, all of the 'going-one-better in eschatological eloquence . . . the end of history, the end of the class struggle, the end of philosophy, the death of God, the end of religions, the end of Christianity and morals . . . the end of the subject, the end of man, the end of the West, the end of Oedipus, the end of the earth, *Apocalypse now*',[28] all give evidence of the failure of Kant's project to banish the apocalyptic tone from philosophy.

Furthermore, Derrida suggests, the apocalyptic tone is most evident when the explicit identity of the writer is uncertain, when the voice seems to come from nowhere. The implications of this claim are profound. For if, as deconstruction has always tried to demonstrate, authorial presence is a fiction that can be dissolved, then is there not an apocalyptic moment in all writing? Derrida unsurprisingly contends there is:

> Wouldn't the apocalyptic be a transcendental condition of all discourse, of all experience itself, of every mark or every trace? And the genre of writings called 'apocalyptic' in the strict sense, then, would be only an example, an exemplary revelation of this transcendental structure.[29]

Thus, even the contemporary 'enlightened' critics of apocalypse denounce the tradition in tacitly apocalyptic terms. 'The end approaches', Derrida wryly concludes, 'but the apocalypse is long-lived.'[30]

But if apocalypse is both everywhere and interminable, perpetually defeating the attempt by Kant's thought-police to banish it, its implications for Derrida are not precisely the same as its earlier defenders had thought, especially in the religious tradition. For there is a subtle shift in Derrida's interpretation of the term, which expresses the typically postmodernist suppression of one of its janiform faces. In an extended analysis of the command 'Come' in the Apocalypse of John, he draws on Blanchot's and Levinas's radical separation of prescriptive and descriptive statements.[31] The injunction to come, he claims, can never be transformed into a meaningful statement about the world. Ethics and ontology are not the same, the performative function of the former is incommensurable with the constative one of the latter. Thus the command to come 'could not become an object, a theme, a representation, or even a citation in the current sense, and subsumable under a category, whether that of the coming or of the event'.[32] It is beyond being, beyond visible appearance, beyond the unveiling promised by revelation.

As a result, the apocalyptic *tone* does not really prefigure an apocalyptic *event* in the sense of an ultimate illumination following the catastrophe. According to Derrida,

> here, precisely, is announced – as promise or as threat – an apocalypse without apocalypse, an apocalypse without vision, without truth, without revelation . . . of addresses without message and without destination, without sender and without decidable addressee, without last judgement, without any other eschatology than the tone of the 'Come' itself, its very difference, an apocalypse beyond good and evil.[33]

And if no event can terminate the constant sense of waiting in dread for the climactic conclusion, then the true catastrophe is 'a closure without end, an end without end'.[34]

In a recent gloss on this essay, John P. Leavy Jr has argued that Derrida's strategy is to introduce just enough of the apocalyptic to act as a kind of immunization against its full realization.[35] It thus serves as a kind of apotropaic device, warding off evil like images of genitals and circumcision rites designed to prevent castration or painted eyes to keep away the evil eye. Combining the two terms in a tongue-twisting neologism, he comes up with 'apotropocalyptics' to indicate the mixed quality of the results. We are, in other words, on that familiar Derridean territory where *pharmakon* means both poison and cure. Leavy then further connects apotropocalyptics to another Derridean coinage, 'destinerrance', which suggests the impossibility of messages ever reaching their assigned destinations.

From the point of view of deconstruction, such an outcome is a source of apparent comfort, because it forestalls final totalization. But in the larger context of postmodern apocalyptic fantasizing, the emotional effect it produces is closer to saturnine resignation, what one observer has called its pervasive 'rhetoric of bereavement'.[36] Thus, for example, Baudrillard has described the current mood in the following terms:

> It is no longer spleen or fin-de-siècle wistfulness. It is not nihilism either, which aims in some way to normalize everything by destruction – the passion of *ressentiment*. No, melancholy is the fundamental tonality of functional systems, of the present system of simulation, programming and information. Melancholy is the quality inherent in the mode of disappearance of meaning, in the mode of volatilization of meaning in operational systems. And we are all melancholic.[37]

Lyotard, when pressed to describe the affective tone produced by his 1985 postmodern exhibition at the Centre Pompidou 'Les Immatériaux', replied, 'a kind of grieving or melancholy with respect to the ideas of the modern era, a sense of disarray'.[38] It was, moreover, a melancholy laced with a certain degree of free-floating manic hysteria, which commentators were quick to notice.[39]

Such admissions provide us with an important clue to the apocalyptic imaginary as a whole, and not merely its postmodern variant. That is, melancholy may well be the best term to describe the underlying mental condition accompanying fantasies of termination, while mania captures the mood engendered by belief in a rebirth or redemptive unveiling after the catastrophe. Although I am not usually prone to psychologizing cultural phenomena, the fit between the apocalyptic mentality and these pathologies is too striking to ignore.[40] They become even more explicit if we turn to the classic psychoanalytic text on the theme, Freud's 1917 essay on 'Mourning and Melancholia'.[41]

For Freud, normal mourning follows the loss of a loved person or an abstract surrogate, such as fatherland or liberty. Never considered patho-logical or warranting treatment, it runs it course when reality testing demonstrates the objective disappearance of the loved one. This realization allows the slow and painful withdrawal of the libido cathected to it, which restores the subject's mental equilibrium. Once the work of mourning (*Trauerarbeit*) is done, Freud claims, 'the ego becomes free and uninhibited again',[42] able to cathect with new love objects.

Melancholia apes many of the characteristics found in normal grief, such as profound dejection and loss of interest in the outside world, but it adds one that is all its own: 'a lowering of the self-regarding feelings to a degree that finds utterance in self-reproaches and self-revilings and culminates in a delusional expectation of punishment'.[43] The remarkable fall in self-esteem experienced in melancholia, but not in mourning, expresses, so Freud conjectures, a split in the ego, in which one part is set against another. The punishing part he identifies with the conscience because 'in the clinical picture of melancholia dissatisfaction with the self on moral grounds is far the most outstanding feature'.[44]

The target of the punishment is somewhat more difficult to identify than the source, for if one listens carefully to the patient, his reproaches are not really directed against himself. Instead, they seem aimed at the lost loved object with whom the melancholic now unconsciously identifies. As Freud famously put it, 'thus the shadow of the object fell upon the ego, so that the latter could henceforth be criticized by a special mental faculty like an object, like the forsaken object'.[45] The result is a regression into narcissism, where the love object may no longer be around, but the love-relation with its internalized surrogate can remain. That is, part of the subject's erotic cathexis of the object regresses to identification with it, while another part sadistically punishes it for its alleged failings, sometimes even leading to suicidal fantasies and deeds. What the melancholic subject cannot do is separate himself or herself sufficiently from the lost object to be able to give it up when it is objectively gone.

Freud also notes another feature frequently accompanying the melancholic syndrome, which is relevant to our general analysis: its frequent, although not universal, transformation into manic elation. 'The most remarkable peculiarity of melancholia', he writes, 'and one most in need of explanation, is the tendency it displays to turn into mania accompanied by a completely opposite symptomology.'[46] Superficially similar to the working through of grief in normal mourning because it seems to show the lost object is no longer the object of a libidinal cathexis, mania actually continues to manifest some of the same traits evident in melancholia. In particular, it discharges a surplus of energy freed by a sudden rupture in a long-sustained condition of habitual psychic expenditure. Mania is like melancholia, Freud hypothesizes, because it also derives from the regression of the libido into a narcissistic state of self-identification.

In *Group Psychology and the Analysis of the Ego*, he would return to the relationship between melancholy and mania.[47] Here he admitted that he lacked a fully satisfactory explanation of how they were linked, but argued that they expressed two sides of the same coin. In melancholia, the ego was attacked by what he now called the ego ideal, whereas in mania, the two were fused together. In both cases, the working through based on the ego's ability to test reality is now thwarted. And the periodic oscillation between the two states, producing the psychotic syndrome of manic-depression, could lead to a perpetual failure to deal with the world in rational terms, meaning, among other things, the acknowledgement of the separateness of self and other.

Although Freud's explorations of mourning, melancholy and mania were tentative and have continued to invite further refinement by such analysts as Melanie Klein,[48] they can still help us to make sense of the apocalyptic imaginary. For there can be little doubt that the symptoms of melancholy, as Freud describes them, approximate very closely those of apocalyptic thinking: deep and painful dejection, withdrawal of interest in the everyday world, diminished capacity to love, paralysis of the will, and, most important of all, radical lowering of self-esteem accompanied by fantasies of punishment for assumed moral transgressions. The cycle of depression and mania is furthermore repeated in the oscillation between the two faces of the janiform syndrome we have seen intensified when apocalypse and centurial or millennial mysticism coincide.

These similarities are perhaps most evident in the religious version of apocalypse, where divine retribution for sins fits well with Freud's description of a split ego, one side sadistically punishing the other for its alleged failings. These failings are consciously understood as sin, but unconsciously, if Freud is right, express the melancholic's self-blame for the loss of the love object, a loss he unconsciously thinks he desired. The source of the blame is then projected outwards and returns as an attack on the battered ego of the sufferer. Although there are reality checks which happen whenever concrete predictions of the end of the world are disappointed, the feelings of doom can be triggered again by traumatic events – wars, earthquakes, plagues, other 'signs' from heaven – that reignite the process of splitting and self-punishment.

In the case of scientific apocalyptic thinking, it is harder to defend a one-dimensionally psychopathological interpretation, because there is always enough evidence of the kind secular, 'enlightened' minds take seriously to support dire extrapolations and projections. And no one but the most polyannish believer in the myths of progress could discount such evidence out of hand. But insofar as virtually every prediction, as far as I know, has been contested by at least some other scientists who read the data differently, the preference for the worst possible scenario, which leads to apocalyptic fantasies, may in part be explained by some of the same mechanisms that determine religious anxieties about the end of the world. That is, they may well be overdetermined in a way that suggests no single explanation will suffice to make sense of this persistent power.

Although the language of sin and redemption is no longer very fashionable among such thinkers, fantasies of retributive destruction for our aggressive domination of nature still are. However much secular critics protest against the identification of nuclear war with a meaningful Judgement Day, they nonetheless often employ other metaphors that suggest similar anxieties to those haunting religious doom-sayers.[49] It is also important to remember that the critique of technological hubris was easily appropriated by earlier thinkers like Ernst Jünger and Martin Heidegger, who had no trouble infusing their critique with irrationalist, mythic energies.[50]

As for the more cynical and anti-redemptive postmodernist voices in the apocalyptic chorus, they too, as we have already noted, often explicitly stress the melancholic tone of their fantasies. Even more obvious is the manic component in much of their theorizing, which is expressed in Lyotard's fascination with libidinal intensities, Derrida's valorization of infinite, unconstrained linguistic play, and Baudrillard's celebration of the hyperreal world of simulacral overload. The postmodern whirl often seems so breathlessly speeded up that there is rarely even time for that occasional testing of reality that slows down the apocalyptic fantasizing of traditional religious adherents. The result is that grim exaltation of 'apocalypse forever', noted by Scherpe as typical of the de-dramatized postmodernist version of the syndrome.

Mentioning the refusal to test reality refers us back to Freud's distinction between mourning and melancholy, for it is precisely the ability to do so that distinguishes the former from the latter. Insofar as apocalyptic thought remains caught in the cycle of depressive anxiety and manic release, it can thus justly be called the inability to mourn. The work of mourning, it bears repeating, has two distinguishing characteristics that set it apart from melancholy: it is conscious of the love-object that it has lost, whereas melancholy is not, and it is able to learn from reality testing about the actual disappearance of the object and thus slowly and painfully withdraw its libido from it. The love-object remains in memory, it is not obliterated, but is no longer the target of the same type of emotional investment as before.

Melancholy, in contrast, seems to follow the logic of what Freud calls elsewhere disavowal or foreclosure (*Verwerfung*), in which inassimilable material seems to be cast out of the psyche and reappears in the realm of a hallucinatory 'real'. Unlike neurotic repression, in which such material remains in the psyche and can be worked through via transferential re-enactments, foreclosure throws it out (*ver-werfen*'s literal meaning) so that it cannot be successfully symbolized and integrated. Instead of being able to reincorporate the lost object in memory, the melancholic is neither able consciously to identify what actually has been lost nor work through its libidinal attachment to it. Instead, he remains caught in a perpetually unsublated dialectic of self-punishing fear and manic denial. 'The complex of melancholia', Freud tells us, 'behaves like an open wound, drawing to itself cathectic energy from all sides . . . and draining the ego until it is utterly depleted'.[51]

The questions that such reflections raise are obvious: what is the object (or objects) whose loss cannot be confronted by apocalyptic thinking and why does it (or they) remain so resolutely disavowed, so resistant to conscious working through? Here the honest analyst must falter, for we are dealing with cultural phenomena of such complexity and with so long a history that no simple answer can be confidently advanced. Unlike other cases in which the inability to mourn has been adduced to interpret collective phenomena, such as the German reaction to the loss of Hitler,[52] it is difficult to locate a specific historical trauma which resists the mourning process. Still, some speculation may be warranted, if only to suggest possible ways to deal with the problem.

In a recent essay comparing archetypes of apocalypse in dreams, psychotic fantasies and religious scripture, the psychoanalyst Mortimer Ostow has contended that all share a common premise: 'the messianic rescue brings the individual into a paradise, usually recognizable as a representation of the interior of the mother's body. The trip to mother-paradise is often obstructed and made hazardous by dangerous and ferocious creatures, representing father, siblings, or both'.[53] If, as is often argued, monotheistic religions like Judaism and Christianity sought to replace their mother-goddess predecessors with a stern patriarchal deity, then perhaps the lost object can be understood as in some sense maternal. The pervasive marriage imagery in apocalyptic literature emphasized by M.H. Abrams would thus have a more precise and more fraught meaning than merely 'God's reconciliation with His people and with the land'.[54] Mourning would mean working through the loss produced by the archaic mother's disappearance. An inability to renounce the regressive desire to reunite with the mother in a fantasy of recaptured plenitude, when accompanied by the unconscious self-reproach that her death was covertly desired, would result in melancholia instead.

These psychodynamics have often been applied to religious phenomena by commentators like Jean-Joseph Goux, who ties the prohibition on incest with the mother to other taboos, such as that on images so important to Judaism and certain ascetic strains of Christianity.[55] Lyotard has also treated the same theme in an essay entitled 'Figure Foreclosed', which explicitly links Freud's analysis of melancholia with the Jewish taboo on sight and the refusal of the mother.[56] A further connection, he suggests, is with the inability to provide positive symbolic representation of what has been lost, which ties this entire complex to the characteristic domination of the sublime over the beautiful in postmodernism.

But perhaps the most elaborate attempt to explain melancholy in terms of the inability to mourn the death of the mother has been made by Julia Kristeva in her recent meditation on depression entitled *Black Sun*.[57] Going beyond Freud, she claims that it does not involve an actual object, such as a real mother, but rather what she calls the 'Thing', which is more fundamental and more elusive. She defines it as 'the real that does not lend itself to signification, the center of attraction and repulsion, seat of the sexuality from which the object of desire will become separated'.[58] Gerard de Nerval's metaphor of a 'black sun' from his 1854 poem 'El Desdichado' captures its unrepresentable absence: 'the Thing is an imagined sun, bright and black at the same time'.[59] The melancholic is mesmerized by the Thing, which he mourns without respite, like a disinherited wanderer who does not know where his home was. Resisting symbolic representation, the 'Thing' remains encrypted in the psyche, walled up without any ability to be expressed linguistically and worked through. Instead, melancholy produces a feeling tone of despair – perhaps like that apocalyptic tone attacked by Kant and defended by Derrida? – which is literally at a loss for words.

For Kristeva, the alternative to melancholy requires negotiating two stages in which a relation with an object is substituted for one with the ineffable 'Thing'. First, the individual, of whatever gender, must actually 'kill' – or more precisely, separate from – the mother to achieve psychic maturity.[60] 'For man and for woman the loss of the mother is a biological and psychic necessity, the first step on the way to becoming autonomous', she writes. 'Matricide is our vital necessity, the sina-qua-non of our individuation'.[61] When such a break does not take place and the subject narcissistically identifies with the mother instead of 'killing' it through separation, then the results are pathological: 'the maternal object having been introjected, the depressive or melancholic putting to death of the self is what follows, instead of matricide'.[62]

The second step involves a working through of the guilt produced by the matricidal act, which Kristeva claims involves linguistic identification with the father. Reminiscent of Lacan's controversial notion of the 'name (no)-of-the-father', this argument subtly departs from it on one point: 'the supporting father of such a symbolic triumph is not the oedipal father', Kristeva claims, 'but truly that "imaginary father", "father in prehistory" according to Freud, who guarantees primary identification'.[63] But in both cases, the ability to identify with the father's prohibition on narcissistic identification with the mother is the source of psychic health. Whereas the melancholic disavows negation, denies the signifier and seeks impossible union with the lost 'Thing', the successful mourner of matricidal separation is able to find a symbolic way to work through the fateful deed. Certain types of art in particular, Kristeva contends, are able to provide such an avenue of escape, especially if they avoid the silent hypertrophy of images, which she explicitly identifies with the apocalyptic imaginary.[64]

Whether or not such arguments are a retreat from her earlier distinction between a maternal semiotic and paternal symbolic language I shall leave to serious students of Kristeva's *Oeuvre*, who also may want to debate her suggestion in *Black Sun* that a return to Christian symbolization can provide an antidote to the melancholy of postmodernism. What is important for our purposes is the link she forges between melancholy and 'an unfulfilled mourning for the maternal object'.[65] For what she helps us to understand is the often fiercely misogynist tone of much apocalyptic thought. That is, narcissistic identification with the mother, whose necessary 'death' has not been mourned, results in that reversal Freud has argued is characteristic of melancholy in general. Cast out of the psyche rather than symbolically integrated, the identified-with mother returns, as it were, as the avenging 'whore of babylon' and 'mother of harlots' so ferociously reviled by John of Patmos and his progeny.[66]

That such associations may be more than adventitious is suggested by evidence from previous episodes in the history of the apocalyptic imaginary. During the last *fin de siècle*, apocalyptic fantasies were often explicitly tied to anxieties about the erosion in what was assumed to be woman's primary role as a mother. As Bram Dijkstra has demonstrated in *Idols of Perversity*, once the ideal of the 'household nun' was undermined and women's sexuality unleashed, many artists and intellectuals projected images of sadistic fury onto women, who were figured as viragos, gynanders, vampires and other instruments of doom.[67] The German artist Erich Erler's 1915 etching 'The Beast of the Apocalypse', in which a blood-soaked nude wreaks her vengeance, exemplifies the melancholic inability to integrate the anxieties generated by unconscious ambivalence about the mother's loss.

Although the scientific version of the apocalyptic imagination is harder to reduce to such speculations about disavowed lost mothers, the time-honoured personifications of mother earth and mother nature suggest that even here something comparable may be at work. Feminist historians of science, such as Evelyn Fox Keller and Susan Bordo, have demonstrated the extent to which the modern scientific enterprise drew on violent images of separation from the mother to legitimate itself.[68] It is thus tempting to interpret the apocalyptic moment in the critique of technological and scientific hubris as a convoluted expression of distress at the matricidal underpinnings of the modernist project, indeed of the entire human attempt to uproot itself from its origins in something we might call mother nature.

If we succumb to this temptation, and agree that the lost love-object disavowed by the apocalyptically prone melancholic is, in some rather ill-defined way, the mother, then the next question is why has it been so hard to mourn her loss? Why have apocalyptic fantasies continued to thrive even in the ostensibly post-religious imaginaries we have called scientific and postmodernist? Here we are on even shakier ground than before, as collective psychological speculations of this magnitude can only be offered in the most tentative way. Still, two potential answers come to mind.

The first concerns the continued presence in what we might call the real world of the object whose apparent loss we cannot mourn. That is, whereas in the case of an individual's working through his or her loss of an actual parent, the passage of time is enough to allow the realization of genuine absence to achieve its work of consolation, in the case of the collective 'loss' of mother surrogates such as the earth, no such solution is possible. For the earth, however wounded by our depredations, is still around to nurture us. There is no reality testing that permits us to let go of the libidinal investment we seem to have in an object that has not fully disappeared. Thus, the guilt at secretly wanting to destroy what we love can never be fully worked through because the crime is always freshly enacted and always regretted anew.

The second explanation operates on a different plane. Taking a cue from Derrida's contention that the apocalyptic tone can never be abolished from philosophy, it suggests that mourning as a complete working through of lost material is itself a utopian myth. That is, the hope of finding a means to transcend the repetition and displacement characteristic of apocalyptic melancholia is necessarily doomed to failure. For it is, *pace* Kristeva, as impossible to reincorporate all disavowed material into the cultural unconscious and then work it through as it would be to achieve perfect mental equilibrium on the individual level. Nor may it always be healthy to strive for a perfectly worked through mourning in which none of the unrelieved grief associated with melancholy is retained.[69] To believe otherwise is to fall victim to the dialectical fantasies of perfect sublation that post-structuralist theory has so vigorously disputed. Melancholia is thus less an illness to be overcome than a permanent dimension of the human condition, and perhaps so too are the apocalyptic fantasies that can be marshalled so easily by a myriad of different stimuli.

This might be an appropriate place to end this paper on the repetition of endings, but I want to postpone the inevitable with one final thought. It is less perhaps a bang than a whimper, a whimper of protest, that is, against the too ready acceptance of the gloomy implications of these last arguments. For although the task of undoing the domination of mother nature may be far more difficult than some well-intentioned ecofeminists suggest, there are degrees of mastery and modes of alternative relations that provide some source of genuine hope. If there has been real progress in gender relations in the last century, and I think by many meaningful indicators there has been, it may well be the case that we have also learned something about the costs of violating mother earth. Although I do not want to be too sanguine, there may be some warrant for hope concerning the future of the collective melancholy that fuels apocalyptic fantasies.

Likewise, for all the well-justified post-structuralist scepticism about fully redemptive scenarios of reconciliation, it is important to distinguish between regressive nostalgia and the mourning process *per se*. Whereas in the former, the lost object remains a source of continuing libidinal investment, in the latter, it has been replaced by a thought-object in memory, one which no longer commands the same amount of fruitless yearning. Kristeva, I think, is persuasive in contending that symbolic acceptance of a necessary matricide can replace endless mourning for an encrypted or disavowed 'Thing' which resists representation. The suppurating wound of melancholia can finally heal, even though a scar remains to remind us of what has been sacrificed. Mourning need not mean complete dialectical sublation, but rather a willingness to tolerate its impossibility. Only if the ability to mourn allows us to work through what we have lost can we get beyond the saturnine disavowal on which apocalyptic fantasies so hungrily feed. Only then will the end of a century or even a millennium no longer be an occasion for sublime terror and become instead merely an arbitrary moment in an artificial chronology that we have deliberately created and know as such. No revelations lurk on the other side of the apocalypse, just the banal, but still valuable project of enlightenment whose horsepower may not be as powerful as that of its opponent, but which may in the long run have more stamina to stay the course.

NOTES

1 M. Blanchot, *The Writing of the Disaster*, trans. Ann Smock (Lincoln, Nebraska, 1986), p. 42.
2 According to Henri Focillon, the relationship between the two is not, however, intrinsic or inevitable. See his *The Year 1000*, trans. Fred D. Wieck (New York, 1969), p. 50.
3 For a very technical explication of the linguistic workings of this text, see David Hellholm, 'The Problem of Apocalyptic Genre and the Apocalypse of John', *Semeia* 36 (1986).
4 Hillel Schwartz, *Century's End: A Cultural History of the Fin de Siècle from the 990s to the 1990s* (New York, Doubleday, 1990), p. 31.
5 A number of articles in the popular press have commented on the upsurge of apocalyptic thinking, e.g. Bill Lawren, 'Apocalypse Now', *Psychology Today* (October 1989); Jeffrey L. Scheler, 'Will Armageddon Start in Iraq?', *The San*

Francisco Chronicle (16 December 1990), p. 13.

6 Schwartz, *Century's End*, p. 201.

7 See, for example, C.A. Patrides and Joseph Wittreich (eds), *The Apocalypse in English Renaissance Thought and Literature: Patterns, Antecedents and Repercussions* (Ithaca, 1984); Louise M. Kawada (ed.), *The Apocalypse Anthology* (Boston, Rowan Tree Press, 1985) or Saul Friedländer *et al.* (eds), *Visions of Apocalypse: End or Rebirth?* (New York, 1985).

8 Amos Funkenstein notes that 'it is very clear that the apocalyptic tradition does not exclude eternal return, at times even alludes to it under the influence, perhaps, of Iranian tradition'. See his 'A Schedule for the End of the World: The Origins and Persistence of the Apocalyptic Mentality' in Friedländer, *Visions of Apocalypse*, p. 50.

9 M.H. Abrams, *Natural Supernaturalism: Tradition and Revolution in Romantic Literature* (New York, 1971), p. 37f. Dominick LaCapra has recently noted that for all his celebration of the symbolic overcoming of differences in a wide variety of forms, which valorize the consummation of the marriage, Abrams himself 'tends to repeat the apocalyptic paradigm in an almost obsessive way, in wave upon wave of plangent high seriousness, until the allowed story he tells becomes almost hollow – eroded and made a bit tedious and even senseless'. See his *Soundings in Critical Theory* (Ithaca, 1989), p. 100.

10 Michael Barkun, 'Divided Apocalypse: Thinking About the End in Contemporary America', *Soundings* LXVI, 3 (Fall 1983), pp. 257–280.

11 Norman Cohn, *The Pursuit of the Millennium* (London, 1957).

12 See Spencer R. Weart, *Nuclear Fear: A History of Images* (Cambridge, Mass., 1988), p. 397.

13 Ibid., p. 260.

14 For a discussion of such books, see John Elson, 'Apocalyse Now?', *Time* (11 February 1991), p. 88.

15 Barry Commoner, *The Closing Circle: Nature, Man and Technology* (New York, Norton; 1971); Robert L. Heilbronner, *An Inquiry into the Human Prospect* (New York, Norton, 1974); Jonathan Schell, *The Fate of the Earth* (New York, 1982).

16 Elaine Showalter, *Sexual Anarchy: Gender and Culture at the Fin de Siècle* (New York, Viking, 1990), p. 176.

17 Barkun, 'Divided Apocalypse', p. 278.

18 Derrida, to be sure, has resisted incorporation into the discourse of post-modernism. See his remarks recorded by Ingeborg Hoesterey in her introduction to *Zeitgeist in Babel: The Postmodernist Controversy*, ed. Ingeborg Hoesterey (Bloomington, Ind., 1991), p. xii. What he apparently dislikes about it is its implied notion of linear historical periodization. But Derrida's work has certainly figured prominently in the discourse of postmodernism, which cannot be fully grasped without taking it into account.

19 For an account of the linkage in eighteenth-century Britain, see Morton D. Paley, *The Apocalyptic Sublime* (New Haven, 1986).

20 Frank Kermode, 'Apocalypse and the Modern' in Friedländer *et al.* (eds), *Visions of Apocalypse*. A similar apocalyptic current ran through certain Western Marxist theorists of the same era, such as Ernst Bloch and Walter Benjamin. For an account, see Anson Rabinbach, 'Between Enlightenment and Apocalypse: Benjamin, Bloch and Modern Jewish Messianism', *New German Critique* 34 (Winter 1985); and Michael Löwy, *Rédemption et Utopie: Le Judaïsme libertaire en Europe centrale* (Paris, PUF, 1988). In fact, apocalyptic fantasies were common coin among many German intellectuals during the Weimar era. See Ivo Frenzel, 'Utopia and Apocalypse in German Literature', *Social Research* 39, 2 (Summer 1972).

21 Yve-Alain Bois, 'Painting: The Task of Mourning', *Endgame* (Boston, 1990), p. 30. Bois is referring to the belief that abstraction was the final reduction of painting to its essence, after which nothing more could be done. There were, to be sure, more literal modernist attempts to depict apocalypse, for example, by the German Expressionist Ludwig Meidner. See Carol S. Eliel, *The Apocalyptic Landscape of Ludwig Meidner* (Los Angeles, 1989).

22 Klaus R. Scherpe, 'Dramatization and De-dramatization of "the End": The Apocalyptic Consciousness of Modernity and Post-Modernity', *Cultural Critique* 5 (Winter 1986–87), p. 122.

23 For a suggestive reading of the *posthistoire* discourse, see Lutz Niethammer, 'Afterthoughts on Posthistoire', *History and Memory* I, 1 (Spring/Summer 1989). The relation between history and apocalypse, it should be noted, is more complicated than may appear at first glance. Hans Blumenberg has contended that the 'historicization of eschatology' in the early Christian era did not mean putting the moment of redemption in the historical future, but rather believing that it had occurred in the past. That is, disappointed initial hopes for a Second Coming led to the consoling belief that all that was needed for personal salvation had been already provided by the First Coming, which allowed the faithful to gain heaven by acting on the basis of Jesus's message. See *The Legitimacy of the Modern Age*, trans. Robert M. Wallace (Cambridge, Mass., 1983), chapter 4. If this is true, then the postmodernist belief in *posthistoire* should also be understood as denying past as well as future consolations.

24 Derrida, 'Of an Apocalyptic Tone Recently Adopted in Philosophy', *Semeia* 23 (1982). Derrida acknowledges in this essay the prevalence of apocalyptic concerns elsewhere in his work, such as *Glas*, *La Carte postale* and the essays 'Pas' and 'Living On' (pp. 90–91). 'The Ends of Man' is available in *Margins of Philosophy*, trans. Alan Bass (Chicago, 1982). It deals with the theme of the last man and the end of metaphysics in philosophers like Heidegger and Nietzsche. He treats the theme again in his essay on 'nuclear criticism', entitled 'No Apocalypse, Not Now (Full Speed Ahead, Seven Missles, Seven Missives)', *Diacritics* 14, 2 (Summer 1984). Here the three apocalyptic discourses – religious, scientific and postmodern – all mingle in the shadow of the nuclear holocaust.

25 Kant, 'Von einem neuerdings erhobenen vornehmen Ton in der Philosophie' in A. Buchenau, E. Cassirer, B. Kellerman (eds), *Schriften von 1790–1796 von Immanuel Kant*, vol. 6 of *Immanuel Kants Werke*, ed. E. Cassirer (Berlin, Cassirer 1923), pp. 475–496.

26 The distinction between knowledge and thought is based on the crucial opposition in Kant between the synthetic *a priori* judgements of pure reason and the speculative ideas that metaphysics had claimed it could provide. Only in practical reason, the moral reasoning discussed in the second *Critique*, are such ideas given to us, but they can never be grounded in synthetic *a priori* judgements.

27 Derrida, 'Of an Apocalyptic Tone Recently Adopted in Philosophy', p. 80.

28 Ibid.

29 Ibid., p. 87.

30 Ibid., p. 89.

31 In so doing, Derrida curiously forgets what he has argued elsewhere: that there can be no absolutely categorical distinction between prescriptive and descriptive language games (between the Greek fascination with ontology and the Jewish obsession with ethics). See his critique of Levinas for precisely this failing 'Violence and Metaphysics: An Essay on the Thought of Emmanuel Levinas', *Writing and Difference*, trans. Alan Bass (Chicago, 1978). Instead, in this essay he sounds very much like Lyotard, who follows Levinas more rigorously in such works as *The Differend: Phrases in Dispute*, trans. George Van Den Abbeele

(Minneapolis, 1988).

32 Derrida, 'Of an Apocalyptic Tone', p. 93.

33 Ibid., p. 94.

34 Ibid., p. 95.

35 John P. Leavy Jr, 'Destinerrance: The Apotropocalyptics of Translation' in John Sallis (ed.), *Deconstruction and Philosophy: The Texts of Jacques Derrida* (Chicago, 1987).

36 Eric L. Santner, *Stranded Objects: Mourning, Memory and Film in Postwar Germany* (Ithaca, 1990), p. 13. Santner argues that much postmodernism represents itself as a healthy mourning for the lost hopes of the modernist project, but as he notes in the complicated case of Paul de Man in particular, the mourning appears endless. That is, de Man's insistence that language itself necessitates a never-ending mourning for its inability to achieve plenitude leads to a valorization of repetition that is closer to melancholy than mourning *per se*. It is, to be sure, a melancholy shorn of its affective charge and abstracted from any link with actual lived experience and the human solidarity that might be its antidote.

37 Jean Baudrillard, 'Sur le nihilisme', *Simulacres et simulation* (Paris, 1981), p. 234.

38 J.-F. Lyotard, 'A Conversation with Jean-François Lyotard', *Flash Art* (March 1985), p. 33.

39 John Rajchman, 'The Postmodern Museum', *Art in America* 73, 10 (October 1985), p. 115.

40 For a different attempt to psychologize the apocalyptic mentality, see Robert J. Lifton, 'The Image of "The End of the World": A Psychohistorical View' in Friedländer *et al.*, *Visions of Apocalypse*. He relates it to paranoid schizophrenia, as in the case of Schreber. Cohn, *The Pursuit of the Millennium* also stresses paranoia (p. 69f.).

41 Sigmund Freud, 'Mourning and Melancholia', *Collected Papers*, vol. 4, ed. Ernest Jones (New York, Basic Books, 1959). There is a vast pre-Freudian literature on the theme of melancholy, from literary, pictorial, theological and medical points of view. For helpful overviews, see Raymond Klibansky, Erwin Panofsky and Fritz Saxl, *Saturn and Melancholy: Studies in the History of Natural Philosophy, Religion and Art* (London, 1964); Reinhard Kuhn, *The Demon of Noontide: Ennui in Western Literature* (Princeton, 1976); Wolf Lepenies, *Melancholie und Gesellschaft* (Frankfurt, 1972).

42 Freud, 'Mourning and Melancholia', p. 154.

43 Ibid., p. 153.

44 Ibid., p. 157. This essay provides one of the earliest accounts of what he would later call the superego.

45 Ibid., p. 159.

46 Ibid., p. 164.

47 S. Freud, *Group Psychology and the Analysis of the Ego*, trans. James Strachey (New York, Bantam 1985), p. 82f.

48 See in particular, Melanie Klein's 1940 paper, 'Mourning and its Relation to Manic-Depressive States', *Contributions to Psychoanalysis, 1921–1945* (London, Hogarth Press, 1973). For a general overview of the literature, see Lorraine D. Siggens, 'Mourning: A Critical Survey of the Literature', *International Journal of Psychoanalysis* 47 (1966), pp. 14–25, and the more recent bibliography in Neal L. Tolchin, *Mourning, Gender, and Creativity in the Art of Herman Melville* (New Haven, 1988).

49 See, for example, Schell, *The Fate of the Earth*, pp. 127 and 174.

50 For a good account of this aspect of their work, see Michael E. Zimmerman,

Heidegger's Confrontation with Modernity: Technology, Politics, Art (Blooming-ton, Ind., 1990).

51 Freud, 'Mourning and Melancholia', p. 163.

52 See Alexander and Margarete Mitscherlich, *The Inability to Mourn: Principles of Collective Behavior*, trans. Beverley R. Placzek (New York, 1975) and Santner, *Stranded Objects*.

53 Mortimer Ostow, 'Archetypes of Apocalypse in Dreams and Fantasies, and in Religious Scripture', *American Imago* 43, 4 (Winter, 1986), p. 308.

54 Abrams, *Natural Supernaturalism*, p. 45.

55 Jean-Joseph Goux, *Les iconoclastes* (Paris, Senill, 1978).

56 Lyotard, 'Figure Foreclosed', in Andrew Benjamin (ed.), *The Lyotard Reader* (Oxford, 1989).

57 Julia Kristeva, *Black Sun: Depression and Melancholia*, trans. Leon S. Roudiez (New York, Columbia University Press, 1989). For a helpful analysis, see John Lechte, 'Art, Love and Melancholy in the Work of Julia Kristeva' in John Fletcher and Andrew Benjamin (eds), *Abjection, Melancholy and Love: The Work of Julia Kristeva* (London, 1990).

58 Ibid., p. 13.

59 Ibid.

60 For a similar argument cast in the less dramatic terms of object relations theory, see Jessica Benjamin, *The Bonds of Love: Psychoanalysis, Feminism, and the Problem of Domination* (New York, 1988), pp. 211f.

61 Kristeva, *Black Sun*, pp. 27–28. She borrows Klein's notion of the 'depressive position' to indicate the first stage of breaking with the mother. It should be noted that, according to Klein, this is a normal and not pathological moment in human development, despite the seemingly pejorative label. For a suggestive application of this and other Kleinian categories to moral and social phenomena, which illuminates the issues addressed in this paper, see C. Fred Alford, *Melanie Klein and Critical Social Theory* (New Haven, 1989).

62 Ibid., p. 28.

63 Ibid., p. 22.

64 Ibid., p. 224.

65 Ibid., p. 61.

66 As Kristeva puts it, 'in order to protect mother I kill myself while knowing – phantasmatic and protective knowledge – that it comes from her, the death-bearing she-Gehenna . . . Thus my hatred is safe and my matricidal guilt erased. I make of Her an image of Death so as not to be shattered through the hatred I bear against myself when I identify with Her, for that aversion is in principle meant for her as it is an individuating dam against confusional love' (ibid., p. 28).

67 Bram Dijkstra, *Idols of Perversity: Fantasies of Feminine Evil in Fin-de-siècle Culture* (New York, 1986).

68 Evelyn Fox Keller, *Reflections on Gender and Science* (New Haven, 1985); Susan R. Bordo, *The Flight to Objectivity: Essays on Cartesianism and Culture* (Albany, NY, 1987).

69 For an interesting defence of this position, which uses Roland Barthes's treatment of his mother's death in *Camera Lucida* to modify Freud, see Kathleen Woodward, 'Freud and Barthes: Theorizing Mourning, Sustaining Grief', *Discourse* 13, 1 (Fall–Winter 1990–1991).

Chapter 3

The elementary ethics of everyday life

Agnes Heller

I

When Emmanuel Levinas placed our relationship to the Other at the very centre of ethics, he found little echo among modern moral philosophers. His gambit seemed to be outdated and explained by his religious inspirations alone, if noticed at all. Philosophies like that of Levinas were initially rejected, or at least neglected, as idiosyncratic and marginal affairs.

There are three approaches in Levinas's work (as well as in similar approaches) of which modern mainstream moral philosophies were suspicious.

First, it has been taken for granted that modern culture is decentred, at least since Max Weber formulated his ingenious theory about the differentiation of cultural (value) spheres. As is well known, Weber compared the modern world to the Olympus of polytheism; every person (every authentic person, at least) chooses his or her divinity in the pluralistic universe; different people choose different gods. Every sphere has its own – immanent – morals, and people who dwell within one sphere cannot carry these sphere-immanent morals into another sphere. This decentring of values results in the decentring of morals. Certain theorists, first and foremost Habermas, propose an alternative interpretation of Weber. According to Habermas, Weber meant to locate a separate single sphere of morals alongside all other cultural spheres. With regard to the present issue, the two interpretations do not differ; one way or another, ethics has no centre in either of them. Regardless of whether ethics is understood as one sphere among all others or whether one attributes to each sphere an ethics of its own, morals is itself fully subjected to cultural changes in both cases.

Second, knowledge and paradigms change. Though knowledge can still be regarded as cumulative, there is no centrepoint that knowledge might approximate. The vision of approximating a centre is metaphysical; there is no centre. Perhaps our knowledge still approximates, but we do not know *what* it should approximate; as a result, it approximates nothing. If there is no centrepoint for knowledge to approximate, how can there be a centrepoint in ethics to approximate?

Third, since there is nothing to approximate, the objectivity (or inter-subjectivity) of both true knowledge and of the rightness of norms must be established first. A few alternatives are offered on how this could be achieved; among them a kind of computation concerning maximum utility was once quite famous; nowadays rather different forms of discourse are recommended. What the participants in a discourse will agree upon will be called 'true' if the agreement concerns knowledge; and it will be called 'right' if the agreement concerns norms. The form (the discourse) produces the content (the truth of the true or of the good). All kinds of discourse ethics explore moral problems in this direction, though they can disagree in many things, first and foremost in matters of a fair or just procedure. As a result, pre-discursive moral intuitions are treated as if they were kinds of a pre-scientific knowledge.

One cannot expect great opposition to the proposition that prior to the nineteenth century there was (still) a centrepoint in ethics, and that the relation to the Other occupied at least a major place in this centre. It would be rather difficult to deny this. After all, Plato says that the good person is the one who prefers suffering wrong to doing wrong to others, and Aristotle defines justice first as the sum total of all the virtues in relation to the others. Furthermore, in Christian ethics, love (charity) is the main virtue, and Leibniz insists that we call certain acts morally evil because they cause physical evil (that is suffering) to other human beings (or living beings in general). One could say that Kant made a Copernican turn here too, insofar as he reversed the traditional relationship between the good (as end) and the morally right (as moral law). This turn ushered in modern moral philosophy insofar as, from now on, it seemed that form is responsible for constituting the content (that is, the formula of the categorical imperative constitutes the maxims and the maxims the acts), or at least that the form needs to test the content of inherited or intuited maxims. However, Kant also did his (theoretical) best to preserve the moral centre. It was the major asset of the formula of the categorical imperative that it offered such a centre: everyone is supposed to be able, and be in full authority, to test his or her maxims using the categorical imperative. The categorical imperative is not only a device, it also presents the centre; everyone knows *what* needs to be, or rather, ought to be, approximated. By contrast, Kant insisted that approximation in knowledge is to take place in the process of infinite regression alone, where the end (the *what*) of the approximation itself remains unknown, not only *de facto*, but also in principle (the thing-in-itself). Briefly, in Kant, knowledge became decentred, whereas morality remained emphatically well-centred.

For Kant the difference between ethics and knowledge was not the difference between two kinds of discourses. It was absolute, and absolutely essential.[1] In the case of morals, the person is related to transcendence (transcendental freedom determines); in the case of knowledge everything is, and remains, immanent. One is related to transcendence practically, to immanence theoretically. If one changes this scene and begins to discuss two kinds of discourses (theoretical and practical), morality loses its direct relation to transcendence and becomes reduced to, or transformed into, a kind of knowledge. In moral discourse, persons who are situated in similar cultures find out together which norms are reasonable or rational and which are not. Moral discourse says little about action, and even if it does, it is *not* an action. The most evil of men can have the best or most correct opinions in the situation of discourse.

Since practical discourse cannot become substantive (and generally I see this as an asset), it must remain silent about virtues, particularly about the other, the very other *for* whom one lives ethically (provided that one lives ethically at all); for the latter has, as indicated, absolutely nothing to do with one's participation in practical discourse. It must remain silent about the most important, the very source of morals, for the source(s) of morality is (are) not, and cannot become, subject-matter(s) of discourse; they are prior to discourse.

By the transcendent character of morality I understand that preliminary questions such as 'Why should I be moral?' or 'Why is it good to be good?' or 'Does it make sense to be good?' are in moral matters wrongly put, because they are all asking us to give reasons for being or becoming good. We often ask questions about things where reasons cannot be found or given. The problem with the above questions is certainly not that they insist on giving reasons where no reasons can be given, but something entirely different. When someone poses such a question, that person has already begged the moral questions. These questions are not moral questions: they rather indicate the termination of moral inquiry. Preliminary epistem-ological or historical interrogation that might give a more solid foundation in science or philosophy of science (though not always) keeps the same interrogator constantly outside the moral centre. This is so, because the above questions constantly decentre the real moral questions; the latter can no longer be asked. Whatever answers are given to those questions, they will never become the 'preliminary' questions that lead up to ethics, for one cannot trespass the threshold between knowledge and action with this kind of baggage; one is supposed to drop the baggage of these questions before the threshold.

The real moral question that cannot be asked after the enquiry becomes decentred by all the (morally) wrong ones (for example by this one: 'What good does it do to be good?') are as follows: 'What should I do?', 'What is the right thing for me to do?' These are in essence moral questions, for they always aim at the centre of the person who raises them; and do so on each and every occasion. The centre of the person is unlike the standpoint of the person; 'my centre' reads 'my responsibility'. As far as 'perspective' (standpoint) is concerned, my centre is the other's centre, and vice versa; if this were otherwise, moral questions could not be put at all.

Moral questioning starts with a gesture. This gesture is transcendent, for one cannot attempt at its rationalization without cancelling it. Founded in transcendence, moral questioning proper is the solid immanent foundation of the moral. It cannot be rationalized, but it grants rationality. Moral rationality has to have recourse to this foundation.[2]

All this was not meant to refute discourse ethics. Philosophy cannot be refuted. In addition, there are many morally fruitful insights in discourse ethics, they only need another (a moral) foundation. Furthermore, all this was not meant as a dithyramb against modern ethics in general. After all, many philosophers have felt uneasy about the self-complacency of mainstream modern thinkers and their practice to subject moral enquiry under the authority of speculative reasoning. I mention here only Alasdair MacIntyre's work or Judith Shklar's book *Ordinary Vices*, particularly its first chapter on cruelty. Still, the attempt to bring the practical under the tutelage of the speculative has marginalized all other lines of enquiry prior to yesterday.[3]

There is either well-centred morals or there is none. If such a centre were to be lost, law (legal regulation) would replace morals entirely. It does not depend on moral philosophers whether or not there is, or there remains, morals. But it does depend on moral philosophy whether the kind of morals that exist will be illuminated by speculative reflection, or whether this, speculatively not extremely rewarding, task will be left to everyday actors, to writers or religious preachers alone.

Philosophers (and sociologists) began to decentre morals in the process of sincere reckoning with the modern historical condition. The question was not whether modern historical conditions have entirely destroyed the moral intuitions that once centred morals and the reflection on morals, for it was obvious that they have not. On this point philosophers and sociologists normally agree. The primary question was (and has remained) whether these moral intuitions and gestures, these acts of centring, should be treated as remnants, as leftovers from pre-modern ages, already marked for destruction and self-destruction. The secondary question was (and has remained) whether those traditional and 'irrational' ways of centring morals need to be swept away, or, conversely, whether they are the most precious things that can be preserved, if they need to be, or even should be, within the modern social arrangement. Finally, the question is whether it is worth while to speak about all these gestures philosophically. I put my bet on the survival of these moral intuitions and gestures, and I think that there are things that can be said about them and that they are also worth being said. Perhaps true moral reflection has become pedestrian or at least lacking in the esoteric touch. But, after all, morals are the same for everyone – experts and laypeople alike. Whatever else belongs to moral philosophy, morals begin in everyday life, in the life that everyone shares.

II

We came to the conclusion that an authentic practical discourse is circular. First, one accepts (with a gesture) that one should be a moral being (one should be decent or good), and only then does the question of 'What is the right thing for me to do?' arise. The essential difference between the moderns and the pre-moderns is certainly not that the moderns do not need a gesture but that they rationalize ethics. The opposite is closer to the truth. Although there is an initial gesture where there are moral beings (the acceptance of morals as an absolute through taking responsibility), only moderns need to be aware of the gesture-character of this gesture. This is so, because in the pre-modern worlds the gesture of taking responsibility cannot be isolated from the answer to the question of 'What is the right thing for me to do?'. As long as ethics is traditional, all children learn from their parents and other this-worldly as well as other-worldly authorities that they should be good and how they should be good, simultaneously. Yet modernity's dynamics requires that men and women constantly query and test the contents of most traditional moral customs and virtues. Not only philosophers, but everyone learns how to reject traditional virtues, to make interpretations of virtues, to make decisions that rules and precepts are wrong and how to open the way for new ones and embrace them as right instead. It has been often stated that this never-ending query results in nihilism, and this might be so. De-legitimizing discourse on ethics can deconstruct morals, yet only if it succeeds in replacing and discrediting moral gestures fully. Moderns need to remind themselves constantly of the transcendent, absolute character of the first gesture, in order to remain able to protect morals from being colonized by sheer immanent/cognitive claims.

The absoluteness of the initial moral gesture now rests fully on the resolve of each individual to be a decent person, to be a good person. With the absoluteness of the initial gesture granted, one can proceed to discuss all the moral choices, dilemmas, virtues, etc., that are constantly opened up by this resolve. In a post-conventional world, questions like 'How can I be moral?' are no longer organically embedded in the tradition; this is why one always has to keep in mind that their immanence is related to transcendence. This is why in the modern world of contingent existences, I understand this first gesture (in Kierkegaard's spirit) as an existential choice. One chooses morals existentially, if one chooses oneself as a good (decent) person. It is only after this choice that a person can raise the question of 'What is the right thing for me to do?'. This question reads as follows: 'How can I become what I already am, namely a decent person?'. The immanent/cognitive questions are asked about the conditions of goodness (in various situations), yet never about goodness itself.

Since it is the absolute gesture that centres life, and it centres life no less now than it had done five hundred or a thousand years ago, we cannot expect grand changes here. Dramatic changes have occurred in the conditions of making our original choice good. To be more precise, 'making a choice good' means now exactly the same thing as it meant before. It refers to the approximation of the centre (being entirely good), where the centre is never hit. The new conditions do not change the relation between centre and approximation, but they do change certain ways through which one approximates this centre. The all-encompassing new element consists in the centrality of the value of freedom in modern times. Since freedom has assumed the position of a universal value, it belongs to the good life of everyone to enjoy freedom. One could say that since the existential choice of oneself as a decent being is already a gesture of full moral autonomy, it implies implicitly the respect for the moral autonomy of all others. Yet, though this is implicitly so, one needs to make it explicit. Furthermore, the value of freedom requires not just the respect of moral autonomy, but also the recognition of other kinds of liberties, such as personal, economic, political and the like. If one begins to answer the question of 'how can I be (what I am) a decent person?', one needs to make explicit how the autonomy, and all the kinds of liberty of others, can be recognized and respected.

The existential choice of goodness is the gesture of taking responsibility. Responsibility, in general, is one of the fundamental moral concepts; every kind of responsibility is at bottom a moral one. Taking responsibility is also the matter of a person's dignity; one respects another person's dignity if one treats him or her as a responsible being.

We normally assume that everyone is responsible for one's own actions, though not to the same extent (with certain exceptions); yet not everyone takes responsibility for those actions even in the most elementary sense. The word 'responsibility' stems from 'responding' (in several languages). The person who responds truly, takes responsibility; the person who does not respond truly, avoids responsibility (but is, for that matter, not less responsible). One can avoid responsibility mainly by remaining silent, with lying (denying, accusing someone else), and rationalizing. One can take responsibility in pride and in shame; one avoids responsibility normally if taking responsibility would cause pain or unpleasantness of a kind.

Whenever one takes or avoids responsibility (in this primitive sense), one already faces others. The concrete Others who press the actor to take responsibility can be just or unjust persons, dignified moral actors but also aggressive and frightening bullies. Only angels would take responsibility in each and every single case. But if one seriously means the business of approximating the moral centre, one should take responsibility in every case when another human person would suffer should one fail to do so. The smallest schoolchildren with some moral sense know that one does not lie to the teacher about a mischief committed in class if another child might be punished instead of the perpetrator. Already, in this simple case, there are more Others facing the actor than one, and, at least indirectly, taking responsibility for one's action goes together with taking responsibility for other human persons.

Dostoevsky said somewhere that every human being is responsible for all others; and if everyone knew this, there would be paradise on Earth at once. This dictum does not refer to the simple case of taking responsibility in retrospect (that is, for something that we have done), but about prospective responsibility in the sense of 'being in charge'. Responsibility in the sense of 'being in charge' is always responsibility for the others. We normally take responsibility in this sense for a few others, but we do not take responsibility for all. 'Taking responsibility' is here the starting point, whereas the terminus is 'to live up' to the responsibility taken as long as others need us, and, incidentally, also throughout our whole life. In this case, once again, 'being responsible' on the one hand and 'living up to responsibility' on the other are not synonymous interpretations of responsibility. One assumes that parents are responsible for their small children; but from this it does not follow that they will live up to this responsibility. An elected government is responsible for keeping its promises, but it does not follow that it will genuinely live up to this responsibility. There is a duplication of questioning/responding (in the sense of responsibility) in such a case. The gesture of taking responsibility can already be expressed as a kind of a response to a question. Traditionally, one can express this 'response' in taking a solemn oath – for example, in the marriage ceremony of 'till death us do part'. Apart from the original expression of responding, one must respond to the question 'afterwards'; then it turns out how and to what extent one has lived up to one's promises.

A person who has chosen himself or herself as a decent person, will be as sincere as possible whenever he or she takes up a responsibility in the sense of 'taking charge'. This follows from everything previously said. Here, contrary to the merely retrospective kind of responsibility, there is always a direct relation to others(s). What one actually decides is whether one stands for self-election to become answerable for the good life of other persons, and whether one is ready to do one's best to make other(s) suffer as little as possible. How far one lives up to this responsibility is another, although related, matter. In the first case, we speak about the sincerity of the resolve to aim at the moral centre, whereas in the second case we speak about the kind and the distance of approximation.

Though Dostoevsky's dictum, that we all are responsible for all other human beings, refers to prospective responsibility, it cannot be fully understood in its terms. As we saw, prospective responsibility is about taking responsibility and living up to it. But how can one take responsibility, in the above sense, for all human beings simultaneously? How can you take all human beings into your charge? Unless one accepts empty gestures and emotional outpourings on the theme of the suffering of humankind as manifestations of moral responsibility – which would be foolish – the answer is that one cannot. But Dostoevsky does not propose everyone's taking up responsibility for everyone else; he mentions becoming eventually conscious of having had such a responsibility all along. Consciousness of responsibility and living up to responsibility are not identical terms. But if one does not live up to this responsibility, what kind of responsibility can that be? What would happen if everyone knew that everyone is responsible for everyone else, if no concrete act might be traceable as the result of this enormous consciousness?

Something certainly would follow from such an enormous consciousness, and this 'something' was spelt out by Dostoevsky in plain words: Paradise on Earth. If everyone were conscious about his or her responsibility for everyone else on Earth, everyone would centre himself or herself in a moral sense. And if everyone (all others separately and together) lived and acted towards their moral centre, everyone could also actually arrive at this centre. This is what we could call Paradise on Earth. Yet a paradise on earth contradicts ethics. Dostoevsky does not mention moral beings standing in the draught of transcendence (which is just a metaphor for people who are simply good without asking the question of 'What for?'), but transcendence pure and simple. Thus Dostoevsky cancels ethics, similarly to all moral philosophers who superimpose a cognitive discourse upon morals, with the difference that he cancels morals in reverse. Sheer cognitive ethics transforms the transcendent elements of morals into immanent ones, whereas Dostoevsky transforms its immanent elements into transcendent ones. Moral responsibility is engendered by a gesture, but it does not remain a gesture.

III

All of us know many good, decent persons. They are decent both in everyday life and in borderline situations. Sometimes the heroes of certain borderline situations can fail the average tests of moral righteousness in daily life; if they do, we may rest assured that they have not chosen themselves as decent persons and their heroism was either ideologically or cognitively founded or simply self-serving. By contrast, sometimes the most forthcoming, friendly and charitable persons fail the average test in borderline situations; if they do, we may rest assured that they have not chosen themselves as good persons, and that their friendly and charitable demeanour resulted from their inclinations alone.

The latter discrepancy is rather rare, whereas the first is frequent. After all, everyday life is ethically demanding, complex and variegated; all kinds of moral conflicts appear here; moreover, there are occasionally borderline situations in everyday life. It is true that stepping outside the everyday framework is demanding, because the specific feature of the new conditions need to be learned. Yet the same is required when someone moves from one everyday culture into another. If one joins an institution (for example, begins to work in a factory or in a government office), one has to find out what other people expect one to do before one can decide whether something is right or wrong. What is demanding here is not a primary, but a secondary moral process, for it is not the moral attitude that needs to be changed, rather the good practice of already acquired moral aptitudes requires more learning, new information, some exercise.

Moral phronesis, as the readiness to deal with each and every moral situation concretely, requires constant practice and development in daily life. Outside the pale of everyday life phronesis will not be suspended, everyday practice is mobilized in full. It is lazy thinking that has to be avoided.

The decent person cares for others. This is the most elementary starting point of all morals; it remains beyond explanation. For if one asks the question of 'Why should I care for others?', then, whatever the answer will be, one must raise new questions again and again, *ad infinitum*. Morals, as mentioned, begins with a gesture in regard to which no questions can be asked.

Care for other human beings: this is the universal orientative principle of morals. It is universal, because in all spheres, in all forms of life and in all kinds of activities people can care for each other as well as not. The principle is orientative not because its content is meagre (for it is rather rich, dense and condensed), but because it does not spell out how one should care for other human beings. It is left to the discretion of each and every individual to find out how one can best care for this human being or another.

'Care for other human beings', as the universal orientative principle, is also open to several interpretations. 'To care' can be interpreted as 'to love' in an emotional way; if so interpreted, 'Care for other human beings' could read: 'It is a morally good thing if one loves at least a few human beings emotionally.' 'To care' can also be interpreted as practising charity, as it can also mean 'take responsibility' for others, that is, to assume prospective and not only retrospective responsibility for them. And there are many other ways in which one might further interpret this universal orientative principle.

We all know that we are not confronted with this dense, at the same time very vague, orientative principle alone. We have inherited a host of representative explications of this principle. Such explications are not applications, yet they mediate between the universal principle, on the one hand, and the concrete situation, in which we are caring for concrete other persons in practice, on the other.

It is entirely wrong to believe that moderns have thrown the whole baggage of this tradition out the window. Only two things changed here. I have already mentioned both of them. First, among the traditional interpretations of the universal orientative principle, only those could be preserved which were compatible with the recognition of the other person's freedom and full moral autonomy. Second, interpretations that were rooted in the pre-modern world lost their moral relevance. I can exemplify both issues in one. In a world of asymmetric reciprocity, care for other human persons emphatically included interpretations which dealt with the master–servant relationship. Since the social arrangement of symmetric reciprocity has taken the place of the social arrangement of asymmetric reciprocity, such interpretations became irrelevant at least in countries where modernity has already taken strong roots.

In what follows, I shall enumerate a few orientative principles. All of them are interpretations and concretizations of the universal orientative principle: 'Care for other human beings', as well as of its negative formulation: 'Do not harm another human being on purpose.'

1. Have proper regard for other persons' vulnerability. Among others, this principle stipulates that we do not offend another human being in his or her person and in anything he or she holds dear (that we do not show contempt for other persons, unless morally justified, that we do not ridicule other persons or put them to shame, with the same qualification, and so on.) Furthermore, it stipulates that we express our feelings of love, sympathy and respect towards other persons, that we help the other person to 'save face' and that we respond to another person's need for our person sincerely.

2. Have proper regard for other persons' autonomy. Since this is the principle that gained the uppermost status of modernity, many a traditional stipulation has become radicalized under its guidance. For example, do not violate another person's body, do not violate another person's soul, do not manipulate others, do not keep others under tutelage, help others to achieve greater autonomy. Due to the special standing of the orientative principle concerning autonomy in modernity, three of its orientative sub-principles are interpreted in a strongly constitutive–imperative manner, such as: 'Do not violate another person's body and soul, do not manipulate others or keep them in tutelage because of their race, sex or membership in other human groups.'

3. Have proper regard for other persons' morality. That is, one has to pay attention to the moral merit of others, one has to learn how and when to pass moral judgements, and one has to learn how (and when) to forget and when to remember.

4. One should have proper regard for other persons' suffering. A decent person notices the suffering of others; a decent person does his or her best to alleviate another person's suffering. A decent person offers a part of his or her time, money and energy for the alleviation of such suffering that can be remedied.

All these orientative principles sound, and indeed are, simple and quite traditional. However, the few non-traditional (modern) principles among them modify each and every principle in the catalogue, even if their wording does not change the wording of traditional ones. The principles do not need to be compatible with one another in practice, that is, in single cases; they are after all not principles of a system. There can be conflict between them. But all of them have to be formulated such that the formula should be compatible with freedom and autonomy.

The orientative principles enumerated above were said to be nothing but interpretations or explications of the universal orientative principle: 'Care for other human beings – do not harm another human being on purpose.' It is obvious that the universal principle itself is not incompatible with possible sub-principles which, for their part, are incompatible with the sub-principles that stipulate autonomy. There is no reason for being embarrassed in regard to this discovery. The universal principle of moral orientation is the *arche* of morals. It is the meta-principle. As meta-principle, it is valid for all morals; it is not historical insofar as it is valid in all human histories where there are morals. The interpretations of the *arche*, the sub-principles, introduce history into the supra-historical. This is why they can mediate between the master principle (the *arche*) and all the always new and changing concrete situations in which individuals decide.

IV

The universal orientative principle of morals with all its interpretations and explications (the sub-principles) points at the centre of all moral intentions, judgements and considerations: a person takes responsibility for other persons. There is no reciprocity involved yet. One takes responsibility (for others) irrespective of the circumstance whether others take responsibility for you. In this sense, the starting point of the moral attitude (not of moral knowledge, of course) is 'monological'. You do not do your best to alleviate another person's suffering because the other person did (or does) her best to alleviate yours, and you do not have a regard for another person's vulnerability because this person once had (or is having now) regard for your vulnerability. This non-reciprocal character of the initial moral gesture needs to be emphatically underlined. Moral philosophies just too often tie the foundation of morals to reciprocity; for example, we do not murder others, for we do not want to be murdered. Social contract theories, and not only of the Hobbesian but also of the Lockean kind, are rooted in such or in similar considerations. The Kantian categorical imperative (which has nothing to do with reciprocity at all) is also frequently interpreted in this spirit, particularly by British and American philosophers. Though the golden rule of justice is truly based on reciprocity and formulates it, reciprocity itself would be empty (void of content) and non-sensical (void of the readiness to give content) without presupposing something beyond reciprocity first. After all, justice is a virtue; one cannot have justice (as a virtue) before having morals (readiness for acquiring virtues) first. Every attempt at founding morals on the considerations of reciprocity is utilitarian, even if non-utilitarian philosophers do it. And utilitarianism runs the same risk as all merely cognitively based ethics do – it decentres morals and thereby deconstructs it.

If a philosophy starts with rules, it will also start with reciprocity; for ethical rules, or at least the most fundamental ethical rules, are rules of reciprocity. If one begins moral philosophy with the universal orientative principle (which is not a rule), one does not begin with reciprocity. But after having scrutinized the initial gesture, one soon arrives at the problem of reciprocity. Almost all rules of everyday ethics that guide human intercourse can be described in terms of reciprocity.

Practising reciprocity is giving and receiving. This sentence is on closer scrutiny a tautology, for what else can reciprocity be but giving and receiving? Where one party gives and the other does not receive, there is no relationship. Where one party gives and the other only receives, there is a relationship but no reciprocity. One of the most elementary ethical norms is that reciprocal relationships are preferable to non-reciprocal relationships. If you take something from someone, you should also give something to the same person.

One can give and receive in so many ways and forms that discussing them all would result in discussing practically everything. You can give and receive a piece of bread, advice, encouragement, a kiss, a promise, a kingdom, a kick, a wound, a bad time or a blow. In terms of the elementary norms of human intercourse, whatever you get, you return in kind – good for the good things, bad for the bad ones. There may be merit in failing to return the bad things (particularly) in cultures imprinted by some ethical religions, yet it is always a debit to fail to return a good one. A person who receives and does not give in kind is in debit. If that person is in debit for too long a time, he or she loses face. A person who received a good thing and returns a bad one, is considered to be a scoundrel in all cultures without exception (in an 'in-group' situation).

The different levels, modes and forms of giving–receiving are meticulously specified and refined in every known culture. They are sometimes also surrounded by rites and ceremonies. If you are familiar with the norms of giving and receiving down to the minutest details, and if you follow the norms meticulously (returning precisely what is required and how), then you match the yardstick of what is termed *equal*. But how can you equalize such absolutely different things as getting a piece of land and giving loyalty; receiving a piece of bread and saying 'God bless you' (giving a blessing); receiving a sum of money and providing the giver's nephew with a lucrative position? Quite obviously, it is not only in commodity exchange that quali- tatively different 'things' are quantified in the exchange. All acts of giving and receiving quantify the qualitatively different things, services, gestures. What you are *not* supposed to return is exactly the *same* thing that you have received. For example, what you give to your friend for her birthday could be anything, but certainly not the same thing you have received from her for your birthday. Many virtues and vices are crystallized out of the practices of reciprocity. Misers fail to give when they should; the ungrateful ones receive but do not repay or, what is worse, repay the good with bad. The generous lavishly give without expecting an equal return; the grateful ones give more than they receive or at least exactly that much. Honesty and dishonesty are also closely related to acts of giving and receiving. So is justice.

Reciprocity can be symmetric and asymmetric. Pre-modern societies were grounded in asymmetric reciprocity, whereas modern society is grounded on symmetric reciprocity. In the first case, inequality is constituted as the essence of the person, whereas in the second case, as the appearance of the person (that contradicts its essence). Aristotle described the pre-modern arrangement in the well-known remark that men are born masters and born slaves; and we could add that a few slaves were to become free men whereas free men could be enslaved (e.g. as prisoners of war). Rousseau described the modern arrangement with the succinct paradox: all men are born free; but they are everywhere in chains. This exclamation reads also as an injunction: become what you really are, namely free; that is, manifest your substance.

This radical turn-around in the basic social arrangement has not annulled traditional forms of reciprocity in giving and receiving, nor did it cancel traditional virtues such as gratitude, generosity or justice (or traditional vices, such as greed, miserliness, stinginess, injustice). The rules of reciprocity underwent the same transformation as the interpretations/explications of the universal principle of orientation. In modern times, rules of reciprocity have to include the quest for symmetricity. The quest for symmetricity does not make it normative that everyone give or receive in kind, for such a norm would cast out many forms of reciprocity at once. Furthermore, inequality remains, although it takes other forms, and as a result, equality expresses itself in all reciprocal relations though the proportional disproportionality of the substantive content of things given or received. The essential change took place on the level of role equalization. In modern society, at least as far as its model goes, no one is born into a place that prescribes ahead all the major roles one is going to play in the game of reciprocation throughout one's entire life. Nowadays roles can always be switched and reversed. The receiver of grants can become, in turn, the giver of grants, and after having been battered, a woman can go to court and make the man pay compensation. The most simple (and everyday) manifestation of this change is perceptible in the simplification (and equalization) of greetings and addresses. After all, greetings and addresses are the most elementary rules of giving/receiving/reciprocating in everyday life.

The primacy of the *arche* (master principle) of morals will be evident if we pay attention to that which is not permitted in the game of giving/receiving. First it is an ugly thing to break the chain of giving/receiving when it is up to us to reciprocate. This follows from the rules of the game. Yet there are several other things that are not permitted, which appear ugly and utterly wrong and have nothing to do with the rules of the game.

- It is always wrong to use the rules of reciprocation for instrumentalizing others.
- It is wrong if someone does something for another while having in mind the kind of thing, service or favour that she or he expects in return, or does it in

order to receive the thing she or he desires without disclosing this purpose to the receiver.

- It is wrong if someone asks a favour of someone whom she or he despises or vilifies.
- It is wrong if someone pretends feelings in order to make the other party inclined to do a service, a favour, or be willing to transfer things to him or her.
- It is wrong if the reciprocity offered for things received or services rendered is a pretence (genuine gratitude is legitimate reciprocity); it is wrong if one renders services or gives things *in order* to be reciprocated with feelings.

Certainly, everyone knows that these things are wrong. It even sounds ridiculous to make mention of them. But why is the game of reciprocity disqualified or judged ugly, and sometimes even wicked, in the former cases (and a few other ones)? The answer is obvious. It is not the game of giving/receiving/reciprocating that the ugly and wicked players infringe. They play the game so that they annul, disregard, immunize or positively infringe the *arche* of morals, that is, the universal orientative principle. They do not care for other human beings at all; they do not care whether they cause them suffering. This is why they instrumentalize others.

V

I started this article with Max Weber's diagnosis of modernity: there are many deities and a host of plural values in it. Each person chooses his or her own deity. Virtues are always related to values. Still, there remains the astonishing fact that no virtue pluralization follows from value pluralization. Needless to say, decisive shifts in abstract values accompany decisive shifts in the status of virtues and vices. The birth of modern society witnessed the most spectacular devaluation of a supposed eternal abstract value, that of social hierarchy, alias the natural, the best, the divine world order. Many a virtue went down with this value. However, all these developments did not result in the noticeable pluralization of virtues. One can now promote any value with constancy and courage; people choose one value or another; but to ask whether they choose constancy or courage is a ridiculous question. And to whatever value one may be committed, generosity is invariably a virtue and meanness invariably a vice.

Candour, truthfulness, trustworthiness and sincerity are equally age-old virtues; mutual understanding gets shipwrecked if truthfulness is wanting. The 'virtues of truthfulness', as I am going to call them, are 'two-way' virtues. As such, they are the most common in immediate (person-to-person) relationships, in particular, in personal attachments. There is no meaningful personal reciprocal attachment without the practice of these virtues. This is how they are directly related to the source of morals, the universal orientative principle. One can best care for other persons if one cares intensively, day-to-day, and in many ways, for at least a few human persons. This happens in personal attachments alone.

But if we want to describe what those 'virtues of truthfulness' actually require from us, or how these virtues are to be practised, difficulties will arise. The network or web of mini-practices in personal emotional attachments requires a kind of person-to-person hermeneutics; it is impossible to sum up the essence of those practices; to circumscribe them would require much space. It is far easier to enumerate the attitudes and the practices which are entirely incompatible with the virtues of truthfulness. Those virtues are absent: if one does not show what one is (or believes oneself to be); if one never discloses oneself to any human being, never tries to make oneself transparent to a single 'other'; if one habitually conceals the motives for one's actions and attitudes; if one acts or behaves with pretence (for reasons other than to avoid evil consequences); if one does not trust anyone; if one habitually suspects others and attributes bad motives and intentions to them; if one habitually withholds knowledge or information from others; if one makes promises without intending to keep them; if one habitually makes promises without considering whether or not one can keep them; if one discloses confidential information (for reasons other than avoiding evil consequences).

Let us recall Leibniz's chain of thought: acts are regarded as morally evil if (because) they cause physical evil. People may not be killed or mutilated, impoverished or made sick by the mere absence of the virtues of truthfulness (although they can be). But the most lasting, the most incurable, spiritual wounds are caused exactly as a result of this absence. The total absence of the virtues of truthfulness in one of the parties of an intimate human relationship, where the other party to the relationship assumes, expects, or takes their presence for granted, is totally devastating. A person who goes through such an experience can lose confidence, self-confidence and the ability to trust for life. Sometimes people cheat the feelings and confidence tricksters are normally not wicked, just self-serving, inconsiderate or indifferent.

Decent persons require courage when it comes to doing the right thing. Decent persons are the ones who raised the question of 'What is the right thing for me to do?' to be able to approximate the centre of their life. Let us assume that such a person has already discovered the right thing she should do, the right thing here and now. Then that person should just shut her eyes and let go of the rail. This particular act of decision, the act of courage, is unlike the pattern of 'finding out what the right thing is'; it is also unlike the 'existential choice pattern'. In and through a decision that person chooses not herself but some thing (the thing to do), and rational deliberation is suspended. That person begins to do the right thing while isolating herself from her past, and also from all the cognitive thought experiences concerning her future, for she acts no matter what the consequences of her actions may be for her own life. But first and foremost, she sets herself free from all determinations which lie in the past, and from everything she has achieved so far. Yet she does not isolate herself from the world and from the future (as it happens in an initial, existential choice); she rather turns towards both the world and her future passionately. She lets go of the rail in order to swim towards something. The gesture of moral courage is not identical with the gesture of self-sacrifice. In making a moral decision, in letting oneself go, one is aware of exactly what one leaves behind, but one cannot know what one is going to gain or lose in the future. After all, it was when he went after his father's donkeys that Saul won his kingdom.

Cowardice is not a moral transgression. And still, the greatest evils in life (moral evil, and physical evils caused by moral evil) could have been avoided through the exercises of simple courage. Dictators and tyrants owe their powers not to wickedness, but first and foremost to cowardice. And this is also true of the tyrants in the everyday life of civil society. Civic courage, the most courageous courage, cleans the way for the practice of all the other virtues.

To reflect on moral issues in contemporary everyday life may be spiritually unrewarding, because one undertakes to speak about something that everyone knows. But this modest work needs to be performed if for no other reason that mainstream philosophy is now sitting on the speculative high horse. It 'knows' that out of all the moral virtues and moral issues only justice has remained; it 'proves' that morals has become entirely relativized; it deduces moral norms from utility maximization or it ties them to rational discourse. It is this that philosophy deconstructs morals theoretically, and having done so, happily or unhappily buries the already mummified corpse. But morals cannot be deconstructed with merely cognitive means, for knowledge and morals are, at least in their origin, heterogeneous. Morals is absolute – it was, it is, and it remains. Perhaps, there will be a world without morals; but this world will also be without justice, though not necessarily without laws also. A world like this we cannot imagine, for it would be entirely different from ours. As long as ours lasts, philosophy will be able to account for the kind of morals that we still (and already) have, that is, what we practice – just by modestly following the traces of decent persons.

NOTES

1 The mediation of morals and cognition (freedom and nature) through reflective judgements (the beautiful and the teleology of nature) does not change the absolute centring of morals, but rather it brings nature closer to, and in harmony with, this centre.
2 Whether the foundation by gesture is a single event or whether the same event is repeated in every gesture, is a major interpretandum in moral philosophy.

3 Jacques Derrida has begun to explore matters in this spirit. See, e.g., 'The mystical foundation of Justice', *Cardozo Law Review*. See also Raimond Gaita's recently published book, *Good and Evil: An Absolute Conception*. My own books, *The Power of Shame* (London, Routledge & Kegan Paul, 1985), *General Ethics* (Oxford, Blackwell, 1988) and especially *Philosophy of Morals*, were committed to this standpoint.

Chapter 4

European rationality

Niklas Luhmann

I

However one judges the cultural situation of present-day world society, what appears as specifically modern has been shaped by European traditions. One may question on a structural level whether and how far the change from a primarily stratified to a primarily functional differentiation of society has been carried through in many regions. Nevertheless, the development in this direction came from Europe. On a semantic level one may have differing evaluations regarding the resistance of old cultures, their future, their capacity for renewal and self-assertion in the face of the demand that they become 'modern' in an European sense. However, only Europe has produced descriptions of the world and of society which take into account the experience of a radical structural transformation of society since the late Middle Ages.

The geographical label 'Europe' is of course a term of embarrassment. It gives the illusion of uniformity where at first sight only difference is visible. However, these are only superficial impressions and terms. In the following I shall therefore attempt to demonstrate the distinct unity of a European tradition by means of the theme of rationality. This is first of all a question of the unity of a historical–semantic development which accompanies the transition to modern society. This process provides its own commentary and oscillates between self-subversion (in phases under headings like critique, nihilism, postmodernism) and utopian renewal. But even this 'dissension' can be still comprehended as unity, that is to say, as the process of learning in relation to the uncomprehended phenomenon of modern society. And unity is understood as a distinct unity in the sense that it differs from whatever conceptions of rationality may exist today outside of Europe.

If we accept this self-estimation, which remains to be clarified, then it could be understood to amount to this – that European rationality differs from other comparable semantics through its use of distinctions. This can involve a working through of its own history, as for example in Hegel's logic and theory of history; or a multiplicity of other distinctions which divide rationality itself or distinguish it from other, equally justified world orient-ations such as feeling or the imagination. This leads us finally to the thesis that only from the perspective of a rationality conscious of difference can the difference between the European and other world semantics be observed and described. The admiration for China during the century of the Enlightenment would thus be no accident. And the reflective advantage of European rationality does not have to mean that reflexion on a self-declared superiority has to amount to a self-valuing Eurocentrism. The opposite is also thinkable, as admiration for the no longer attainable naivety and authenticity of world descriptions of other provenance.[1]

At this stage these are only vague suppositions. Much thus depends on whether it is possible to describe the specificity of a rationality oriented to distinctions in a conceptually more exact fashion.

II

The history of European rationality can be described as the history of the dissolution of a rationality continuum which had joined the observer in the world with the world. If the observer is seen as thinking creature (*animal rationale*), then what is involved is the convergence of thought and being. If he is seen as acting creature, then what is involved is the convergence of action and nature, that is, naturally given purposes. In any case the totality of things and the ends of movements (*téle*) are the bearers of what occurs in the world. The activity of intelligence according to Aristotelian–thomistic doctrine is directed to things (*ad rem*) – and ends there. And the possibility of comprehending what is and what occurs as visible order or of attributing it in Christian belief to the knowledge and will of the Creator allows this convergence to be declared good. *Ens et verum et bonum convertuntur*, as the doctrine of transcendentals stated.

This order, perhaps, already begins to dissolve in the nominalism of the late Middle Ages, certainly in the seventeenth century. Since the seventeenth century the talk of 'ontology' reveals the critical consciousness of the problem. Thought and being move apart, first of all in the form of parallel ontologies with the result that thought can confirm itself through true and through untrue thoughts: whether true or false, I think! Purposes are conceived as subject to choice with the result that motives or interests must be interrogated and nature is reduced to external parameters. The eighteenth-century faith in reason is already based on differences. The Enlightenment sees itself in a world in need of enlightenment. It irrationalizes everything which opposes it. Besides reason there is history, beside Newton Münch-hausen, beside rationality enjoyment, beside a modernity defined by labour, language and science the fantasy of Romanticism, which can present the unity of the world only as an imaginary backdrop – as the magic which presupposes that it is not believed. High-performance rationalities assume the title of rationality although they only cover partial phenomena and serve to orient only functional systems of society, e.g. economic rationality in the relation of means and ends or scientific rationality in the correct application of the laws of nature or legal rationality in decisions based on laws or on conceptionally ordered experience with precedents. Finally, different types of rationality are constructed – for instance, purposive rationality and value rationality – without even posing the question, on the basis of what understandings of rationality do *both* sides of this and similar distinctions deserve the title of rationality? This brings us to Max Weber and Jürgen Habermas. But here, too, the traditional distinction between subject and object or the distinction between the facticity of actions and normative claims is taken as the grounding schema for the posing of the problem. And rather than questioning this, a plurality of forms of rationality is accepted.

Since the nineteenth century we have become more and more accustomed to working with distinctions without posing the question of the unity of the distinction itself. The narrator stages the narration – whether of the novel or of world history – in which he no longer appears and, as we can see in the case of Hegel, can no longer appear.[2] Equally the physicist has no place in the 'universe automate'[3] of classical physics; physically he does not appear at all – neither as observer or as actor. Endless explicit distinctions like matter and mind, state and society, society and community, the individual and the collective, capital and labour are used as instruments of analysis with an option left open (or openly or hiddenly realized) for one of the sides. Politicized distinctions based on the programme of the French Revolution or the socialist movement employ the same style of hiding the question of unity. Holism becomes an intellectual option.[4] Rationality itself can be made the component of a distinction, whose other side must then be something irrational – for example enjoyment, fantasy, imagination.[5] But does the irrational perhaps then serve to protect an inadequate concept of rationality?[6]

At the end of our century one can speak quite generally of an 'erosion of the validity of former cultural oppositions' and correspondingly call for the move from 'what questions' to 'why questions'.[7] And then it is not only a question of what is distinguished but how we distinguish and who distinguishes. Certainly, to the degree that social reflexivity, empathy for others, consideration of their reactions, are built into decisions about action, this undermines the concept of a reason which could guarantee the unity and certainty of the world view.[8]

What happened to the observer? to the narrator? to the describer? to the person who uses distinctions in order to distinguish and designate something? The person, whom one could ask: why this way and not another way?

One possibility is to characterize him as an extra-worldly subject. However, that only leads to the question: who could observe him and how could he be observed if he does not appear in the world? Another possibility is to ignore him, because it is self-evident that all observers must observe in the same way – at any rate if their thought is to be true and their action rational. This leads to the celebrated but now hardly accepted congruence of reference, meaning and truth, whose last advocate was logical empiricism. It presupposes that the world is the same for all observers and that it is determinable (and not, for example: that insofar as it is determinable, it is in each case a different world for different observers, and insofar as it is the same world, it remains indeterminable). Perhaps the most significant attempt at a post-ontological construction of the observer could be described as the philosophy of immediacy. It reaches from the take off of Hegelian logic via the thesis of an immediate (unreflected) relationship to the self to vitalism,[9] philosophy of existence, Heidegger's analysis of Dasein, indeed even to the philosophy of the sign which seeks in the immediate understanding of the sign the only intermittently possible redemption from the endless reference to other signs.[10] Derrida's radical critique of the premiss of presence is the first attempt to overcome this tradition. Less ambitiously we could also ask whether immediacy is not already always mediated by the distinction immediate/mediate and whether it could be available to observation (experience, understanding) in any other way.

A further possibility, the laziest of all compromises, is to agree on 'pluralism'. This is the beginning and at the same time the evasion of the deconstruction of the distinction between subject and object. Each subject is conceded his own point of view, his own world view, his own interpretation – as, for example, the reader with Wolfgang Iser – but only within the frame permitted by the still 'objective' world, the text, etc.[11] In a similar fashion recent epistemology, bowing to inescapable insight, permits 'constructivism' – but not without a certain taking into account of reality.[12] Western rationalism in its final phase could hardly make its own weakness more evident.

Finally, once all this has become doubtful, we could arrive at the idea that the observer is not to be observed. The observer must designate what he observes, i.e. distinguish it from everything else which remains as 'unmarked space'. He himself disappears in the 'unmarked space'; or, in other words, he can only observe from this 'unmarked space' by distinguishing what he observes from everything else, including, that is, himself. And the same would apply if he designated himself as the object of his observation.

Or rather, this applies when observation has only a dual value logic at its disposal. In this case the two logical values at the disposal of the observer are already exhausted when he uses them to designate the one or the other side of the distinction. The logical possibilities of indicating the distinction itself and even more their user are lacking.[13] This means that distinctions as well as observers must be treated as simple objects which have to be distinguished by means of inexplicable distinctions. But if we want to observe and describe how a distinction is used as a distinction or how an observer *qua* observer designates the one and not the other side of a distinction (although he could do it differently), then we need a richly structured logical instrument. And this is not as yet, or only in an extremely formal sense, available.

Nevertheless, at the end of our century we can at least formulate the problem more precisely than before.[14] Historically we can see a clear correspondence between the traditional assumption of an ontologically describable world – with the aid of the distinction between being and non-being – and a merely dual value logic. It presupposes a society in which the differences between different descriptions of the world and of society have not become too great and can be bindingly arbitrated from uncontested standpoints, i.e. from the top or centre of the system. The rest is then corruption, error, blindness. Factually we can see that in the meantime possibilities have developed for which there is as yet no logic, indeed not even a recognized epistemology. What is involved are the possibilities of the observation of observers, possibilities of a second-order cybernetics.

If we abandon the assumption of parallel points of view on a common world, we must ask ourselves first of all whether anyone can act rationally at all if he is observed.[15] For the observer of the observer there has to be limitations on his manner of reaction which the first-order observer with rational ambitions can reckon with. Given this problem, rationality becomes dependent on institutional premises or on premises secured through negotiation, whose own rationality (meta-rationality) can hardly lie in the rationality which they make possible.

To this we must add far more radical problems which are tied up not only with the divergence of interests and goals but with the very structure of observation itself. An observer can observe another observer (who can be himself) with regard to what he sees and with regard to what he cannot see. Applied to the instruments of observation – i.e. to the distinctions used by an observer to designate what he observes – this leads to a differential theory of relativism. One can see what can be designated with certain distinctions which specify *both* sides (e.g. good/evil; more/less; before/after; manifest/latent). One does not see, in the context of distinguishing, what functions neither as the one nor the other side but as the excluded third. The observer is always the excluded third. He is the parasite of his observations in the sense intended by Michel Serres.[16] But exactly *that* is what another observer (a critic of ideology, a psychoanalyst, in short: a therapist) can in turn observe and designate – even if only as a further observer, who only sees what he sees, and does not see what he does not see. In this fashion we can thematize the harmful effects of rationality, the calamity precisely which results from rational calculation and best intentions; the rational fool[17] or, in Paul Valéry's words, the 'maliciousness of the man of reasons'.[18]

So far this interest in observing what an observer is *unable* to observe has not succeeded in gaining epistemological recognition. The so-called debate on the sociology of knowledge took place under the same premise as that which governed discussion in *Theaetetus*: that there can be only one truth, so that statements, which designate true statements as untrue, do not claim validity for two truths but can at best contribute to the elucidation of error. Psychoanalysis likewise has never been recognized as a theory of knowledge but at most as the science of a therapeutic practice. In a corresponding fashion 'relativism', 'historicism', etc., are deplored, and the 'postmodern' (however, in reality: modern) plurality of discourses, deconstructionism and 'anything goes' can only excite attention as 'gay science' and they stylize themselves accordingly. All the same, these forms of presentation have become by now so widespread that one is entitled to ask whether the problem lies not rather on the side of a theory of knowledge and its instruments which still regard such phenomena as deviant.

III

Perhaps there are epistemic obstacles which stand in the way of an advance.[19] The following assumptions could belong to them:

(1) that *cognition* is rational in itself;
(2) that *learning* improves and does not worsen the state of the learning system and its adaption to the environment;
(3) that more *communication* and socially reflected communication (for instance, in the broad context of group dynamics) contributes to agreement instead of having the opposite effect;
(4) that rationality can be comprehended in the form of a *programme* – for example, as maximization of utility or as rational agreement.

The familiar problem of social aggregation of individual preferences already makes such theses questionable. The same applies when one considers the narrow conditions of near-decomposability or, in more recent terminology, of the 'reconstructability' of systems.[20] It may be that a still undeveloped understanding of rationality binds us to such premises. But what are we to do if the discrepancy in relation to modern social structures leads to more and more disappointments with these premises?

If cognition, learning, communication in each case operate with distinctions, consist, that is, in our terminology in observation, it could be helpful to enquire into the rationality specifically of dealing with distinctions. Our starting point accordingly is not a specific programme form (see (4) above) for which no further grounds can be adduced as evidence, but the switching of observation onto a second-order level.[21]

The analysis begins by returning again to the old European rationality continuum, which we characterized with reference to two distinctions: the concordance of thought and being and the concordance of action and nature. As long as the world is presupposed as order, as Kósmos, as creation, as harmony, attention is directed to the concordance and its possible failure which is then to be treated as error or imperfection. Thought and action are then each the object of a dual value logic which observes its object with the aid of the distinction between a positive and a negative value. If we then direct our attention to the distinction between thought and being or between action and nature – a distinction which is made for convergence (and 'made for convergence' means that it *cannot* be a question of the distinction between a positive and a negative value) – then something strange becomes apparent. In order to achieve convergence with *being*, thought must itself *be*. It cannot allow itself to be dissipated into the pure self-reference of an extra-worldly subject, it must allow itself to be conditioned. And action, in order to achieve convergence with *nature*, must itself be *nature*, that is, it must realize its own nature and not only the will, which wills whatever it will. Thought and action are the side of these guiding distinctions which refers to human beings, they are privileged over the other side, i.e. they were themselves what they had to distinguish themselves from. In spite of all the emphasis on the unity of the world as nature or as creation, in spite of all the theories which sought to realize this – i.e. theories of the representation of being in thought or of the imitation of nature in artistic action – the old European concept of the world contained a 'symmetry break'. The observer occupied a privileged position. The rationality continuism was conceived asymmetrically. The favoured position, however, which contains itself and its opposite, was that of the human being engaged in the construction of the world. The old European tradition was thus right in understanding itself as 'humanist'.

This can also be reconstructed from a systems-theoretical perspective. As we know, symmetry losses are regarded in contemporary systems theory as conditions of the evolutionary construction of complex system structures.[22] In terms of a theory of distinction this means that the distinction must recur in what is distinguished, but only on the one side and not the other. The distinction reappears in the distinction. In the conceptuality of George Spencer Brown's calculus of form it executes a re-entry of the form in the form.[23]

Recent semiotics finds itself in exactly the same situation. It is based on the distinction between sign and signified. But since Saussure semiotics also knows that this distinction has no external reference and only describes the functioning of language, the processing of distinctions. Does that mean that we must accept an arbitrary rhetorical use of signs devoid of reference? Or does this suggest that precisely the distinction between sign and signified is not arbitrary but must be handled with the necessary redundancies and according to the measure of tradition?[24] But if this is the case then we must be able to *designate* the unity of this distinction as neither temporally nor objectively arbitrary in its use. This gives the, by now, familiar form of the definition of the sign as the difference between sign and signified. That is to say, the sign would also be a distinction which recurs in itself. [25] And this has led in the meantime to the awareness of the self-critical, self-deconstructive potential of a 'second semiotics', which is obliged to apply its guiding distinction to itself if it is to be able to designate its own form.[26]

These are astonishing, puzzling findings which dissolve all the categories with which tradition with its ontological assumptions had worked, because the categories are now read as distinctions.[27] Thought, which must distinguish itself from being in order to observe and designate it, is itself the distinction between thought and being. It 'is' 'thought'. And action, which confronts nature with a sequence which would not have occurred without the intervention of an action (that is, strives for deviation) itself produces the distinction between action and nature. It could well be that the core problem of European rationality is hidden in this figure of the re-entry of the form in the form, and that this figure indicates the reason why the distinction on its re-entry side had to become reflexive and thus unstable, finally bringing forth the absolute configurations of thought and will through which the European semantics of the subject completed the break with tradition and *demonstrated to itself at the same time that it does not work.*

But what exactly went wrong?

Perhaps it is only the humanism of this tradition, its tie to anthropological concepts, which cannot tolerate the impulse of re-entry. Perhaps thought and action are not suited to tolerate the reappearance in themselves of what they had to distinguish from themselves. Perhaps it is only the intensification of anthropological individualism since the eighteenth century which has made it seem puzzling how action can be rational if one has to presuppose that others follow the same rule, when the infraction of the rule must be rational for them.[28] And perhaps it is only the dwindling plausibility of humanist descriptions of the world and society which has led us into these straits. Perhaps it is only man with his presumption of being the subject of the world who has exploded – leaving behind billions of concrete individuals who, as such, can once again be taken seriously. And perhaps that was the last external demand on man that he emancipate himself; which presupposes that he is seen as a slave *and not in his individuality.*

Let us look first of all at the calculus of form from which we have taken the figure of re-entry. Spencer Brown uses a single operator, the mark (which allows the integration of arithmetic and algebra). It indicates the operative unity of distinction and indication, i.e. the unity of a distinction in which the distinction itself occupies one side. This, however, is introduced only by the argument: 'We take as given the idea of distinction and the idea of indication, and that we cannot make an indication without drawing a distinction.'[29] Only at the end of the calculus is the concept of re-entry formulated, which also includes this beginning. The calculus thus models an operatively closed system, in which a latent re-entry is transformed into an open re-entry without the re-entry itself becoming an object of the calculus either at the beginning or at the end. For beginning and end are distinctions which cannot be distinguished in the beginning and ending system – any more than the universality of the applicability and the elementarity of the operations.[30] Nothing more is involved than the self-explication of distinction in the construction of complexity. And distinction is 'perfect continence', thus corresponding to the closure of the system. There is no outside, no external dependence, no carrying world – other than as components of the distinction between inside and outside. The marginalization of both re-entries seems to serve the purpose of keeping the calculus itself free of paradox while yet recognizing that all distinctions run up against paradoxes as soon as the symmetrical exchangeability of both sides (or the accessibility of each side from its other side) is broken by a re-entry on one of the two sides.

These considerations gain in concreteness if they are explicated with the aid of systems-theoretical conceptuality. Recent systems theory eschews holisms of every kind, including the schema of the distinction between the whole and the part, that is, forms of re-entry which must assume that the parts represent the whole or that they are determined by 'holograms', through which the whole dovetails into the parts. Instead, system theory starts from the distinction system and environment. Thus it does not describe particular objects called systems but orients its observation of the world to a particular (and no other) distinction – precisely that between system and environment.[31] This calls for consistently 'autological' concepts, since the observer must also recognize himself as a system-in-the-environment as long as he carries out observations and connects them recursively. The narrator appears himself in what he narrates. He is observable as an observer. He constitutes himself in his own field – and thereby necessarily in the mode of contingency, that is, with an awareness of other possibilities.

The form of re-entry also follows this theory design. It applies only to the system side, not to the environment side, of the initial distinction and describes the re-entry of the distinction between system and environment in the system. It thus takes the form of the distinction between self-reference and external reference, presuming in the process that it is clear for every system what the difference between 'self-' and 'external' refers to – i.e. the system itself. If necessary, re-entry can be repeated within the distinction between self-reference and external reference. The 'self' then determines itself as a second-order observer, who observes how he himself divides the world by means of the schema self-reference and external reference. The consequence of this is, on the one hand, a 'constructivist' world view, in which the unity of the world is no longer congruent with its determinability via observation based on distinctions; and on the other hand the acceptance of the certainty that every observation in the world makes the world visible – and invisible.

The observation of the operations which accomplish first- or second-order re-entry amounts to the observation of the production and unfolding of a paradox. The outside is only accessible inside. Observation observes the operation of observation; it observes itself as object and as distinction or – if we take the images of Romanticism – as the double (*Doppelgänger*) or as the asymmetry of the mask, in the mirror, from inside and from outside,[32] but always by means of its own operations, i.e. in a highly individual fashion. Its mathematical presentation would require an 'imaginary space', invented solely for this purpose. Certainly, it would not suffice to evade the problem through a 'hierarchy of types', which accomplishes nothing more than a veiling of the paradox with the invention to this end of a distinction between 'levels'.

In this world of magic and irony, of imagination and mathematics, of schizophrenia and individualization, is it possible to look for rationality through observing oneself as observer? Certainly not, if you think that this will enable you to describe the world as it really is and then to communicate to others how they are to think and act correctly. No concept of rationality based on a differential logic will ever lead us back to this position of unity and authority. Never again reason! But one could arrive at the idea that the rule 'observe the observer', together with the development of the appropriate formal instruments, points the way out of the sheer resignation induced by obsolete ideas.

Then one is able to observe what other observers cannot observe, and one can observe that oneself is observed in the same fashion. Formally this can be attributed to a self-referential form.[33] An observer can thus observe how a system produces paradoxes through the distinctions it uses; and which distinctions it then uses in order to 'unfold' these paradoxes, i.e. to decompose them into distinguishable identities and thereby to dissolve them.[34] In other words, there are always distinctions with which a system identifies, because it makes *their* paradox invisible in order to be able to avoid the paradoxes of *other* distinctions.[35] This condition reproduces Spencer Brown's calculus of form with its initial command: draw a distinction, where distinction means the unity of the distinction between distinction and indication, which has already carried out its re-entry without being able to observe it.

IV

These considerations can be condensed into a concept of system rationality based on a theory of difference.[36] Its starting point would be that a system *excludes* itself *operatively* from the environment and *includes* itself in it by means of *observation*. The system does this by making the basis of its own observations its difference to the environment *qua* distinction between self-reference and external reference. What this means is that through differentiation the system becomes as good as completely indifferent in relation to what occurs in the environment; this indifference is used, however, as a shield in order to construct its own complexity, which then can be highly sensitive to environmental irritations insofar as they are registered internally and in the form of information. Rationality could then mean: the reflexion of the unity of the difference between system and environment in the system. But this cannot be carried out dialectically as sublation of the difference, and above all not as the pointer to a more comprehensive system, a 'higher' system, an 'ecosystem'. This reach for the whole was coupled traditionally with conceptions of domination. Both fail to engage with the structural realities of modern society. What this leaves is the possibility that individual autopoiesis be carried on under these conditions of ever greater improbability.

What, however, is specifically European about this? What does this have to do with the specifically modern structures of a world society which, starting from Europe, has grown into a global system of communication?

First of all some demarcations are called for in relation to what this *cannot* mean. Not intended, obviously, is the unperturbed continuation of a rational *télos* of European history, as Husserl envisaged in his late work.[37] Not intended is the continuation of a standpoint of reason from which what does not correspond to it can be characterized as 'irrational'; for the distinction rational/irrational is only a distinction, whose use and for what purpose must be observed. Not intended are 'cultural comparisons' of any kind which either offer only juxtapositions or presuppose an external standpoint, which does not exist. Not intended, finally, are the fashionable fusions of mysticism and rationality with the offer of a confusion of a Far Eastern and European repertoire of ideas.[38] We do not have to exclude apodictically the return to such figures but remain explicitly within the self-distinguishing, dissolving and reconstructing tradition of the European understanding of rationality.

If, socialized in this tradition, one reads texts on the world, society, politics, etc., sent by Chinese or Indian colleagues, one finds that they work categorically. That is to say: they use concepts (just as the European tradition once used categories) in order to divide up reality. The concepts distinguish what they indicate (or so it appears to us) but they do not ground why these and other distinctions are chosen. Western ideas may enter into the conceptuality or its translation but it is employed from the perspective of a first-order observer – as if it were capable of indicating something, which is as it is indicated. Generalizations can get dissipated into ambiguities, perhaps into the contradictory. But this is not noticed or at least not felt to be disturbing, and it has no effect on the intention to describe the world or some of its states immediately.

Nevertheless, we must not make things too easy for ourselves. This tradition is also familiar with self-referential knowledge just as it is familiar with self-referential signs, i.e. symbols. The forms of self-referential knowledge are communicated as wisdom.[39] Wisdom is precisely what arises if knowledge of knowledge, i.e. self-referential knowledge, develops on the level of first-order observation and does not go beyond this level. The origins may well have lain in the practice of divination both in the Near East and in China; further, in their written textualization and in reflexion on failures in the semantic primary material. We cannot, however, exclude other impulses. At any rate the result is bodies of knowledge which (like proverbs) are only practicable in relation to situations. As a kind of compensation for this weakness they oblige the wise men themselves to follow their own wisdom in their conduct of life.[40]

Efforts to eliminate inconsistencies (to systematize) are lacking because the wise man observes himself, tests his wisdom on himself and does not try to harmonize with the views of others or with other possible views of his own. And if this is correct, then we can deduce conversely that systematizations correlate with the transition to second-order observation. Both in the law and in theology wisdom comes to be renounced once inconsistencies become apparent on the basis of the already existing wealth of written texts and give cause to problematize 'hermeneutically' (as it will be called) the manner of observation, while presupposing the constancy of the texts in question. Transcendental philosophy, and with it the figure of the autonomous subject, was perhaps the last European attempt to assure, through the recourse to individual subjectivity and its states of consciousness, an order of knowledge which is cognitively, ethically and aesthetically binding.

Printing in a parallel fashion facilitated the transition to a much more trivial technique of knowledge compared with wisdom, which is now completely based on writing and already prepares for second-order observation. The typical format of Western 'scientific papers' requires that one takes the state of research as starting point.[41] This also saves the necessity of further-reaching reflexion. It is only necessary to offer something new in relation to what is already given in publications. A pedantry touching on scurrility, supervised by editors and referees, takes the place of all reflexion. This, too, can only be practised as first-order observation. Maturana would say: as observation of one's own niche in its interaction with the system.[42] However, the form is chosen so that it is compatible with the contingency of all world descriptions; it draws its justification solely from the momentary state of research, from a historical situation which it, itself, changes. Without being planned in this way, this quite modest text in itself realizes a description of the world, which changes what it describes through its description. It accomplishes the autopoiesis of the scientific system and through it that of the societal system without needing to reflect this in accomplishing the operation. Another level is responsible for reflexion and distinguishes itself as theory of science (or more comprehensively: as theory of knowledge) from immediate practical research and explicates in relation to the momentary state of research what innovations this research offers research.[43] Philosophy has thus become since Hegel its own history, but goes beyond Hegel because this history is that of an observer who can judge it differently and propose other distinctions.

One publishes – not in order to instruct but in order to be observed. The system of the sciences has differentiated itself on a level of second-order observation. The same applies to the market-mediated economic system[44], to politics oriented to 'public opinion'[45], to art[46], indeed presumably to all functionally differentiated systems. And functional systems, not society as a unity, are the operative executors of the rationality of modern society. Our expectations of rationality must therefore accord with system formations which need to secure their autopoiesis not only in part but in fact primarily on the level of second-order observation – for instance, the outbidding rationality of economics and politics (called competition) or the ongoing observation of the observers according to the schema old/new in science and art.

It has been noted that these conditions still mean that the historical situation prescribes to rationalism its problems, i.e. that rationalism still proceeds in a traditionalistic way even though it owes its origins in the seventeenth and eighteenth centuries to the rejection of traditional ties and still seeks to profile itself through the critique of traditionalism. In relation to its own posing of problems rationalism proceeds blindly.[47] This cannot be denied and cannot be overcome even on the level of second-order observation. Rather the second-order observer makes observation, and thereby himself, aware of this problem. One cannot see what one cannot see, but perhaps one can at least see that one cannot see what one cannot see.

A theory which incorporates these considerations can be a theory of *society*. It must, however, anchor itself in the scientific system and accept that it is only a *theory* of society. It will produce a constructivist understanding of reality which takes into account that first-order observation deals not with constructions but with objects. It will no longer recognize any binding representations, rather it will find itself – and not only others – in a polycontexturally constituted world. It will have to make the painful sacrifice of self–interest the more it reflects on its own contexturality, compensated by the certainty (included in the price) that there are other points of departure for rationality and for second-order observation.

But this constructivist, polycontextural concept of rationality must also be part of a distinction, otherwise it could not be described. It is usual to draw this distinction historically, that is, in comparison to old Europe or to other cultures of the old world. This, however, leaves the question which concerns us – the self-understanding of modernity – completely open and leads at best to the already stale slogan of 'postmodernity'. Nevertheless, perhaps it is possible to arrive at more precise conceptions of the 'other side of rationality' – for instance, those that could be indicated by the semantics of paradox, of imaginary space, of the blind spot of all observation, of the self-parasitical parasite, of chance or of chaos, of re-entry or the necessity of externalization with reference to an 'unmarked state'. These would then be conceptions which owe their contours exclusively to the precision with which rationality is fixed and which amount in the last instance to an indirect self-designation of the rational. But also the other way round: the very understandability of the world then becomes un-understandable and the amazement at the functioning of technology increases the more one knows how it functions.

V

We come back in conclusion to questions of form, and that means to the question: how does rationality distinguishes itself? It should be clear that this is not a question of a Cartesian self-confirmation of rationality, which, once secured, can use itself as the point of departure for distinctions (e.g. between true and untrue). On the contrary, the self-confirmation of rationality already presupposes a distinction, otherwise it could not make itself its own theme. However, we cannot presuppose a distinction – this was the result of our analyses in section II – without raising the question: which observer uses it, with what restrictions on selection typical for him, with what blind spot, and to what end? There is no distinction which could exempt itself from such a second-order observation, not even Spencer Brown's distinction between distinction and indication.

But this does not have to mean that the last refuge of a forced abandonment of fixed pre-givens is the regret for their loss. It also does not have to mean that we celebrate the outcome as the victory of rhetoric over ontology and declare that sickness, now that it has become universal, is health.[48] This may point in the right direction, but what is lacking is the reflexion of form; and only this could justify the continuing claim to the title of rationality instead of simply speaking of the 'postrational' in order to hide the embarrassment.[49]

The precondition of every rationality is a distinction which re-enters itself. We illustrated this in the case of Spencer Brown's calculus of form (distinction/indication), with the example of systems theory (system/environment) and with the distinction between sign and signified, choosing these examples in order to comprehend the most complex and familiar terrains of modern intellectuality (mathematics, systems theory, semiotics) with all their traditionally cultivated uncertainties. Once one has grasped this self-implicating form it is easy to find further examples – for instance, the distinction between observation and operation, which implies that observation is itself an operation and that this distinction is itself an instrument of observation; or the distinction between medium and form, which can only assert itself as form in a medium.[50]

What is common to all these instances is not only the form of the re-entry of the distinction in the distinction but also an implicit reference to the historical context in which they are formulated: the experience of modern society. They negate explicitly an orientation to ontological pre-givens, including those of transcendental philosophy. They seek their ultimate guiding principle in difference and consequently regard every search for unity – even if it is within the atoms of modern physics[51] – as the (hopeless) longing to return to the state of nature or even to paradise.[52] They observe with the distance of a second-order observer those who attempt this and already know that they cannot succeed.

But can the form of re-entry of the distinction in the distinction claim to be rational only because it makes this uncoupling possible? Is that not merely a historical specification which registers no more than the failure of all concepts of rationality which are dependent on reference? The form guarantees closure, 'perfect continence', to quote Spencer Brown again.[53] It owes this closure, however, to an initially hidden paradox which needs to be brought into the open, the paradox that the distinction which re-enters itself is the same and not the same. Evidently it symbolizes (but can we say 'symbolizes'?) the paradox of the world. It stops the observer before he undertakes to state something about the world, which could only have the result that the world withdraws before the statement. The paradox of form, seen in this light, would be a representation of the world in the mode of unobservability – but with the demand that the paradox be dissolved through the appropriate distinction, i.e. that the paradox be 'unfolded' through the identification of differences. The other side of the form of rationality, which must be excluded (although it could be indicated), is the paradox of form.

But even indications like 'world' or 'paradox' are only (but do we have to say 'only'? and what is missing if we say 'only'?) components of a distinction. The dependence of indicating on distinguishing would seem to be that problem which has directed the European development towards second-order observation. If we formulate the problem in this fashion it becomes apparent that Far Eastern mysticism (does this European word fit at all?) reacts differently, that is to say, with a *direct rejection of distinguishing*, in especially drastic form in Zen Buddhism's communicative practice with the *koan*.[54] The expectation, inherent in a question, of a specific answer, which *qua* indication of something always actualizes a distinction and must include an other side, is destroyed as expectation – verbally or also physically. This does not amount to a paradox, whose specific form of a to-and-fro without issue is itself, in turn, a form which has an other side, namely the need to unfold the paradox through its conversion into practicable distinctions (the prototype: distinction of types or levels). Rather, the experience is directly related to the absence of difference, and this from the perspective of a first-order observer. Whatever is achieved in this fashion, it is not social elaboration of differences but liberation from the necessity of distinguishing. Confronted with foreign cultures, Europeans are accustomed to transform the un-understandable into the understandable. Global communication has compelled this, especially since the discovery of the Americas which coincided with the invention of printing. To this end we have experts: ethnologists, orientalists, students of comparative religion, psychoanalysts. And we are also accustomed as readers of novels and critiques of ideology to see that others do not see what they do not see. But if we want to hold on to the old world-relation of the concept of rationality rather than follow its modern derangements, then rationality could be regained if we round off those accustomed habits with an autological conclusion, i.e. apply them to their users and thus posit them universally. Then it would be a question of understanding that one does not understand what one does not understand, and of trying out semantics which come to terms with this.

Traditionally this was designated religion. But if this concept is to be retained, then the corresponding expectations will have to be changed. Instead of signalling a potential for certainty, it will involve a potential for uncertainty. Instead of attachment, a potential for freedom: the place of the arbitrary, which nowhere has any place, the place of the imagination.

Translated by David Roberts

NOTES

1 One aspect of this need for (recreatable) authenticity is examined by Dean MacDonnell, 'Staged Authenticity: Arrangements of Social Space in Tourist Settings', *American Journal of Sociology* 79 (1973), pp. 589–603. Artistic attempts at authenticity, spontaneous expression, non-reflexion of being observed, happenings, performances, installations, etc., can also be included here. Cf., for instance, the presentations by Frederick Bunsen in Niklas Luhmann, Frederick D. Bunsen and Dirk Baecker, *Unbeobachtbare Welt: Über Kunst und Architektur* (Bielefeld, 1990), pp. 46ff.

2 See Dietrich Schwanitz, 'Rhetorik, Roman und die inneren Grenzen der Kommunikation', *Rhetorik* 9 (1990), pp. 52–67. The parody of the reappearance of the narrator in the text of *Tristram Shandy* was a possibility which Jean Paul above all did not wish to dispense with – to the disadvantage of the narrative flow of the novel or with the consequence of unfinishability as in *Die unsichtbare Loge*.

3 Thus Ilya Prigogine, 'La lecture du complexe', *Le genre humain* 7/8 (1983), pp. 221–233 (233). For a more detailed critique of this classical conception of the world without physicists, Ilya Prigogine and Isabelle Stengers, *La nouvelle alliance* (Paris, 1979).

4 An option which is then usually recommended as the better. See, as example, Friederich Schlegel, 'Signatur des Zeitalters' (1823) in Wolfdietrich Rach (ed.), *Dichtungen und Aufsätze* (Munich, 1984), pp. 593–728.

5 These are themes which interest Michel Maffesoli, *L'ombre de Dionysus. Contribution à une sociologie de l'orgie* (Paris, 1982) and *La connaissance ordinaire: Précis de sociologie compréhensive* (Paris, 1985).

6 'Irrationality tends to be invoked to protect the too narrow definition of rationality' observes Mary Douglas, *Risk Acceptability According to the Social Sciences* (New York, 1985), p. 3.

7 Cf., in the context of an interdisciplinary semiotics, Dean MacCannell and Juliet F. MacCannell, *The Time of the Sign: A Semiotic Interpretation of Modern Culture* (Bloomington, 1982); the quotation, p. 18.

8 '. . . the reflexivity of modernity actually subverts reason, at any rate where reason is understood as the gaining of certain knowledge', as Anthony Giddens also states. *The Consequences of Modernity* (Stanford, 1990), p. 39.

9 Vitalism cannot use the distinction life/death if it wants to present the immediacy of the relation of being but must seek other counter-concepts such as mechanics, system or even rationality.

10 Thus Josef Simon, *Philosophie des Zeichens* (Berlin, 1989).

11 See here Stanley Fish, 'Why No One's Afraid of Wolfgang Iser' in Fish, *Doing What Comes Naturally: Change, Rhetoric, and the Practice of Theory in Literary and Legal Studies* (Oxford, 1989), pp. 68–86.

12 For one of many examples, see Mary Hesse, *Revolutions and Reconstructions in the Philosophy of Science* (Brighton, 1980).

13 This is the theme of Elena Esposito, *L'operazione di osservazione: Costruttivismo e teoria dei sistemi sociali* (Milan, 1992).

14 See George Spencer Brown, *Laws of Form* (Reprint, New York, 1979); Heinz von Foerster, *Observing Systems* (Seaside, Cal., 1981); Gotthard Günther, *Beiträge zur Grundlegung einer operationsfähigen Dialektik*, 3 vols (Hamburg, 1976–1980).

15 Cf. on this much debated problem, Nigel Howard, *Paradoxes of Rationality: Theory of Metagames and Political Behaviour* (Cambridge, Mass., 1971).

16 *Le parasite* (Paris, 1980).

17 This Amartya K. Sen, 'Rational Fools', *Philosophy and Public Affairs* 6 (1976–77), pp. 317–344.

18 From 'Mélange', *Oeuvres*, vol. I (Paris, 1957), p. 329.

19 The concept of epistemological obstacles comes from Gaston Bachelard, *La formation scientifique: Contribution à une psychanalyse de la connaissance objective* (1938) (Reprint, Paris, 1947), pp. 13ff.

20 See here vol. 4, 1 (1990) of *Revue internationale de systémique*.

21 An objection to this conception of rationality may also be seen in that it has produced two different versions: utility maximization and rational understanding, between which there is no bridge.

22 For irreversibility as the breaking of symmetry between past and future, see Ilya Prigogine, *Vom Sein zum Werden: Zeit und Komplexität in den Naturwissenschaften*; Prigogine, 'Order out of Chaos' in Paisley Livingston (ed.), *Disorder and Order. Proceedings of the Stanford International Symposium 1981* (Saratoga, 1984), pp. 41–60.

23 See *Laws of Form* (1979), pp. 56ff, 69ff. The implications of this concept are not fully apparent in Spencer Brown. Further applications become possible when one sees that self-reference is dependent on distinction and being able to distinguish dependent on self-reference. Then one can show that the copying of the form in the form is the basis of the phenomena of symmetry and of repetition and thus of every directed infinity if the circular process is repeated often enough so that the sequences lose their distinguishability. See Louis H. Kauffmann, 'Self-reference and recursive forms', *Journal of Social and Biological Structures* 10 (1987), pp. 53–72.

24 See the objections to Saussure in Roman Jakobsen. 'Zeichen und System der Sprache' (1962), reprinted in Jakobsen, *Semiotik. Ausgewählte Texte* (Frankfurt, 1988), pp. 427–436.

25 This can be avoided in formulation if the sign is defined as the distinction between the signifier and signified, but this does not solve the problem, it only makes it invisible.

26 See Dean MacCannell and Juliet F. MacCannell, *The Time of the Sign*. Similarly also Julia Kristeva, *Semiotikè: Recherches pour une sémanalyse* (Paris, 1969), pp. 19, 21ff, 278, with the goal of going beyond without abandoning the structue of the sign in the direction of its operative practice by means of 'sémanalyse'.

27 That this has led to attempts at restitution – with the argument: this only shows that we cannot do without metaphysics – is hardly surprising. See, for the case of the 'sign', Josef Simon, *Philosophie des Zeichens*, or, for the return to transcendental philosophy, Gerhard Schönrich, *Zeichenhandeln: Untersuchungen zum Begriff einer semiotischen Vernunft im Ausgang von Ch. S. Peirce* (Frankfurt, 1990).

28 This is the point at which we find the embarrassed theories of a natural social instinct, of a natural 'sympathy', of a coordinated following of rules secured by 'imagination', to which Hutcheson, Hume or Smith look for help. It is another example of the efforts which are required to protect an initially inadequate concept of rationality.

29 *Laws of Form*, 1.
30 Cf. also Joseph Goguen and Francisco Varela, 'Systems and Distinction: Duality and Complementarity', *Int. Journal of General Systems* 5 (1979), pp. 31–43; Ranulph Glanville and Francisco Varela, 'Your Inside is Out and Your Outside is In (Beatles 1968)' in G. E. Lasker (ed.), *Applied Systems and Cybernetics*, II (New York, 1981), pp. 638–641.
31 For a more detailed account, Niklas Luhmann, *Sociale Systeme: Grundriß einer allgemeinen Theorie* (Frankfurt, 1984), pp. 15ff.
32 Read, for example, E.T.A. Hoffmann's *Princess Brambilla*. Cf. also Winfried Menninghaus, *Unendliche Verdoppelung: Die frühromantische Grundlegung der Kunsttheorie im Begriff absoluter Selbstreflexion* (Frankfurt, 1987).
33 See following Spencer Brown, Jacques Miermont, 'Les conditions formelles de l' état autonome', *Revue internationale de systémique* 3 (1989), pp. 295–314, esp. 303ff.
34 That this is the usual procedure of philosophical systems is shown by Nicholas Rescher, *The Strife of Systems: An Essay on the Grounds and Implications of Philosophical Diversity* (Pittsburgh, 1985).
35 For the application to legal history, cf. Niklas Luhmann, 'The Third Question: The Creative Use of Paradoxes in Law and Legal History', *Journal of Law and Society* 15 (1988), pp. 153–165.
36 This is not meant to exclude more abstract concepts of rationality based on the same approach – e.g. a concept of rationality of form which designates and delimits completely abstractly the re-entry of the form in the form.
37 See esp. Edmund Husserl, *Die Krisis der europäischen Wissenschaften und die transzendentale Phänomenologie* (The Hague, 1954). It must be added that one can readily understand and appreciate the attractiveness of this idea at the time of the territorial expansion of fascism and in the immediate postwar period.
38 For a critique it is sufficient to refer to Henri Atlan, *A tort et à raison: Intercritique de la science et du mythe* (Paris, 1986).
39 See the stimulating text of Alois Hahn, 'Zur Soziologie der Weisheit' in Aleida Assmann (ed.), *Weisheit: Archäologie der literarischen Kommunikation*, III (Munich, 1991), pp. 47–57. I agree with these analyses in many respects and would add only the (for me decisive) distinction between first- and second-order observation and thus a stronger historization.
40 See in the European tradition for instance the commandment of purity in Plato's *Cratylos* 396E-397 as the precondition for insight into the connection between things and words.
41 On the history of this form as a result of printing and the differentiation of science, cf. Charles Bazerman, *Shaping Written knowledge: The Genre and the Activity of the Experimental Article in Science* (Madison, 1988).
42 Cf. Humberto R. Maturana, *Erkennen: Die Organisation und Verkörperung von Wirklichkeit* (Braunschweig, 1982), pp. 35ff.
43 And not by chance mainly in the form of journal articles. One of the major examples of this century is Willard van O. Quine, 'The Two Dogmas of Empiricism', reprinted in Quine, *From a Logical Point of View*, 2nd edn (Cambridge, Mass., 1961), pp. 20–46.
44 See Dirk Baecker, *Information und Risiko in der Marktwirtschaft* (Frankfurt, 1988).
45 See Niklas Luhmann, 'Gesellschaftliche Komplexität und öffentliche Meinung' in Luhmann, *Soziologische Aufklärung*, vol. 5 (Opladen, 1990), pp. 170–182.
46 See Niklas Luhmann, 'Weltkunst' in Luhmann, Bunsen and Baecker, *Unbeobachtbare Welt*.
47 Thus Terry Winograd and Fernando Flores, *Understanding Computers and*

Cognition: A New Foundation for Design (Reading, Mass., 1987), esp. p. 77: '. . . the rationalistic tradition . . . tends to grant problems some kind of objective existence, failing to take account of the blindness inherent in the way problems are formulated'. Cf. also pp. 97ff. Similarly, Klaus Peter Japp, 'Das Risiko der Rationalität für technisch-ökologische Systeme' in Jost Halfmann and Klaus Peter Japp (eds), *Riskante Entscheidungen und Katastrophenpotentiale* (Opladen, 1990), pp. 34–60, sees 'in the inbuilt incompetence to take into account nonrational effects of rational decisions' (51) the risk in the preference for rational decisions.

48 This is how I (I!) interpret (interpret!) Stanley Fish, *Doing What Comes Naturally*.

49 E.g. MacCannell and MacCannell, *The Time of the Sign*, p. 121, for a very relevant observation: 'The *postrational* perspective differs from the rational by being that position that cannot honour absolutely the fundamental claims that Reason makes as to the necessity of its divisions; it knows then to be arbitrary.'

50 The point of departure for this unfamiliar conceptuality is Fritz Heider, 'Ding und Medium', *Symposion* 1 (1926), pp. 109–157. Cf. also Niklas Luhmann, 'Das Medium der Kunst', *Delfin* 4 (1986), pp. 6–15 and 'The Medium of Art', *Thesis Eleven* 18/19 (1987/88), pp. 101–113.

51 Here concretely: David Bohm. See for instance 'Fragmentierung und Ganzheit' in Hans-Peter Dürr (ed.), *Physik und Transzendenz: De großen Physiker unseres Jahrhunderts über ihre Begegnung mit dem Wunderbaren* (Bein, 1986), pp. 263–293. Cf. also Ken Wilber (ed.), *Das holographische Weltbild* (Bern, 1986).

52 MacCannell and MacCannell, *The Time of the Sign*, p. 149, also see it this way – with the restrictions (?) evident in the following quote: 'Assumptions of unity at the level of the individual or the community are based on a desire to return to a state of nature.'

53 *Laws of Form*, 1.

54 Cf. here Niklas Luhmann and Peter Fuchs, *Reden und Schweigen* (Frankfurt, 1989), pp. 46ff.

Part II

Creating imagination

Chapter 5

Creativity and judgement: Kant on reason and imagination

John Rundell

INTRODUCTION

Kant's work stands as a watershed in the self-understanding of modernity, especially in the context of the present, but not new, dispute between the moderns and postmoderns. His work is important because in it three currents converge, as well as become separate, which are central to the long history of the Enlightenment. These currents are: a philosophy of the subject with its tendency to reduce its idea of reason to cognitive relations that humans establish with the world; a proto-romantic counter-image of the protean, creative imagination; and the problem of what might be termed unsociable sociability which became thematized from the vantage points of both manners and politics in terms of citizenship and civic virtues. On the one hand, Kant is concerned to give meaning, depth and veracity to the notion of reason, which he does on transcendental grounds, but also to shift reason beyond purely cognitivist formulations. Kant addresses and criticizes the cognitive reductionism of subject-centred reason. On the other hand, he opens reason up, so to speak, to other dimensions of the world that humans establish – the political-ethical and the aesthetic, and he does this by both constructing and denoting the different faculties and their principles that ought to be employed in the distinct domains – the understanding, imagination and reason. The imagination becomes not so much reason's other, but 'an indispensable dimension of the human soul', equal in power and capacity to the other faculties.

In the process of grappling with the imagination's indispensable work in a second encounter with it, in the *Critique of Judgement* Kant implicitly problematizes reason and its transcendental grounding. Moreover, in so opening up reason to this other aspect of the human condition, as well as confronting the imagination *sui generis*, he also argues that reason constitutively addresses the way in which human sociability, and especially its unsociability is formed and played out. In order to throw into relief this set of interrelated problems and issues, I will begin with a discussion of Kant's transcendental construction of the understanding, reason and the imagination in the *Critique of Pure Reason* before turning to the way in which this is transposed in the *Critique of Judgement*. I shall then address the problem of unsociable sociability in the context of the 'sublime' gaps that Kant constructs between reason and imagination. The argument here is that the legacy of Kant's philosophical anthropology points beyond a notion of reason that is constructed transcendentally as well as beyond a notion of the imagination that is pure protean creativity. Its underlying thesis is that reason, and especially practical reason, and the imagination never exist in their own right, but solely in the context of human unsociable sociability, and that this context permanently raises problems and tensions.

THE MYSTERY 'X' AND THE DOOR THAT OPENS INWARD

The *Critique of Pure Reason*, both because of and in spite of the three questions around which reason's interest revolves, concerns two fundamental problems: what is knowledge? and what is reason?[1] In other words, Kant's task is *first* to enquire into the epistemological conditions through which knowledge is not so much attained, as *constructed*, and through this enquiry, *second* to link an epistemological set of problems to the issue of the nature of reason itself. Moreover, Kant's enquiry is *a philosophy with anthropological intent*. By this I mean that part of Kant's own interrogation of the higher faculty of cognition is propelled by a single concern – to elucidate the conditions under which human beings not only construct their world (from their pure categories of space and time to their often impure and practical relations between one another), but also reflect upon these conditions and transform themselves from pre-rational into rational beings. In this sense, the *Critique of Pure Reason*, at a more fundamental level than that of epistemology, is a reflection on the condition of human freedom. By human freedom Kant means the capacity of human beings to critically reflect, judge and thus establish the conditions for their own freedom.[2]

Kant shifts the problem of knowledge from a preoccupation with empirical conditions (phenomena) to that of a human capacity which not only makes this interaction with empirical conditions possible, but also establishes its own conditions and criteria (the noumena). He argues that a theory of knowledge which begins with an assumption of empirical sensibility cannot get beyond intuition and provide knowledge about properties and relations. The faculty of the understanding is, for him, more than merely the faculty making mediate inferences in the form of logical connections; rather he constructs it as the faculty which brings together the diversity of appearances, unifying them according to rules.[3] The task of the faculty of the understanding is to subsume empirical diversity (the manifold of appearances) to rules. In this way, relations between these appearances are also established and illuminated.

More important, though, an epistemology grounded on intuition or appearances fails in its objective. Kant argues that at a fundamental level human beings are representational animals, and can get neither outside nor beyond these representations. The primary representations through which human beings establish both their outer and inner world relations are space (outer) and time (inner). These representations are given life in concepts. The task of the understanding is to provide the means through which a critical reflection upon and validation of these concepts may take place. It is the task of the understanding to make intelligible *a priori* concepts, and it does this by making either analytic or synthetic judgements. It is through these judgements that the rules become known and 'experienced'. To be sure, the role of judgement in Kant's work generally and here in the First *Critique* is both double-sided and central. On the one hand, judgement emerges as 'the faculty of subsuming under rules'.[4] According to him, all acts of understanding can be reduced to judgements which themselves can be abstracted according to four headings, with each containing three moments. The headings, with their moments, are quantity (universal, particular, singular), quality (affirmative, negative, infinite), relation (categorical, hypothetical, disjunctive) and modality (problematic, assertoric, apodictic). These four headings exhaust, for Kant, the forms which judgement takes.[5] On the other hand, judgement is the place where his anthropology of freedom also surfaces. We shall turn our attention to the first side of Kant's notion of judgement.

Kant makes a distinction between what might be termed pragmatic judgement which proceeds by trial and error (and which contains a naturalistic assumption about the presence or absence of a capacity for judgement, that is, some have it, some do not), and transcendentally grounded synthetic judgement. This latter form of judgement proceeds from an anthropological principle of the universality of reason, that is, a reason 'with which every human being is endowed'.[6] Kant assumes and argues that its transposition into a transcendental register is the way to both protect and sustain this principle and claim. As Kant argues, judgement 'must formulate by means of universal but sufficient marks the conditions under which objects can be given in harmony with the concepts. Otherwise the concepts would be void of all content . . .'[7] The condition of sufficiency is given transcendentally by the understanding. In order for there to be content, or more precisely, for content to be given to concepts and for a harmonization of objects and concepts to occur, this content must be brought under the auspices of the faculty of the understanding which itself is the source of the rules and principles through which this harmonization takes place. In other words, concepts and objects harmonize according to rules. It is the task of judgement to ascertain whether the attempted harmonization leads to true or false conclusions (in the case of cognitively derived knowledge), or good or evil actions (in the case of practically orientated knowledge).

At this point in his reconstruction Kant makes a crucial distinction between the twofold employment of reason, that is, the two distinct ways in which the *a priori* rule giving nature of the understanding is played out. He makes a distinction between the mathematical and the dynamical employment of reason during the activity of synthetic judgement. They refer to quantitative and qualitative judgements respectively.

In a mathematical synthesis reason is employed through the construction of concepts without the assistance of empirical data, as these concepts relate to quantitative *a priori* intuitions concerning either space or time. There is, as Kant argues, 'an *a priori* intuitive certainty [and an] evidential force'[8] concerning the division and duration of time and the magnitude of space. In a dynamic synthesis reason is employed as the means by which 'appearances are brought under concepts, according to their actual content'.[9] This entails that reason confronts, subsumes and establishes relations between a heterogeneous number of elements. For Kant, the dynamical synthesis is the means of establishing not only knowledge about the world of physical appearances, but also, and more importantly, philosophical knowledge, the knowledge concerning the three questions with which philosophy ought to deal. Moreover, because it is philosophical knowledge, it is also knowledge concerning the world of practical relations and affairs. Dynamic synthesis is the form through which the co-existence of 'substances in space' (and here by implication Kant also means human beings) and their reciprocal interaction is subsumed under reason.[10] The metaphor which Kant uses to locate his notion of dynamic synthesis is space. In other words, co-existence and reciprocity take place only in spatial forms. In many respects, Kant is alluding to the problem of the community of subjects to which he will turn his attention in the *Critique of Practical Reason* and return to again in the *Critique of Judgement*. The issue of reciprocity and co-existence is addressed epistemologically, at least in the first instance. It does not matter for Kant, at this point, whether reciprocity and co-existence occur in a heavenly or earthly community (*commercium*).

However, Kant is not content to rest on a formal division between two types of synthetic judgements within the faculty of understanding. This distinction serves to prepare the ground for a systematic analysis of the way in which comparisons are made between the substances and elements that co-exist together. Comparison is internal to dynamic synthesis and, for Kant, the act of comparison is both an act of judgement and an act of reflection concerning the nature and qualities of each substance. In the moment of judgement and reflection, substances and elements come together. Epistemology shifts from a static theory of empirically derived knowledge-formation to a dynamic theory of reason in action, that is, as critical reflection, which does not concern itself with objects, but with the conditions under which concepts can be formed. In other words, Kant argues that critical reflection is not a comparison between empirical objects themselves, but between representations. A critical, or what he terms transcendental, reflection refers to 'the objective comparison of representations with each other',[11] which relies on, and is grounded in, the capacity of reason to provide rules unconditionally.

But how do we know this? Kant's move beyond empiricism and logic to the issue of dynamic synthesis goes to the heart of his formulation of reason. In so doing, he also confronts head on the issue of the imagination, and reason's relation to it. The issue of the universal veracity of knowledge, and judgements concerning such veracity, is internal to the problem concerning the transcendental condition of reason. The explicit aim of Kant's critical programme is to provide the conditions, derived from reason, of certitude not only for the empirical world, but also for morals and ethics as well as taste. As already mentioned, the judgements that are enacted are not those that belong to the realm of logic (the analytic), because they add or subtract nothing concerning our understanding of the world. Synthetic judgements, and especially dynamic synthetic judgements, in Kant's argument, rest upon the addition of something else which Kant signals by an 'X'. As Kant asks himself in his introductory comments to the *Critique of Pure Reason*: 'What is here the unknown = X which gives support to the understanding when it believes that it can discover outside the concept A or predicate B foreign to this concept, which it yet at the same time considers to be connected with it.'[12] For Kant this 'X' cannot be experienced; it is certainly mysterious, but its mystery refers to knowledge, or rather concepts that are formed *a priori*. Kant's task, then, is to answer the question 'what is this "X"?', or as he asks himself: 'How are *a priori* synthetic judgements possible?'[13]

Kant answers this question in two sections of the *Critique of Pure Reason* – 'The Deduction of the Pure Concepts of Understanding' (of which there are two versions – a first and a rewritten second version) and 'The Schematicism of the Pure Concept of Understanding'. Kant argues that appearances are nothing but 'sensible representations, which as such and in themselves, must not be taken as objects capable of existing outside our power of representation'.[14] At first glance it appears, as Kant himself suggests, that his 'X' is the representation itself, as we cannot get outside it. On closer examination, though, representations themselves are a synthesis of reason (especially the legislative power of the understanding) and the imagination. In analysing the synthesis itself, Kant views and constructs the imagination as an essential and almost prefigurative dimension in the formation of knowledge. He neither dismisses nor constructs it as simply the world of phantasy or chaotic aberration. Rather, for him, it is 'an indispensable function of the soul without which we should have no knowledge whatsoever, but of which we are scarcely ever conscious'.[15] But how does Kant construct the imagination, and its relation to reason?

Kant suggests that there are four forms of the imagination – the empirical, the associative or reproductive, and the productive, which itself is divided into the figurative (or what can be termed the dynamic) and the schematic (or mathematical). These divisions are important for Kant's attempt to construct a theory of critical reflection on transcendental grounds. For Kant, transcendentality is the means by which he not only moves beyond empiricism and establishes the divisions within knowledge between the sensible and the supersensible, but also establishes the critical employment of reason itself which becomes manifest in the activity of judgement.

Kant argues that there are three moments within the synthetic formation of knowledge: the synthesis of apprehension in intuition, its reproduction in the imagination, and its recognition in a concept. Synthesis is the process whereby diverse forms and appearances are brought together and relations formed between them. In other words, associations are formed between the diverse forms and appearances that determine the meaning of a certain space and the meaning of a certain time. The activity of association, moreover, both assumes and assures the reproducibility of appearances. Kant terms this activity of association the reproductive imagination, and is the first indication of the imagination's power. This reproductive faculty of the imagination is directed to perceptions, impressions of which it must have some knowledge in order to form images. This is what gives to the imagination, for Kant, its empirical nature. In other words, the reproductive imagination 'rests upon empirical conditions'.[16] Moreover, and notwithstanding its empirical orientation, the associative or reproductive imagination guarantees that knowledge (representations) not only endures and continues over time, that is, guarantees relations between past and present, but also forms patterns and associations with other knowledge.

This power of association is the evidence, for Kant, that the reproductive imagination is also transcendental. This is what ensures that, even in the first instance, chaos and indeterminacy are *not* the nature of the imaginary life and its power. The reproductive or associative imagination functions according to *a priori* principles without which the empirical imagination, so Kant argues, 'would never find opportunity for exercise appropriate to its powers, and so would remain concealed within the mind as a dead and to us unknown faculty'.[17]

In other words, both because and in spite of plurality, diversity and difference there is, so Kant argues, an objective ground of synthesis, and by objective Kant means *a priori* and antecedent to all empirical laws of the imagination. This objective ground is what Kant terms the *productive imagination* which aims at unity, an intercourse between sensibility and understanding or cognition, the outcome of which are categories or concepts. It is worth quoting Kant at some length on this:

[By means of the pure imagination] we bring the manifold of intuition on the one side, into connection with the condition of the necessary unity of pure apperception on the other. The two extremes, namely sensibility and understanding, must stand in necessary connection with each other through the mediation of the transcendental function of the imagination, because otherwise the former though indeed yielding appearances, would supply no object of empirical knowledge, and consequently no experience. Actual experience ... contains a recognition ... certain concepts which render possible the former unity of experience, and therewith all objective validity (truth) of empirical knowledge. These grounds of the recognition of the manifold ... are the *categories*. Upon them is based not only all formal unity in the [transcendental] synthesis of imagination, but also, thanks to that synthesis all its empirical employment (in recognition, reproduction, association, apprehension) in connection with the appearances.[18]

It is this process of transcendental synthesizing mediation that makes the imagination, for Kant 'one of the fundamental categories of the human soul'.[19] It is not so much a conduit that facilitates interaction between sensibility and understanding, but rather is constitutive to this interaction. Kant's 'X' can now be named: the transcendental function of the imagination. This suggests that on one level 'the imagination provides [ ] a functional unity for intuitions and concepts',[20] which, while constitutive, is nonetheless only a necessary aid to the understanding and the formation of categories. On another level, though, Kant's discussion of the imagination is suggestive of a power that is both formative and creative in its own right. While this aspect of Kant's discussion of the productive imagination ought not to be overstated, its presence comes forward in some suggestive remarks that Kant makes, especially when he renames it the 'figurative synthesis' in the B Deduction. In fact the productive imagination splits in two to form a figurative or dynamic synthesis and a mathematical or schematic synthesis. As has been noted earlier, a transcendental synthesis occurs in two ways: either 'appearances are brought under concepts according to their actual content' or there is the construction of concepts without the assistance of empirical data. These two ways of employing reason were termed the dynamical and mathematical synthesis respectively. The transcendental function of the imagination follows this basic division within Kant's construction of pure reason, and although a division between the dynamical or figurative synthesis and schemata is not necessarily equivalent to a division between creative and functional dimensions of the imagination, this division within the B Deduction can be used to establish such a contrast. This is in contradistinction to the argument by Rudolf Makkreel, for one, who argues that the figurative synthesis and schematicism are, if not interchangeable, then related as instances through which the transcendental imagination brings 'to bear some of its formative power'.[21] The issue, or point of disagreement, is one of emphasis. The point I wish to make in stressing this difference is that it is the figurative imagination that *remains* essentially problematic for Kant, whereas schematicism is formulated, so it appears, in a way that remains confined to the construction of mathematized relational forms (in the context of either time or space), and which in the end indicate that they are (imaginative) products of the pure understanding; that is, they remain bound to pure reason. This distinction establishes an unacknowledged tension between the productive imagination's functional aspect, and its more properly creative and formative dimension. Let us first look at Kant's discussion of schematicism before turning our attention to figurative synthesis.

As Makkreel points out, 'schemata are *a priori* products of the imagination that mediate between concepts and empirical appearances'.[22] In a transcendental schema there is an intellectual relation, in which things are subsumed to categories, and a sensible relation, which constitutes the universal and empirical condition 'under which the category can be applied to as object'.[23] This combination of the intellectual and the sensible Kant terms the schematicism of pure understanding, which is itself a product of the pure understanding. As Deleuze, in this instance, comments:

> The schema is a spatio-temporal determination which itself corresponds to the category everywhere and at all times it [consists] in *spatio-temporal relations which embody or realise relations which are in fact conceptual.* The schema of the imagination is the condition under which the legislative understanding makes judgements with its concepts, judgements which will serve as principles for all knowledge of the manifold ... [It] schematicises only when the understanding presides, or has legislative power.[24]

The task of the schemata is to mediate between the conceptual universality of the categories – time and space – and the empirical act of intuiting time and space. And it does this 'by translating the rules implicit in the categories into a temporally ordered act of instructions for constructing an objectively determinate nature'.[25] In this context, then, the schemata are primarily functional, they have a basic transcendental synthetic function, which, while belonging to the imagination, is subsumed under and co-ordinated with the rule-giving propensity of the pure understanding.

There is, though, another aspect of schematicism which alludes to a creative power of the imagination in its own right. This is where Kant speaks of the schemata as *pure sensible concepts*. The schema of a pure sensible concept 'is a product and, as it were, a monogram of pure *a priori* imagination, through and in accordance with which images themselves first become possible'.[26] It is distinct from an image which is the work (initially) of the empirically orientated reproductive imagination. But these images, so Kant argues, can only be conceptualized by being connected to schemata. Whether a triangle (which can only exist in thought) or the concept 'dog', these schemata rely on the 'art' and activity of the *synthesizing* imagination. As Kant says, and in a way that indicates he is unaware of the importance of his statement, the 'imagination is the faculty of representing in intuition an object that is *not itself* present'.[27]

Following Castoriadis, in this instance, it can be claimed that this is the creative aspect of the productive imagination, the name to which Kant gives figurative synthesis. What Kant terms schematicism is an attempt to capture what is assumed to be the empirically unknowable, unfathomable and spontaneous nature of creativity itself, the site and power of which is the productive imagination. This is in contrast to Makkreel's hermeneutic reading of Kant in which he argues that the mathematical monogrammatic nature of schematicism can be extended metaphorically to include the notions and activities of reading and interpretation, which require an additional dimension of meaning beyond the categorical rule – boundedness of the schemata's subsumption under the understanding.[28] To be sure, a hermeneutic, interpretative effort is required, but the issue here is creativity *sui generis*. And for a reading of Kant that for the moment 'leans on' Castoriadis's notion of imaginary signification, knowledge is constituted only through a process of imaginary creation which includes representational formation, and yet is not functionally reduced to this.[29]

Hence, while Kant is at pains to point out, against Descartes, that knowledge proceeds mediately through representations which themselves become further objects of representation, there is still a further imaginative dimension of creativity. In the light of Kant's theory of knowledge, but in a way that brings the role of the imagination (and not only reason) much closer to the surface, a tension emerges between the imagination as a creative force and source of reflexivity, and the imagination viewed as constitutive to the understanding.

Kant confronts an abyss, where, were he to fall into it, he would confront chaos and uncertainty. He pulls back onto the ground of certitude. In so doing he circumscribes the nature and role of the imagination, especially its synthesizing power, making it dependent on the understanding. As Makkreel points out, 'ultimately all synthesis is a function of the understanding and its categories. This is the conclusion that Kant arrives at in the Objective Deduction.'[30] This is especially the case in the B Deduction of the second edition of the *Critique of Pure Reason* where Kant diminishes the role of the imagination, particularly in its associative and reproductive senses, which in the first edition (A Deduction) stand independent of the categories. This, then, is the essential point of the above discussion of schematicism, and for separating it from figurative synthesis or the figurative imagination. In the B Deduction the creative and reflexive dimensions of the imagination (whether it be in the form of mathematics, philosophy or art) is subsumed by the functional requisites of the pure understanding, that is, to a notion of reason which provides rules transcendentally for constructing judgements.

This has the effect, as the *Critique of Pure Reason* unfolds, not only of reducing the nature of the imagination to that of cognition (and thus bypassing the issue of fiction and phantasy), but more importantly of driving a wedge between reason and imagination. Reason contains no creative power, only a regulative power which gives rules and standards. The ideal of reason is the archetype, the divinity within humankind. It is not a figment of the brain, nor a product of an external source of authority, nor a creation or invention. As Kant says in one of his summary remarks:

Such is the nature of the ideal of reason, which must always rest on determinate concepts and serve as a rule and an archetype, alike in our actions and our critical judgements. The products of the imagination are of an entirely different nature; no one can explain or give an intelligible concept of them; each is a kind of *monogram*, a mere set of particular qualities determined by no assignable rule, and forming rather a blurred sketch drawn from diverse experiences than a determinate image.[31]

There is, then, a tension in Kant's description of the imagination in both the A and B Deductions, as well as in its relation to reason in the First *Critique* as a whole. On the one side, Kant speaks of the imagination as a monogram, thus alluding to its function as schemata, as well as an indeterminate dimension of human life that casts its own long shadow. This points to some loose fragments within the First *Critique* which remain unacknowledged and unexamined, and yet indicate a direction beyond it. As Makkreel points out, Kant does retain in the second edition 'what is probably the most vigorous affirmation of his early view that the imagination is an independent source of synthesis'.[32] Furthermore, there is also Kant's enigmatic sentence, mentioned earlier, to which Castoriadis draws our attention, which alludes to the creative power of the imagination, and not just its independent existence.[33] Against this, there is the chasm which Kant constructs between reason and imagination themselves. Reason provides rules and principles *a priori*; the imagination invents partly sketched schema that can be rendered only in half-thought and barely spoken. There is an incongruence here, or great divide, which separates what is assumed to be two equally fundamental yet mutually incommunicable dimensions of the subject and which no interpretative effort could fully bridge. As Kant constructs it, there is a Reason which is bound to laying down laws, and there is an Imagination, half-afraid of, half-empowered by, its own creativity. It is these two aspects which will be the concern of the following section, before turning, in the third section, to the unaddressed issue of the anthropology of freedom and its relation to judgement.

THE HARMONY AND DISSONANCE OF THE THIRD *CRITIQUE*

On one level, the *Critique of Judgement* can be seen as a philosophical rendition of a cultural and structural differentiation occurring in modernity that creates an autonomous world of aesthetics freed from the traditional sacred imperatives of religion and separate from the self-reflexive modernizing instituting utopias of science and republican democracy. Like the *Critique of Pure Reason*, the *Critique of Judgement* unfolds as an exposition on the problem of reaching knowledge, or more precisely, forming judgements. In this instance, though, judgement does not proceed theoretically about the way in which humans construct knowledge of nature and judge the veracity of this knowledge. Nor does it proceed practically in a way that concerns the transcendental condition of the norm of freedom, and, thus, how good conduct is judged (an exposition that takes place in the *Critique of Practical Reason*). Instead, the form of knowledge created is that about aesthetics, which refers to objects of nature, which are deemed to be beautiful, or objects either created by human beings or imputed by them to Nature the characteristics of which are deemed to be sublime. In the latter case, the object cannot convey sublimity; to characterize something sublime is to 'speak' of something beyond the object itself. Kant argues that the judgements appropriate to this very specific form of activity – aesthetic creation and the formation of aesthetic sensibility – are aesthetic judgements.

In the *Critique of Judgement* Kant uses the problem of judgement as the pivot around which to locate the two central issues (that is, aesthetic sensibility and aesthetic creation), which he wishes to address on transcendental grounds. While Kant's apparent aim is to develop a critical theory of taste, nonetheless in developing this he also redeploys the transcendental construction of the imagination and its relation to the understanding which we find in the First *Critique*. For Kant, this is necessary if he is to go beyond both psychological and empirical-physiological constructions of the idea of beauty and sublimity which were present in the eighteenth century.[34] Kant argues, against Burke in this instance, that notions and judgements of beauty or sublimity cannot be derived from empirical sensation, delight, gratification or pain. For, as he says,

> if we suppose that our liking for the object consists entirely in the object's gratifying us through charm or emotion, then we also must not require anyone *else* to assent to an aesthetic judgement that *we* make; for about that sort of liking each person rightly consults only his private sense. But if this is so, then all censure of taste will also cease . . . For if taste did not have *a priori* principles, it could not possibly pronounce on the judgements of others and pass verdicts approving or repudiating them with even the slightest semblance of having the right to do so.[35]

Kant assumes that his formulation of a critique of taste through aesthetic ideas is the linchpin which holds the issues of aesthetic creation and the formation of aesthetic sensibility, and hence the entire text, together.

And yet the *Critique of Judgement* remains a fundamentally unsatisfactory work. A careful reading of it indicates that these two central issues, far from being two sides of a single coin, break down into two divergent and complex problems, each with its own direction. Put briefly, what I term aesthetic creation refers to that dimension of Kant's argument which deals with the creation of aesthetic objects, as well as an emphasis which is given to the role of the productive or creative imagination, and is discussed by him from the vantage points of the beautiful and the sublime. What I term the formation of aesthetic sensibility is a shorthand expression for that aspect of Kant's discussion which deals with three interrelated activities which can be brought together under the more general term of communicability. First, there is the 'act' of coming to a subjective judgement about taste; second, the possibility that there can be real or potentially universal agreement about this taste or judgement; and third, both the first and second *together* refer to the issue of the plurality and diversity of taste and the public articulation of this in the one social space – the public sphere. In the context of communicability Kant anticipates or constructs a modernity conscious of itself, or a self-reflexive modernity in the face of a restlessness in which all fixity is dissolved and there is constitutive recognition and acceptance of a plurality and diversity of perspectives, dispositions and tastes. This is internal to his idea of the public. He overlays this with a quest for the modern version of the 'holy grail' – a transcendentally constituted certitude in the face of dynamic, reflexively orientated plurality and difference.

The text breaks down, so to speak, because here Kant is pursuing a double warrant of freedom. He wants to construct a subject who has freedom to create and to judge. Aesthetics becomes the paradigm through which this double warrant is both posited and generated. From the vantage point of judgement the activity of freedom is a condition in which particularity is first given and reflected upon. In the course of this reflection universals are discovered under which the particularities can be subsumed.[36] In other words, the difference between universality and particularity is recognized and reflected upon, and a judgement made in the light of this recognition. (This has been termed the formation of aesthetic sensibility above.) For creativity, the activity of freedom is the capacity of 'the imagination to sustain the mind in free activity'[37] (what has been termed aesthetic creation).

The construction of aesthetic creation in terms of the nature of the productive imagination, and the transcendental grounding of communicability are both problematized, but from different directions. The construction of aesthetic creation is problematized once the sublime is introduced, and in a way that opens onto the unconstrained activity of the productive imagination. Moreover, the transcendental grounding of communicability is problematicized from a different vantage point entirely, an anthropological one. The issue of the plurality of taste takes place in the context of Kant's continuing reflections on practical reason, not only from the vantage point of autonomous freedom – the core of the problem of judgement – but also from the vantage point of what he terms 'the sociability that befits our humanity',[38] which is a combination of a 'universal *feeling of sympathy*, and the ability to engage universally in very intimate *communication*'.[39] What Kant terms here sociability, or *unsociable sociability* in 'The Idea of Universal History . . .', is the undercurrent of practical anthropology that informs the *Critique of Judgement*. His concern is the substantive dimensions and images of not only good conduct, but of conduct in general, and is orientated not only to the subject's own capacity as a freely judging autonomous being, but also as a subject who lives and acts among and with others, that is, who may also love as well as be violent. It is Kant's recognition of the dimension of intersubjectivity and its historicity, which constitutes what has been termed his 'Second Copernican Revolution'.[40] The dimension of unsociable sociability has an effect, too, on how the idea of the creative imagination may be viewed.

On another level, then, the issue of transcendentality, which Kant addresses in relation to aesthetic creation and the formation of aesthetic sensibility, as well as the undercurrent of an anthropology of unsociable sociability entails that the *Critique of Judgement* becomes more than merely the seminal text concerning the *differentia specifica* of modern aesthetics. I shall begin by locating Kant's notion of aesthetics within his transcendental system and method before turning to the problem of aesthetic creation. I shall then, finally, turn to the issue of communicability in the context of the undercurrent of unsociable sociability. Together the creative imagination and unsociable sociability indicate a dimension of Kant's work that opens beyond the Third *Critique*, and in a way that lays an unexploded charge against transcendentality itself.

Harmony on a transcendental scale

There are four places in the Third *Critique* where Kant spells out the location and nature of judgement in terms of its place within his transcendental system as a whole – the Preface, the first and second Introductions and the Dialectic of Aesthetic Judgement.[41] The problem he addresses is whether judgement has *a priori* principles, like understanding and reason, and if so whether they are regulative or constitutive. In the context of aesthetics the issue is not about how *a priori* cognitive judgements are possible where a harmonization occurs between concepts and objects, but how aesthetic judgements are. Kant argues that the question of judgements of taste is beyond, or more precisely, different to, cognitive questions. Aesthetic apprehensions take place without the aid of concepts of the understanding which function as objective principles. The task of judgement is not to apply objective principles derived from elsewhere (the understanding or reason), but rather to provide its own concept, which cannot be an objective rule. The principle peculiar to judgement must be derived regulatively and heuristically, as a principle in use, so to speak. The peculiarity of judgement, then, is 'the ability to think the particular as contained under the universal'.[42] It is an activity viewed not so much from the vantage point of the subject (as this would give to it an overly phenomenological hue), as from the way in which the subject may claim a rationality for his or her own particular judgement. The type of judgements appropriate to this type of activity is reflective where the universal for the particular must be found, rather than determinative, where the universal or rule or principle is already given. In this context, a series of distinctions is already emerging which indicate that the set of problems faced in the Third *Critique* are qualitatively different from those of the First *Critique*. The change of perspective from an objective to a subjective relation to judgements (which, Kant assumes, completes his system) entails a different strategy and language about them. Mathematical and dynamical judgements are, in the First *Critique*, determinative, and hence their synthetic quality is to provide rules under which the work of the imagination is also subsumed. Kant's move to the idea of reflective judgement also entails that the *procedure* of the imagination's subsumption under the understanding is looked at anew, but, as in the First *Critique*, from *within* the transcendentality of reflective judgement itself.

For Kant, the universal principle for reflective judgement must stand on transcendental ground. Reflective judgement requires a principle which it can neither borrow from experience nor from elsewhere. As Kant says, 'this transcendental principle must be one that reflective judgement gives as a law, but only to itself'.[43] Kant identifies this principle as the finality or purposiveness of nature. What Kant means by this is that nature, in all its multiplicity, is capable of being regarded *as if* it presents a coherent and unified system.[44] This gives judgement the ability to compare empirical presentations with one another. And for Kant, this is fundamentally different to the functional formation of schemata in the First *Critique*. Rather, the principle behind reflective judgement is that 'nature has adhered to uniformity that we can grasp',[45] not mechanically, 'like an instrument guided by the understanding and the senses', but in a way that presupposes a harmony in nature that is beyond functionality. This presupposition of a harmony in nature ensures that, for Kant, nature is apprehended, in his terms *technically*, rather than schematically. What Kant means by this is that nature can be viewed as having a power to purposively produce things which have no purpose or end to them. Rather, they simply exist. Reflective judgement cannot work without this idea of purposive purposelessness. As Kant says, 'the principle of a purposive arrangement of nature is a system – an arrangement [made] as it were for the benefit of judgement . . . Judgement makes *a priori the technic of nature* a principle of reflection;'[46] and in a way that neither explains it nor adds anything to our understanding of nature. 'Rather judgement makes this technic its principle only so that it can, according to its need[s] reflect in terms of its own subjective law, and yet in a way that also harmonises with natural laws in general.'[47] In this way, Kant can go on to argue that the sense of purposive purposelessness belongs to the subject's power to reflect, and not to the object itself. The purposiveness does not lie in an inferred purpose of nature's products but rather in 'nature's harmonising with what the subjective conditions of judgement are under which empirical concepts can cohere to [form] a whole of experience'.[48] The purposelessness is experienced as the art of nature and results in a feeling of pleasure, which is not simply a sensuous one derived from the state of the subject. Rather, this feeling of pleasure is governed by the transcendental principle or inference of the purposive purposelessness of nature.

Kant's notion and formulation of reflective judgement generates his own quite specific idea of art from *within* his transcendental system. For him, the presupposition of nature's harmony is the means through which we can regard nature as art, and how our notion of art (and hence the beautiful) is formed. In a way, there is a double harmony present – one which *is* the purposive purposelessness of nature, a harmony *in* nature which itself is doubled to become a 'harmony in reflection between the presentation of the object and the lawfulness inherent in the empirical use in general of the subject's power of judgement'.[49] This 'double' harmony occurs both between the object and the subject and within the subject. The subject combines the faculties (one of which becomes subordinate in the formation of cognition, cf. the First *Critique*) – the imagination and the understanding – which stand separately yet harmoniously conjoined in a reflective judgement. The imagination, which apprehends the object's form, agrees with the exhibition of a concept. As Kant states:

> In an aesthetic judgement of reflection . . . the basis determining [it] is the sensation brought about, in the subject, by the harmonious play of the two cognitive powers [involved] in the power of judgement, imagination and understanding; [they are in harmonious play] when, on the given presentation, the imagination's ability to apprehend, and the understanding's ability to exhibit, further each other.[50]

This construction of harmony allows Kant to generate and locate an aesthetics of taste transcendentally, and which at the same time cannot be reduced to cognitive principles. Judgements of taste, nonetheless, are as rational, or as *reasoned* as the cognitive, but they emerge from a different deployment of the faculties. The idea of purposive purposelessness in nature generates an appreciation of the object without cognitive or utilitarian intent, what Kant terms *without interest*. The result is a reflective judgement of taste. As Kant states: 'Taste is the ability to judge an object, or a way of presenting it, by means of a liking or disliking *devoid of all interest*.'[51] It is the feeling and appreciation of viewing objects free of interested intent that enables them to be termed, in Kant's view, beautiful. From the perspective of its quality, an object can be termed beautiful if it is not judged according to either its empirical utility or goodness or its agreeable enjoyment.[52] In a way, for Kant, finding or naming something beautiful is to suspend it in space and, by analogy, time.[53]

In first addressing the problem of reflective judgements in transcendental terms, and from the vantage point of his system as a whole, Kant announces and introduces the analytic of the beautiful as a *second-order issue*. The beautiful, moreover, remains the centre of Kant's aesthetics because it attains a systemic and methodological priority over all other aesthetic terms, especially the sublime, because of the transcendentality that anchors it.

Leaving the issue of the sublime to one side, momentarily, it is worth enquiring whether his idea of harmony assumes a similar image of the imagination to that developed in its reproductive and productive capacities in the First *Critique*, especially when the issue of creativity is raised. In many ways, this comes to the fore in his discussion of aesthetic ideas, which is an attempt to secure the issue of creativity and the imagination within his transcendental perspective. It is to this that we now turn.

White notes/black notes

Kant defines aesthetic ideas as those presentations of the imagination that cannot be brought adequately under a concept. However, as his discussion unfolds, his idea of the beautiful can neither be the vehicle for, nor sustain, his investigation of what I have termed aesthetic creation. Within the category of the beautiful, the imagination has a precise function. It is one of the indispensable, yet intricately linked dimensions through which the feeling of pleasure arises when we witness the *form* of nature, its purposiveness without purpose. Imagination and the understanding combine in a free play that does not presuppose a determinate concept. As he says 'the beautiful in nature concerns the form of the object'[54] which expands our appreciation and concept of nature beyond its mere utility to an idea of nature as art. Yet, Kant argues that the notion of the beautiful is simultaneously bounded – the question is: by what? Kant argues that it is not only the relation between the understanding and the imagination which is in free play; the imagination itself is also free, by which he means spontaneous *and* lawful. Here there is, in fact, a slippage away from the idea of harmony to a reversal of the relation between the understanding and the imagination in the First *Critique*. In an aesthetic reflective judgement of the beautiful the understanding serves the imagination. This is what gives the imagination its lawful freedom so that it does not roam beyond the hedgerows of the English garden, or dwell too long on the embellishments of the Baroque or the Rococo. Rather, beauty is about rest and contemplation. In this sense, it is white, pure and prone to exemplariness (and thus the ever-present danger of perfection especially when it is appreciated *technically*. Kant inadvertently constructs a relation between beauty and technique). As Kant states, in one of his summary remarks:

> only a lawfulness without a law, and a subjective harmony of the imagination with the understanding without an objective harmony – where the presentation is referred to a determinate concept of an object – is compatible with the free lawfulness of the understanding (which has also been called purposive without a purpose) and with the peculiarity of a judgement of taste.[55]

Peculiar indeed! We shall have recourse to return to this peculiarity below. As we shall see, this idea of harmony is indicative of something else.

The idea of aesthetic creation only enters *tout court* when Kant discusses the sublime. For Kant, the sublime is white *and* black, combining purity with horror and nefariousness to produce a world where the passions dwell in tense relation – furious love, calm hatred. Often it is the underworld *sui generis*. As such it is always played in a minor key. While judgements of the sublime, too, are made without interest, the *condition* of sublimity is one of unease, of restlessness, of dissonance. The dissonance is experienced not between the imagination and the understanding, but between the imagination and reason which orientate themselves either to the faculty of cognition or the faculty of desire. In the former, a mathematical sublimity is constructed; in the latter, a dynamical one. In the category of the sublime Kant moves onto the ground of reason proper, giving to it a creative dimension, in a way similar to the creative dimension of the imagination that emerges in figurative synthesis. In the unease experienced in this discord, there is always the danger of chaos and illusory redemption. The condition of sublimity is experienced, then, in terms of awe, anxiety, fear and fright and can result in a trembling genuflection before the powers of either nature or humankind.

In his construction of the idea of the sublime the central, propelling image is one of infinity. As Kant puts it, the condition of the sublime emerges once human beings confront something beyond nature's purposeful purposiveness, and impute to it something which is entirely their own. This imputation is the idea of infinity. It either expands our idea of nature, of nature's art, or transcends it. Its main expression is in Kant's discussion of the mathematical sublime, which is more central to this part of our reconstruction than his discussion of the dynamical sublime.

The sense of unease or agitation, so central to Kant's formulation of the sublime, is caused by an incongruency between imagination and reason. Unlike the beautiful, which is indicative of a harmony in free play between the imagination and the understanding, the mathematically sublime is indicative of a dissonant free play between the imagination and reason. This is in stark contrast to mathematical synthesis in which finitude is its measure. In the First *Critique*, the imagination is brought under the understanding, the faculty of providing rules, in schemata. In the mathematically sublime the productive imagination is expanded beyond the functionality with which Kant imbues it in the First *Critique*, and takes on the transfunctional, creative dimensions associated with the figurative imagination. In the context of the *Critique of Judgement* the imaginary component of the mathematical or schematic synthesis is loosened from its cognitive dimension. The free play between reason and imagination does not result in harmony, but conflict. It is violent, cruel.

In Kant's construction of the mathematically sublime, it is not the imagination that becomes unbounded and demonstrates it power. Rather it is reason that constructs the ideal of the infinite through which nature is fictionalized. The imagination can only expand in order to pursue this sense of infinity, and yet it can never reach it. This results in the simultaneous feeling of pleasure and displeasure emerging out of the imagination's sense of its inadequacy. Sublimity, then, is the condition where reason and imagination co-exist in a relation of disequilibrium where both pleasure and displeasure are simultaneously expressed. And, for Kant, the idea of uneasy simultaneity is crucial – the imagination's pursuit of reason's idea of infinity entails that the imagination must pursue excess, that it must expand beyond reasonable limits, and yet the existence of reason's idea of the infinite itself gives rise to a law which the imagination can both strive towards, and potentially conform to. The feeling of displeasure, more, of unease, arises from not only a sense of the imagination's inadequacy but also from its pursuit and embroilment in excess which becomes an abyss in which the imagination may lose itself. Ever fraught with danger, the mathematically sublime unleashes a violence upon the subject (otherwise termed displeasure) that is at the same time purposive. The simultaneity of pleasure and displeasure is the means through which a comprehension of an object which is apprehended through the power of reason, which itself becomes unbounded, occurs.[56]

In the context of the mathematically sublime, Kant constructs an image of creativity which emerges out of violence, or more specifically, an unease emerging out of a struggle between two opposing forces. The bearer of this creativity is the genius. Although Kant's construction of the genius occurs in the 'Deduction of Pure Aesthetic Judgements', which pertains to the beautiful *and not the sublime*, nonetheless some affinities emerge, especially when the image of creativity shifts from the unexplored idea of *reason's* creativity to that *of* the imagination's.

Kant attempts to locate aesthetic creation on the ground of the beautiful when he states that 'judging beautiful objects to be such requires taste; but fine art itself, i.e. *production* of such objects, requires *genius*'.[57] However, despite this attempt his notion of genius extends beyond its quasi-naturalism and establishes more than an elective affinity with the mathematical sublime. It is not so much that mathematics and aesthetics, while creative acts, are lonely ones undertaken by an isolated, alienated creator/genius (in a forerunner of romanticism); rather, they point to the imagination's power to expand beyond its natural limits. The imagination is freed from laws of association and the constraint of rules imposed by the understanding. In the manner of the First *Critique* where the imagination is seen as 'the faculty of representing in intuition an object that is not itself present', Kant reiterates in the *Critique of Judgement* that the subject (genius) finds a reference in itself to something in the subject and outside it[58] – the imagination's capacity to both invent and reorder reality, a life beyond its merely empirical power of analogy and association.

The imagination [here] displays a creative activity and puts the faculty of intellectual ideas (reason) into motion – a motion, at the instance of a representation, toward an extension of thought, that while germane, no doubt to the concept of the object, exceeds what can be laid hold in that representation or clearly expressed.[59]

In other words, Kant confronts head on not only the problem of the creative power of the imagination, but also its untranslatability – the problem, that is, of defining the undefinable that must admit 'a communication without any constraint or rules'.[60] As he says later in the same paragraph, 'when the aim is aesthetic, then the imagination is free, so that over and above that harmony with the concept, it may supply, in an unstudied way, a wealth of undeveloped material for the understanding which the latter disregarded in its concept'.[61]

Kant revisits the great divide that he had posited as separating reason and imagination in the closing pages of the First *Critique*. However, in the context of the *Critique of Judgement*, Kant constructs this as a genuine problem of communicability between two fecund worlds. It is not a question of a dead space between them, but of a gap needing to be filled; that is, of how a presentation (or image) is to be re-presented. Because creativity is ultimately defined transcendentally as the 'free play of the imagination',[62] its product can be grasped only barely and inadequately in language or symbolically. The association often demanded to make sense of these creations is, for him, a poor substitute or fabrication of what the creative artist had in mind, and what is required of the audience in its reception of the artist's creation. On the one side, creativity demands, so to speak, an expansion of concepts, symbols and forms in order to construe what its meaning might be. These expanded concepts, symbols and forms are termed by Kant the aesthetic attributes of an object, and it is these, on the other side, to which the audience's imagination must be attuned. The aesthetic attributes must quicken the mind [of the audience], opening it to 'an immense realm of kindred presentations'.[63] The 'sublimity and majesty of creation' can neither be presented nor received in a single coherent concept, but only in what Kant terms an aesthetic idea. Aesthetic attributes are *products* of (on the part of the artist/genius) and also *produce* (on the part of the audience) an aesthetic idea. It

[is] presentation of the imagination which is conjoined with a given concept and is connected, when we use imagination in its freedom, with such a multiplicity of partial presentations that no expression that stands for a determinate concept can be found for it. Hence it is a presentation that makes us add to a concept the thoughts of much that is ineffable, but the feeling of which quickens our cognitive powers and connects language, which otherwise would be mere letters with spirit.[64]

Kant faces the interstice between reality and unreality (the surreal) and between certainty and uncertainty. At this point two incongruities emerge. On the one side there is an incongruity between the creative imagination and concepts/symbols through which its products are presented, and on the other between the artist (or his or her product) and the audience. The latter points our attention to the possibility of a conflict of interpretations, not so much over the beauty of the object, as its *meaning*. And it is this double problem of meaning and the conflict of interpretations between which Kant is caught. He moves to suppress the first and to resolve the second. The issue of creativity is reined in because Kant is primarily interested in a good judgement. This means that the text breaks in two at this point, with the issue of creativity and its products once again left dangling in the air.[65] Here, if we read Kant's discussion of the genius in #49 alongside his discussion of the mathematically sublime (notwithstanding their different location within Kant's transcendental system), there is a sense that creativity and interpretation (or judgements of taste) are eruptions into and violations of an empty space – that is, violent acts that denote an unease, a dissonance generated by the incongruity between imagination and concepts/symbols.[66] It is to this problem of incongruity of judgement that we now turn.

HARMONY IN COUNTERPOINT?

Apart from free creativity Kant is also preoccupied with a second warrant of freedom – the freedom to make rational judgements. The fact that, in Kant's view, reason is compelled to venture beyond 'the field of its empirical employment'[67] and critically confront the limits of all knowledge and human experience indicates that its ultimate aim lies beyond knowledge and cognition. The ultimate aim of reason, for Kant, is freedom.

As his formulation of pleasure indicates, the notion of freedom that Kant has in mind is not one which is fuelled by the dictates of desire. Nor is it one that subordinates freedom either to a happiness derived from the performance of right virtues (as it is, for example, with the Epicureans and the Stoics), or to the avoidance of pain through a rational control and remaking of habits which results in the calculation of pleasure (cf. Locke). Rather, freedom for Kant is exercised by a critical judgement which is also a reasoned judgement.[68]

In the light of our reconstruction of the Third *Critique*, though, there is always the possibility of an incongruity between artist and audience, as well as between members of the audience. Kant's attempt to address this problem of competing aesthetic judgements can be viewed from the vantage point of what I have termed communicability. As mentioned above, this is an umbrella formulation that refers to forming a subjective judgement about taste, the recognition that there is a diversity of tastes and opinions about taste, the possibility that there may be universal assent about taste, and finally that plurality and diversity of taste assumes, for Kant at least, their articulation in a public sphere free from domination. Furthermore, the anthropological dimension to Kant's work makes its presence felt most strongly in this aspect of the *Critique of Judgement*. Here, he continues to posit his two propositions in the *Critique of Pure Reason* that humankind's existence is corporeal, indeterminate and finite in a corporeal, finite and indeterminate world. Simultaneously, this existence is constituted publicly with other selves, discursively, through the linguistic form of interaction. In other words, for Kant, we speak our existence rather than conceptually construct or think it. To speak our existence is to interact publicly – this is for him our ultimate goal.[69] The same argument underpins Kant's 'What is Enlightenment?', where the struggle to be freed from self-incurred tutelage or immaturity only occurs in a double yet initially self-supporting way. Critical self-reflexivity presupposes a public sphere, and the primary constitutive dimension of a public sphere is critical enquiry, the right to ask questions, to agree and to disagree. The linguisticality of the interactions is not the issue here, although it is linked to Kant's notion of *reason* (a dimension that Habermas takes up in his theory of communicative action). Rather, what concerns us is the way in which Kant's notion of communicability itself is a double-sided one that contains the dimensions of both critical reflection and transcendentality. Each ultimately refers to an underlying anthropological image of autonomy.

The image of enlightenment, that is, the release from self-incurred tutelage through the self-legislating use of one's own reason, is central to Kant's notion of communicability. This image is what he terms the *sensus communis* and involves three capacities or maxims which place it both beyond nature and humans' encounter with their first 'natural' world, that is, their everyday existence. The first capacity is to think for oneself and thus have an active critical relation to both the taken-for-granted everyday and specialized forms of knowledge and opinion. The second is the capacity 'to think from the standpoint of someone else', beyond the parameters of one's own particularistic perspective. It indicates, as Kant says, 'a broadened way of thinking', a capacity to think from 'a universal standpoint'. The third maxim or capacity is to think consistently, or more accurately to develop a consistent way of thinking that combines as a matter of course the first two capacities.[70] Together they constitute the *condition* of enlightenment. In the context of the *Critique of Judgement*, rather than 'What is Enlightenment?' the *sensus communis* becomes a public sphere (a paradigm for one of the many possible publics) in which critical reflection occurs without preconditions and constraints. This entails that participants cannot claim privileged positions either as specialists or as rulers or leaders who 'require anyone *else* to assent to an aesthetic judgement that [they] make'.[71] Nor is a critical reflection established 'by gathering votes and asking other people what kind of sensation they are having'.[72] A judgement of taste acquires a validity which, as Kant argues, 'must rest ... on an autonomy of the subject who is making a judgement about the feeling of pleasure'.[73] Two specific features emerge. First, the meaning of communicability is thrown into relief: each singular judgement has a universality, a right to exist, the construction of which is not dependent on 'a logical universality governed by concepts'.[74] 'Taste lays claim to autonomy',[75] and, by extension, plurality on the ground of freedom. This means, that, second, *a priori* proofs can provide neither the *basis* for judgement according to taste, nor the reasons for a change of mind, a change of perspective or a change of heart.

Kant, however, finds *this* particular version or meaning of universality unsettling and unsatisfactory. In this context of a plurality of tastes he searches for a certitude by which the claim for a sound judgement can be made. It is at this point that we can reintroduce the peculiarity of Kant's notion of harmony as he moves on to the ground of transcendentality once more.

As our discussion of reflective judgement above indicates, Kant assumes that he has solved transcendentally the problem of taste, of the activity of coming to judgement, through the harmony between the understanding and the imagination. In searching for certitude Kant claims that the subject who judges reflexively refers the faculty of understanding to aesthetic ideas. This has the effect of harmonizing judgement in the realm of the sensible (objects) with the supersensible (ideas). As Kant says:

> taste, as a subjective power of judgement contains a principle of subsumption; however, this subsumption is not one of intuitions under *concepts*, but, rather, one of the *power* of intuitions or exhibitions (the imagination) under the *power* of concepts (the understanding), insofar as the imagination *in its freedom* harmonizes with the understanding *in its lawfulness*.[76]

It is this transcendentally constructed idea of harmony that enables Kant to argue that singular judgements of the beautiful can be shared or are, as he says, 'universally communicable'.[77] In this construction the '*sensus communis*' means the 'universal communicability' of the experience of harmonization.

Castoriadis has argued, however, this construction only works if Kant assumes that the idea of the finality or purposiveness of nature is rendered not only transcendentally, but also teleologically.[78] Teleology is necessary to complete the argument that is left dangling, truncated, after his discussion of the sublime, as well as the genius. At the close of paragraph 30 he says 'the only deduction we will have to attempt is that of judgements of taste, i.e. judgements about the beauty in natural things; that will suffice for a complete solution of the problem for the whole aesthetic power of judgements'.[79] As Kant is aware, however, beauty resides more in the eyes of the beholder than in the object itself. This means that, for him, beauty has a purpose, if not utilitarian which indicates a finality, not for nature, but for humankind. The final purpose of the beautiful is not beauty but the moral good of humankind. It is a symbol of morality.[80] An ethical core is central to the *Critique of*

Judgement and is addressed by him in teleological terms whereby humankind becomes the ultimate goal or purpose of nature beyond nature itself.

Kant assumes that he brings together his double aim of showing the formation of aesthetic sensibility and aesthetic creativity through the idea of reflective teleology. He assumes that in explaining or demonstrating a reflective teleology of nature it is also possible to explain simultaneously the origin of reflective judgement. The key argument is located in 'The Methodology of Teleological Judgement', and especially in the paragraphs which address the question as to whether things in nature can have a purposive, subjective organization. Kant's aim in paragraph 82, in enquiring whether nature establishes a hierarchical chain of purposes, is to show that unknowable ultimate goals cannot be demonstrated. Rather, we can only refer to a final goal or cause, if we refer to a supersensible substratum, which is humankind, because it also refers to the condition and use of human reason. Humankind, then, is the final goal of a teleologically organized nature. Furthermore, because this teleology relies on *our* use of our reason, it is not determinate or mechanical, but rather indeterminate. And it is this indeterminacy which prompts Kant to ask, in paragraph 83, 'what is it, within [humankind itself], that is a purpose and that [it] is to further through his connection with nature?'.[81] He goes on to answer that 'this purpose must either be such as can be fulfilled by nature in its beneficence, or else [must] be [humankind's] aptitude and skill for [pursuing] various purposes for which [it] can use nature (outside or within . . .). On the first alternative the purpose of nature would be humankind's *happiness*, on the second [its] culture.'[82]

As has been pointed out by Howard, this answer can be read in two ways which are indicative of a deep tension in Kant's work as a whole.[83] From the vantage point of 'On a Common Saying: "This may be true in theory, but it does not apply in practice"', it can mean that the goal may be a product of nature (or what Kant also terms Providence), which acts subsumptively like a determinate judgement. Yet in paragraph 83 Kant repeats his argument from the *Critique of Practical Reason*, outlined above, that happiness cannot be the basis of humankind's 'purpose in nature'. Nature promises humankind nothing – especially not happiness.

Kant, then, puts forward another argument which is much closer to that posited in his 'Idea of Universal History from the Point of View of a Citizen of the World'. Nature's ultimate purpose 'is a formal and subjective condition, namely [humankind's] aptitude in general for setting [itself] purposes, and for using nature (independently of [the element of] nature in [humankind's] determination of purposes) as a means [for achieving them] in conformity with the maxims of his free purposes generally'.[84] Humans act purposively in their relation to nature, develop skills and transform it (and from what Kant says in 'The Idea of Universal History' this is the easier task), as well as address their own unsociable sociability – their capacity to conduct war and do evil – by developing civil society. In each, they develop culture.

Nevertheless, Kant's account of 'the terrible tribulations that war inflicts on the human race', of 'the trouble that results from violence' and 'the shining misery' of insatiability ends up subsuming reflective judgement under teleological judgement. Nature achieves its ultimate purpose – civilized, cosmopolitan humankind – by inflicting all manner of cruelties and evil. In humankind's misery, suffering and unsociableness human beings *learn* practical reason. In this context, Kant, through his already constructed idea of harmony can reintroduce the notion of happiness as a subordinate or conditional moment of a culture of citizenship. Happiness is the harmony of nature's ultimate purpose with that of humankind in its perpetual and peaceful coexistence with itself.[85]

However, Kant's solution to the issue of reflective judgement and creativity suppresses the unresolved tension within the text itself, which has come to the surface in the incongruity between the imagination and its products and the interpretative void between the interlocutors (indicated by the void between the artist and his or her audience). Reflective teleology is a constrained way of addressing this double incongruity and filling its gap.

There is, however, an indication in Kant's work of another direction that constructs a path which does not rely on a teleology, and gives a substantive twist to his transcendental formulations. This is evident in the passage quoted earlier, in which he argues that the imagination can only be 'caught' in concepts in multiple ways and in ways which transform dead letters into living spirit, or, as he says, 'which quicken our cognitive power and connect language . . . with spirit'.[86] Kant's use of this term 'spirit' is indicative of an unacknowledged substantivization of his transcendental philosophy. Moreover, it is a substantivization without which his subject-centred philosophy as a whole cannot stand. Fundamentally, it involves a specific anthropological construct or human self-image which anchors it. It is this image, rather than teleology, that propels his philosophy forward and fills the gap, so to speak, between the imagination and reason's exhibition of it. In a stronger sense, though, an anthropology, or specific human self-image 'invents' Kant's meaning of reason and imagination in which universality and transcendentality combine and coalesce. In both the *Critique of Judgement* and in his critical work as a whole it can be argued that the incongruency or gap is filled and utilized by an anthropology which I term a *critical citizenship in the context of unsociable sociability*.[87] This complex formulation is an attempt to capture the double-sided nature of Kant's project. Given the constraints of this essay, the broad outlines of this reconstruction can only be sketched.

Kant posits a subject who critically reflects. This subject also stands in relation to others, often in a mutually hostile and antagonistic way. Yet these subjects must solve together the problem of antagonism and hostility. For Kant, the solution is the universalization of the regime of practical reason, which he terms *citizenship*. It has its own institutional form (the constitutional republic) and norms of good conduct (civic virtues). By means of both the inner and outer life of the subject (including his or her mediated and intersubjective relations) is constituted. This is the theme of *The Metaphysics of Morals* – Doctrine of Right and Doctrine of Virtues, *Anthropology From a Pragmatic Point of View* (through which he constructs the human self-image of critical citizenship in its multiple dimensions), as well as his so-called political-historical writings once these writings are stripped of their teleological elements. The image of critical citizenship that I attribute to Kant can perhaps best be summed up in the lengthy final paragraph of 'What is Enlightenment?', where he states:

> But only a ruler who is himself enlightened and has no fear of phantoms, yet who likewise has at hand a well-disciplined and numerous army to guarantee public security, may say what no republic would dare to say: *Argue as much as you like and about whatever you like, but obey!* This reveals to us a strange and unexpected pattern in human affairs (such as we shall always find if we consider them in the widest sense, in which nearly everything is paradoxical). A high degree of civil freedom seems advantageous to a people's *intellectual* freedom, yet it also sets up insuperable barriers to it. Conversely, a lesser degree of civil freedom gives intellectual freedom enough room to expand to its fullest extent. Thus once the germ on which nature has lavished most care – man's inclination and vocation to *think freely* – has developed within this hard shell, it gradually reacts upon the mentality of the people, who thus gradually become increasingly able to *act freely*. Eventually, it even influences the principles of governments, which find that they can themselves profit by treating man, who is *more than a machine*, in a manner appropriate to his dignity.[88]

Kant's anthropology contains two values which capture and constantly refer to its complex and double-sided nature – autonomous freedom and friendship. The value of autonomous freedom is indicated by the condition and activity of critical reflection, which he also terms enlightenment. In this way, the self-image of citizenship is related to the question of standards and the universality of those standards. According to Kant, everyone should be able to take a 'yes' or 'no' position to statements about the world. In other words, they should be able to take a critical relation to them. This entails that the notions of judgement and autonomous freedom are both central and interrelated. As we have seen, the issues of judgement and autonomy are already laid out in the *Critique of Pure Reason*. In many respects this is what the First *Critique* is about. It is also the subject matter of the much later Third *Critique*, indicating the continuity in Kant's project of establishing both the reality and ground of a reason 'with which every human being is endowed',[89] a reason which concerns opinions, knowing and believing. This image then refers to the capacity of social actors to reflect, to ask questions, upon the nature of opinions, belief and knowledge, and to make judgements about both these reflections and opinions, beliefs and knowledge.

Kant establishes a hierarchy between opinion, belief and knowledge on the grounds of the certainty of truth, both subjectively and objectively. For Kant truth cannot be established on the ground of opinion. Belief may be subjectively, but not objectively sufficient. It is only when, so Kant argues, 'the holding of a thing to be true is sufficient both subjectively and objectively'[90] that there is knowledge. It is the act of making a rational judgement concerning the veracity of knowledge which constitutes, for him, the meeting place between objectivity and subjectivity. And in terms of this reconstruction, an ideal of critical citizenship is established which is the ground that allows the meeting between objectivity and subjectivity to take place. What makes the judgement rational, and hence successful, is when it is derived not only from a reason, that is from principles from which there can arise the rejection of what is learned – but also from a universalizable value horizon (autonomous freedom) which is related to a specific human self-image. *Sensus communis* is the participation in this universalizable value idea.

In addition, there is also the value of friendship which indicates the form through which intersubjective relations should be both established and conducted in the context of potentially mutual hostility. This value is alluded to in Kant's notion of harmony, but which can be transposed into an idea of friendship in 'The Doctrine of Virtue'. This idea captures the mediation and interaction of symmetrically reciprocal intersubjective relations. Kant takes as his horizon and image of friendship the Christianized concept of love, which he secularizes through his own modernization of the category of freedom. Love and practical reason (here termed respect) join hands without *interest*, that is, without invoking claims to patrimonial authority or treating the other as a means to an end (wealth, power or honour). As Kant states: 'The principle of *mutual love* admonishes [people] constantly to *come closer* to one another; that of the *respect* they owe one another, to keep themselves *at a distance* from one another.'[91] Together they avoid the excesses of a love which results in a stifling claustrophobia or of a respect that results in a reserved or aloof remoteness.

The key category of this practical love of humankind is benevolence. Its maxim is the 'duty of mutual benevolence, in accordance with the principle of equality'[92] where benevolence is the desire to do good which results in either beneficence, gratitude or sympathy. In doing good, one not only recognizes the mutuality of others, but also enacts a benevolent attitude to oneself.

Kant's prized treasure is friendship: 'Considered in its perfection [it] is the union of two persons through equal mutual love and respect.'[93] It is 'the complete confidence of two persons in revealing their secret judgements and feelings to each other, as far as such disclosures are consistent with mutual respect'.[94] Reminiscent of Rousseau's utopia of the Elysium in *La Nouvelle Heloise*, where difference and mutuality coalesce without strife, friendship, for Kant, is the affirmation that human beings are made *for* society. In the garden of friendship men and women cultivate each other, and not only themselves. While often burdened by the pragmatics of everyday life, this form of moral friendship is both a utopia and an existing form which serves as a cultural reference point, stylized as a 'form of life' not only for philosophy, but also for literature. Moreover, this notion of friendship, once generalized beyond the sphere of 'subjective spirit', indicates an intersubjectivity formed according to symmetrical reciprocity. It combines an idea of plurality (difference) with a universalizable notion of respect through which this difference is preserved. The combination of freedom and friendship, the result of which might be termed *autonomous respect*, provides the outer limits beyond which plurality should not traverse, and the benchmark for reasoned judgements (critical reflections) about good conduct (what Kant terms virtues).

Together or separately these orientating values, with their reference to the anthropological self-image of critical citizenship in the context of unsociable sociability, suggest how a critical judgement may be enacted in ways that require recourse to neither transcendentality nor teleology. Although the following suggestion is definitely against the grain of Kant's own critical philosophy, it is not against its *spirit*. Judgements have recourse to values which themselves are neither transcendental nor teleological. Nor are they secure. They are historical creations (in Castoriadis's terms, imaginary significations), which also simultaneously refer to a specific human self-image through which relations to others and to self are constituted. It is this human self-image, with its own historically specific values, to which judgements either implicitly or explicitly refer and through which everyday habit, common understanding or competing value ideas are irrationalized. This activity of critical judgement which refers to value ideas can be termed, following the work of Agnes Heller in this instance, 'double quality reflection'. Briefly, and in a way that points to a direction beyond this paper, double-quality reflection is a combination of empirical and transcendental self-reflection, the transcendental moment of which 'is due to the *standpoint* of the particular reflection, which is also non-empirical (an idea, an abstract norm and so on)'.[95] The important point here is that Heller's construction of the transcendental moment refers to the standpoint or perspective of the questioner/interlocutor (what, elsewhere, she has termed attitude). In this sense, and more importantly, the transcendental moment is not identified by her as a particular procedure of thinking and evaluating. Perhaps it is better described as the proto-value through which the activity of double-quality reflection takes place and in the context of this reconstruction the proto-values are autonomous freedom and friendship.

Yet this reconstruction is in danger of leaving Kant's citizen as only a benign subject who, in the context of unsociable sociability, politely acknowledges strangers on the boulevard of promised dreams. This is far from Kant's intention, as well as the intention of this reconstruction. This image of benignity leaves in tact, in a suppressed way, the tension between reason and imagination, and in a way that ignores a series of competing dimensions emerging from the discussion of the sublime. When taken together, the beautiful and the sublime present us with a series of self-images which are more nuanced and more multi-dimensional than what appears at first sight. If, as I have suggested above, the 'gap' between reason and imagination can be filled anthropologically, then an anthropology of critical citizenship does not exhaust a construction of *the* human self-image. In closing, and in a way that indicates the horizon beyond this paper, this anthropological dimension is an as yet unexplored legacy of Kant's discussion of the sublime in both its mathematical and dynamical qualities. By posing the issue of the incongruity thus, the image of the sublime (of chaos, unease and disharmony) is given over to an anthropological context and a series of competing self-images which are available, and which social actors may draw on as they create and interpret the world. These images can also range from those which construe humans as *cruel* (and not only violent and aggressive) in ways through which violence and aggression may be stylized and expressed. Alternatively, they can be construed in terms of an image of love, in which, for example, an intense sociality may be constituted and expressed in an ecstatic simultaneous state of self-suspension and involvement in another outside oneself.

From these self-images are projected phantasies or utopias in which reason or imagination are viewed *metaphorically* as predominant in any particular cultural tradition. In other words, the human self-images are prioritized and stylized according to different historical contexts. In this way, too, Kant's lodestone notion of creativity is broadened, and shifts from a proto-romantic image of protean, radiant energy to one of competing anthropological perspectives, which themselves provide the vantage point from which judgements can be made. It is through these that the forms and meaning of reason are invented, as well as the meanings that the imagination has attributed to it. This means that the meaning of reason and imagination alter. The human self-images become their home, their permanent sites, out of which orientations towards the world in terms of either *reasonings* or *imaginings* take place.

NOTES

1 Immanuel Kant, *Critique of Pure Reason*, trans. Norman Kemp Smith (London, Macmillan Press, 1978), p. 635 where Kant states: 'All the interests of my reason, speculative as well as practical, combine in the following questions:
  '1.What can I know?
  '2.What ought I do?
  '3.What may I hope?'
2 Cf. Kant, ibid., 'Transcendental Doctrine of Method', pp. 571–669. This aspect of Kant's argument has been explored by F.P. Van de Pitte in his *Kant as Philosophical Anthropologist* (The Hague, Martinus Nijhoff, 1971). See also 'Civil Society as the Public' in my *Origins of Modernity* (Cambridge, Polity Press, 1987).
3 Kant, ibid., p. 303.
4 Ibid., p. 177.

5   Ibid., footnote 9 and footnote 10, pp. 106–119.
6   Ibid., p. 658.
7   Ibid., p. 179.
8   Ibid., 196. See also pp. 583ff. For a critique of Kant's transcendental treatment of space and time see E. Durkheim's Introduction to his *Elementary Forms of Religious Life*, where he argues that they are collective representations and thus creations of a specific social collectivity and M. Elias's *Time: An Essay* (Oxford, Blackwell, 1992).
9   Kant, ibid., p. 583.
10 Ibid., pp. 235–236.
11 Ibid., p. 278.
12 Ibid., p. 51. See also p. 192.
13 Ibid., p. 55.
14 Ibid., p. 134.
15 Ibid., p. 112.
16 Ibid., p. 143.
17 Ibid., p. 132.
18 Ibid., p. 147.
19 Ibid., p. 146.
20 Rudolf Makkreel, *Imagination and Interpretation in Kant* (Chicago, The University of Chicago Press, 1990), p. 21.
21 Ibid., p. 30.
22 Ibid.
23 Kant, op. cit., p. 182.
24 Gilles Deleuze, *Kant's Critical Philosophy*, trans. Hugh Tomlinson and Barbara Habberjam (London, The Athlone Press, 1984), p. 18.
25 Makkreel, op. cit., p. 31.
26 Kant, op. cit., A142, B181.
27 Ibid., p. 165, B152.
28 Cf. Makkreel, op. cit., pp. 32–42.
29 Cornelius Castoriadis, *The Imaginary Institution of Society* (Oxford, Polity Press, 1987).
30 Makkreel, ibid., p. 28.
31 Kant, ibid., p. 487.
32 Makkreel, ibid., p. 28. Kant states that 'synthesis in general . . . is the mere result of the power of the imagination, a blind but indispensable function of the soul, without which we should have no knowledge whatsoever, but of which we are scarcely ever conscious' (A78, B103, p. 112).
33 'Imagination is the faculty of representing in intuition an object that is *not itself present*' (B151, p. 165).
34 Cf. W.J. Hipple, *The Beautiful, the Sublime and the Picturesque in Eighteenth Century British Aesthetic Theory* (Carbondale, The Southern Illinois University Press, 1957); P.J. McCormick, *Modernity, Aesthetics and the Bounds of Art* (Ithaca, Cornell University Press, 1990); J. Engell, *The Creative Imagination* (Cambridge, Mass., Harvard University Press, 1981).
35 Kant, *Critique of Judgement*, trans. with an Introduction by Werner S. Pluhar (Indianapolis, Hackett Publishing Company, 1987), pp. 139–140.
36 Ibid., p. 18.
37 Ibid., p. 131.
38 Ibid., p. 231.
39 ibid.
40 W.J. Booth, 'Reason and History: Kant's Other Copernican Revolution', *Kant Studies* 74, 1 (1983), pp. 56–71.

41 This part of the argument also follows closely that of P.J. McCormick, *Modernity, Aesthetics and the Bounds of Art*, op. cit.
42 Kant, ibid., p. 18.
43 Ibid., p. 19.
44 Kant argues in the first Introduction that reflective judgement 'must assume that nature, with its boundless diversity has hit upon a division of this diversity (into genera and species) that enables [ ] judgement to find accordance among the natural forms it compares, and [so] enables it to arrive at empirical concepts, as well as at coherence among these by ascending concepts that are more general [though] also empirical. In other words, judgement presupposes a system of nature even in terms of empirical laws and does so *a priori* and hence by means of a transcendental principle' (ibid., note 21, p. 400).
45 Ibid., p. 401.
46 Ibid., p. 402.
47 Ibid.
48 Ibid., p. 405.
49 Ibid., p. 30.
50 Ibid., p. 413.
51 Ibid., p. 53.
52 Cf. also #58.
53 Ibid., pp. 28–29.
54 Ibid., p. 98.
55 Ibid., p. 92.
56 Cf. #46–47, for the preceding discussion see also #23–28.
57 Ibid., p. 179. On the creative loneliness of the creative genius see #47 and the *Critique of Pure Reason*, esp. p. 580.
58 Ibid., p. 229.
59 Kant, trans. Meredith (Oxford, Clarendon Press, 1964), p. 177. The Meredith translation captures the better sense in this instance.
60 Ibid., p. 180.
61 Kant, trans. Pluhar, ibid., p. 185.
62 Ibid., p. 217.
63 Ibid., p. 184.
64 Ibid., p. 185.
65 Cf. C. Castoriadis, 'The Greek Polis and the Creation of Democracy' in *Philosophy, Politics, Autonomy*, trans. David Ames Curtis (New York, Oxford University Press, 1991), esp. pp. 96–98. As Castoriadis points out, Kant's theory of aesthetics forces him 'to go beyond his strictly dualistic approach and to consider what late neo-Kantians (for example Rickert) would call *das Zwischenreich des immanenten Sinnes* (the in-between realm of immanent meanings)' (p. 98).
66 This image of the genius can be transposed into either the ascetic or romantic revolutionary who can quite easily do infinite violence to others and themselves. Certainly Kant is no Jacobin, nor does he stand on the ground of the redemptive paradigm. He argues that art and genius (and here we also mean the genius for politics) require training (civilization) and that its unfettered creativity should be made subordinate to cultural demands which themselves are demands for sociability and its responsibilities. Cf. #50. One of the difficulties of Kant's position is that he gives up the more classical ideas of wisdom and *phronesis*, and despite the deployment of the language of virtues, constructs good or sound judgement (as a version of a theory of action) in post-virtue terms.
67 Kant, *Critique of Pure Reason*, ibid., p. 630.
68 Cf. *Critique of Practical Reason*, pp. 174–195.

69 See also 'The Discipline of Pure Reason in Respect to its Polemical Employment', *Critique of Pure Reason*, pp. 593–612.

70 Kant, *Critique of Judgement*, #40, esp. pp. 160–162. Kant argues that the first is the maxim of understanding, the second that of judgement, and the third that of reason. For our purposes this division is not as important as it is for Kant.

71 Kant, *Critique of Judgement* (Pluhar trans.), ibid., p. 139.

72 Ibid., p. 144.

73 Ibid.

74 Ibid.

75 Ibid., p. 146.

76 Ibid., p. 151.

77 Ibid., p. 162.

78 C. Castoriadis, 'The Greek Polis and the Creation of Democracy', op. cit., p. 96.

79 Kant, ibid., p. 143.

80 Ibid., cf. #59.

81 Ibid., p. 317.

82 Ibid.

83 Dick Howard, *From Marx to Kant* (Albany, State University of New York Press, 1985), chapter 5, esp. pp. 140–142.

84 Kant, ibid., p. 319.

85 Ibid., pp. 323–324.

86 Ibid., p. 185.

87 This is not the only anthropological image that can be posited. There are two others that are present which I will term cruelty and love. While it is beyond the scope of this paper to elucidate them further, it can be argued that Kant addresses these in terms of unsociable sociability (war and evil, especially radical evil, cf. 'Perpetual Peace' and *Religion Within the Limits of Reason Alone*), and the forms which love can take and its orientating values ('Doctrine of Virtue'). He subsumes and subordinates both cruelty and love to an anthropology of 'critical citizenship' with its own values of autonomous freedom and citizenship. Cf. my concluding remarks below.

88 Kant, 'What is Enlightenment?', *Kant: Political Writings*, edited with an Introduction and notes by Hans Reiss, trans. H.B. Nisbet (2nd edn, Cambridge, Cambridge University Press, 1991), pp. 59–60.

89 Kant, *Critique of Pure Reason*, p. 658.

90 Ibid., p. 646.

91 Kant, *The Metaphysics of Morals*, Introduction, trans. and notes by Mary Gregor (Cambridge, Cambridge University Press, 1991), p. 244.

92 Ibid., p. 245.

93 Ibid., p. 261.

94 Ibid., p. 263.

95 Agnes Heller, *General Ethics* (Oxford, Basil Blackwell, 1988), p. 28., and 'The Elementary Ethics of Everyday Life', pp. 48–64 in this volume.

Chapter 6

Imagination in discourse and in action

Paul Ricoeur

INTRODUCTION: FOR A GENERAL THEORY OF IMAGINATION

The question considered in this essay can be stated in the following terms: Can the conception of imagination, first set out in the context of a theory of metaphor centred around the notion of semantic innovation, be expanded outside the sphere of discourse to which it originally belonged?

This question is itself part of a wider investigation of which I earlier gave the ambitious title of the 'Poetics of Volition'. The present essay represents one step in the direction of this 'Poetics':[1] the step from the theoretical to the practical. It seemed to me that the test of any claim to universality made by a theory constructed within the sphere of language would be to investigate its capacity of extension to the practical sphere.

We shall therefore proceed as follows. First, we shall review some classical problems inherent in the philosophy of imagination and shall briefly sketch a possible solution worked out within the framework of a theory of metaphor. The tie between imagination and semantic innovation, the core of our entire analysis, will therefore be proposed as the starting point for further development.

The second part will deal with the *transition* from the theoretical sphere to the practical sphere. A certain number of phenomena and experiences will be selected and ordered in accordance with their respective functions at the interesection of the theoretical and the practical: fiction helping to re-describe the action which has already taken place, fiction as belonging to an individual agent's plan of action, or fiction creating the very field of intersubjective action.

The third part will be situated at the very heart of the notion of the *social imaginary*, touchstone of the practical function of the imagination. If the key figures of *ideology* and *utopia* are heavily stressed here, this is because they echo, at the far end of the trajectory we shall follow in this essay, the ambiguities and the contradictions mentioned in the first part of our study. Perhaps it will then become apparent that these ambiguities and contradictions are not the drawbacks of the *theory* of the imagination alone but are constitutive of the *phenomenon* of imagination as such. Only the test of generalization will give weight and substance to this hypothesis.

A philosophical investigation applied to the problem of imagination inevitably encounters from its very outset a series of obstacles, paradoxes, and checks which perhaps explain the relative eclipse of the problem of imagination in contemporary philosophy.

To begin with, the general problem of imagination suffers from the disrepute in which the term 'image' is held following its misuse in the empiricist theory of knowledge. The discredit suffered by 'psychologism' in contemporary semantics – in the eyes of logicians as well as linguists – also attaches to references to imagination in the theory of 'sense' (in this regard we have only to mention Gottlob Frege and his distinction between the 'sense' of a proposition or a concept – 'objective' and 'ideal' sense – and the 'representation' which remains 'subjective' and merely 'factual'). Behaviourist psychology is similarly anxious to eliminate images, which it holds to be private, unobservable mental entities. Then, too, the zealous pursuit of popular philosophy of creativity has to no small degree contributed to discrediting the imagination in the eyes of 'analytical' philosophers.

Behind this repugnance expressed by philosophers for welcoming the 'return of the outcast', there lies a doubt rooted deeper than a passing mood or a question of circumstances. This doubt was forcefully articulated by Gilbert Ryle in his *Concept of Mind*. Does the term 'imagination' designate a single, coherent phenomenon or a collection of experiences only distantly related? Tradition conveys at least four main uses of the term. It indicates first of all the arbitrary evocation of things which are absent but which exist elsewhere; this evocation does not imply any confusion of the absent thing with things which are present here and now.

Following a usage close to the preceding one, the same term designates portraits, paintings, drawings, diagrams, and so on – all of which have their own physical existence but whose function is to 'take the place of' the things they represent.

Stretching the meaning still further, we term images fictions which bring to mind not absent things but non-existent things. These fictions, however, range from dreams – products of sleep – to inventions possessing a purely literary existence such as dramas and novels.

Finally, the term image is applied to the domain of illusion, that is, to representations which for an outside observer or for later reflection, are addressed to absent or non-existent things but which, for the subject and in the instant in which this subject attends to them, call for belief in the reality of their object.

What then do the awareness of absence and illusory belief or the nothing of presence and pseudo-presence have in common?

The theories of the imagination handed down by philosophical tradition, far from clarifying this radical equivocacy, are instead themselves divided over what is to be taken as paradigmatic in this wide range of basic significations. For this reason, there is a tendency to construct in each instance univocal – but rival – theories of the imagination. The range of variation found in these theories can be measured along two different axes: with regard to the object, the axis of presence and absence; with regard to the subject, the axis of fascinated consciousness and critical consciousness.

Along the first axis, the image corresponds to two opposing theories, illustrated by Hume and by Sartre, respectively. At one end of this first axis the image is referred to the preception of which it is merely the trace, in the sense of a lesser presence; all theories of reproductive imagination tend towards this pole. At the other end of the same axis, the image is thought of essentially in relation to absence, of other-than-present; the various key figures of productive imagination – portrait, dream, and fiction – all refer in different ways to this fundamental otherness.

The productive imagination and even the reproductive imagination, to the extent that it includes the minimum initiative consisting in evoking the absent thing, also both lie along a second axis, where the distinguishing factor is whether or not the subject of imagination is capable of assuming a critical awareness of the difference between the imaginary and the real. Theories of the image then take their place along an axis – noetic this time instead of noematic – where the variations are ordered according to the degree of belief involved. At one end of the axis – that defind by a complete lack of critical awareness – the image is confused with the real, taken for the real. Here we see the power of lies and errors decried by Pascal; it is also *mutatis mutandis* Spinoz's *imaginatio*, infected with belief as long as a contrary belief has not dislodged it from its primary position. At the other end of the axis, where critical distance is fully conscious of itself, imagination serves instead as the instrument of the critique of reality. Husserlian transcendental reduction, as the neutralization of existence, is the fullest illustration of this. The variations in meaning along the second axis are no less ample than those mentioned above. What is common to the *state of confusion* characterizing a consciousness which inadvertently takes as real something which for another consciousness is not real and the *act of distinction*, possessing a high degree of self-awareness, by which a consciousness posits something at a distance from the real thereby producing otherness at the very heart of its experience?

This is the knot of contradictions which appear when we survey the shambles of the theory of the imagination today. Do these contradictions betray a weakness in the philosophy of the imagination or do they denote a structural trait of the imagination itself which philosophy will have to account for?

IMAGINATION IN DISCOURSE

What new approach to the phenomenon of imagination does the theory of metaphor offer? What it offers is first of all a different manner of putting the problem. Instead of approaching the problem by way of perception and asking if and how we can move from perception to image, the theory of metaphor invites us to relate the imagination to a certain type of language use, more precisely, to see in it an aspect of *semantic innovation* characteristic of the metaphorical uses of language. This shift in attack is considerable in itself, as so many prejudices were linked with the idea that the image is an appendix to perception, a shadow of perception. To say that our images are spoken before they are seen is to abandon what we initially – but mistakenly – take for granted, namely, that the image is first and foremost a 'scene' being played out on the stage of a mental 'theatre' for the benefit of an internal 'spectator'; but this also means giving up a second point we also mistakenly assume, namely, that this mental entity is the stuff out of which we construct our abstract ideas, our concepts, the basic ingredient in some sort of mental alchemy.

But if an image is not derived from perception, how can it be derived from language?

An analysis of the poetic image, taken as a paradigmatic case, will provide the germ of a reply. The poetic image is something that the poem as a certain work of language sets out in certain circumstances and in accordance with a certain procedure. The procedure involved here is reverberation, to use an expression which Gaston Bachelard borrowed from Eugene Minkowski. But to understand this procedure we first have to see that reverberation comes not from things seen but from things said. The question which must be treated first, therefore, concerns the very circumstances of discourse which serve to generate the imaginary.

I have studied elsewhere how metaphor functions and the important consequences this has for a theory of the imagination. I showed that this functioning is thoroughly misunderstood if metaphor is considered as simply a deviant use of names, a deviation in denomination. Metaphor involves instead a deviant use of predicates in the context of the sentence as a whole. We must therefore speak of metaphorical *utterance* instead of names used metaphorically. The question then turns around the discursive strategy governing the *use of unusual predicates*. Along with certain French and English authors, I want to stress predicative non-pertinence as the means of producing a sort of shock between different semantic fields. It is in answer to the challenge stemming from this shock that we produce a new predicative pertinence which is the metaphor. In its turn, this new appropriateness which is produced at the level of the sentence as a whole provokes, at the level of the individual word, the extension of meaning by which classical rhetoric identifies metaphor.

The value of this approach lies in shifting our attention from problems of change of meaning at the simple level of denomination to problems of restructuring semantic fields at the level of predicative use.

It is precisely at this point that the theory of metaphor is of interest to the philosophy of imagination. The tie between the two theories has always been regarded with a certain suspicion, as is witnessed by the very expression *figurative* language and *figure* of style. It is as if metaphor gave a body, a contour, a face to discourse. But how? It is, in my opinion, in the instant when a new meaning emerges out of the shambles of literal predication that the imagination offers its own special mediation. In order to understand this, let us begin with Aristotle's famous remark that to 'make good metaphor . . . is to perceive the similar'. But we should be mistaken as to the role of resemblance if we were to interpret this in terms of the association of ideas, as the association through resemblance (in contrast to the association of contiguity which governs metonymy and synecdoche). Resemblance is itself a function of the use of unusual predicates. It consists in the *rapprochement* in which the logical distance between farflung semantic fields suddenly falls away, creating a semantic shock which, in turn, sparks the meaning of the metaphor. Imagination is the apperception, the sudden view, of a new predicative pertinence. This could be called *predicative assimilation* in order to stress the point that resemblance itself is a process of the same nature as the predicative process itself. None of this then is taken from the old association of ideas as it relates to the mechanical attraction of mental atoms. Imagining is first and foremost restructuring semantic fields. It is, to use Wittgenstein's expression in the *Philosophical Investigations*, 'seeing as . . . .'.

In this we find what is essential to the Kantian theory of schematism. Schematism, Kant said, is a method for giving an image to a concept. And again, schematism is a rule of producing images. Let us set aside the second assertion for the moment and concentrate instead on the first. In what sense is imagination a method rather than a content? In that it is the very operation of grasping the similar, in the predicative assimilation which answers the initial semantic shock. Suddenly we are 'seeing as . . .'; we see old age as the close of the day, time as a beggar, nature as a temple or living pillars, and so forth. Of course, we have not yet accounted for the quasi-sensorial aspect of images. But at least we have introduced Kantian productive imagination into the field of language. In short, the work of the imagination is to schematize metaphorical attribution. Like the Kantian schema, it gives an image to an emerging meaning. Before it is a faded perception, the image is an emerging meaning.

The transition to the image's quasi-sensorial aspect, usually quasi-optical, is then easily understandable. The phenomenology of reading offers us a sure guide here. It is in the experience of reading that we surprise the phenomenon of reverberation, of echoing or resounding, by which the schema produces images in its turn. In schematizing the metaphorical attribution, the imagination radiates out in all direction, reanimating earlier experiences, awakening dormant memories, spreading to adjacent sensorial fields. As Bachelard before him, Marcus Hester remarks in *The Meaning of Poetic Metaphor* that the sort of image evoked or stimulated in this way is less the free-floating image treated in the theory of association than the 'bound' image engendered by 'poetic diction'. The poet is an artisan working in language, who creates and gives form to images through the medium of language alone.

The effect of reverberation, resonance, or echo, is not a secondary phenomenon. If, on the one hand, it seems to weaken and scatter sense in the case of daydreams, on the other hand, the image introduces into the entire process a note of suspension, an effect of neutralization, in short, a negative moment thanks to which the entire process is placed in the dimension of unreality. The ultimate role of the image is not only to spread meaning over diverse sensorial fields but to hold meaning suspended in this neutralized atmosphere, in the element of fiction. Indeed, it is this element which will appear again at the close of our study under the name of utopia. But it already seems that the imagination is really what we all mean by this term: a free play of possibilities in a state of uninvolvement with respect to the world of perception or action. It is in this state of uninvolvement that we try out new ideas, new ways of being in the world. But this 'common sense' belonging to the notion of the imagination is not fully recognized as long as the fecundity of the imagination has not been connected to that of language as it is exemplified in the metaphorical process. For we then forget this verity: we only see images in so far as we first hear them.

IMAGINATION AT THE INTERSECTION OF THEORY AND PRACTICE

The heuristic force of fiction

The first – and most general – condition for *applying* the semantic theory of imagination outside the sphere of discourse that is semantic innovation is already, within the limits of metaphorical utterance, an *ad extra* application, that is, has a *referential* dimension.

Now this is not self-evident. It may even seem that in its poetic usage language is concerned only with itself and thus has no reference. Did we not just stress above the neutralizing action performed by the imagination in regard to positing existence? Could the metaphorical utterance then have a sense without possessing a reference?

In my opinion, this assertion only tells half the truth. The neutralizing function of the imagination with respect to the 'thesis of the world' is only the negative condition required to free a second-order referential force. An analysis of the affirmative force deployed by poetic language shows that is is not just the sense which is split in the metaphorical process but the reference as well. What is eliminated is the ordinary language reference applied to objects which correspond to one of our interests, our primary interest in controlling and manipulating. By holding in abeyance this interest and the sphere of meaning it governs, poetic discourse allows our deep-seated insertion in the life-world to emerge; it allows the ontological tie uniting our being to other beings and to Being to be articulated. What is articulated in this way is what I call second-order reference and which in reality is the primordial reference.

The consequence for the theory of imagination is considerable indeed. It concerns the transition from sense to reference in *fiction*. Fiction has, so to speak, a double valence as to its reference: it is directed elsewhere, even nowhere, but because it designates the non-place in relation to reality as a whole, it can indirectly point to this reality by means of what I should like to call a new 'reference effect' (in the way that some people speak about 'meaning effects'). This new reference effect is nothing other than the power of fiction to *redescribe* reality. Later we shall see the virulent force of this redescription in the key figure of utopia.

This tie between fiction and redescription has been forcefully stressed by certain thinkers working in model theory and hence outside the field of poetic language. There is a body of work which strongly suggests that models are to certain forms of scientific discourse what fictions are to certain forms of poetic discourse. The feature common to both models and fiction is their *heuristic* force, that is, their capacity to open up and unfold new dimensions of reality, suspending our belief in an earlier description.

It is here that the opposing philosophical tradition concerning images offers stubborn resistance; this is the tradition which holds the image to be a faded perception, a shadow of reality. The paradox of fiction is that striking out perception is the condition for heightening our vision of things. François Dagognet demonstrates this in great detail in *Ecriture et Iconographie* (1973). Every icon is a graphic figure which recreates reality at a higher level of realism. This 'iconic increase' occurs through the use of abbreviations and articulations, as is shown by a careful study of the main episodes in the history of painting and of all types of graphic inventions. Applying the vocabulary of the second law of thermodynamics, we can say that this reference effect amounts to scaling the entropic slope of ordinary perception, inasmuch as perception tends to level out differences and soften contrasts. This theory of the iconic element agrees with Nelson Goodman's theory of generalized symbols in *The Languages of Art* (1968): all symbols – in art and in language – have the same referential claim to 'remake reality'.

Any transition from discourse to praxis stems from this initial extension of fiction outside itself, following the principle of iconic increase.

Fiction and narrative

The first transition from the theoretical to the practical is close at hand. For what certain fictions redescribe is precisely human action itself. Or, to approach the same thing from a different angle, the first way man tries to understand and to master the 'diversity' of the practical field is to provide himself with a fictional representation. Whether this is ancient tragedy, modern drama, novels, fables, or legends, the narrative structure provides fiction with the techniques of abbreviation, articulation, and condensation through which the iconic increase effect is obtained; this, we have noted, has been described elsewhere with regard to painting and the other plastic arts. This is basically what Aristotle had in mind in the poetics when he tied the 'mimetic' function of poetry – that is, in the context of his treatise, of tragedy – to the 'mythical' structure of the fable constructed by the poet. This is a great paradox: tragedy 'imitates' action only because it 'recreates' it on the level of a well-structured fiction. Aristotle is therefore able to conclude that poetry is more philosophical than history which is concerned with the contingent, with the ordinary course of action. Poetry goes straight to the essence of action precisely because it connects *mythos* and *mimesis*, that is, in our vocabulary, *fiction* and *redescription*.

To generalize, may we not extend this remark to any kind of 'recounting', of 'telling a story'? Why have all peoples invented so many apparently strange and complicated stories? Is it merely for the pleasure of playing with the various combinations afforded by a few simple action segments and by the basic roles which corresponds to them – the traitor, the messenger, the saviour, and so on – as structural analyses of stories seem to suggest? Or, based upon this very type of structural analysis, should we not extend the dialectic of fiction and redescription to narrative structure as well? If this comparison is valid, we have to distinguish between the act of narration and the story strucuture, in order to then discern in the narration what is characteristic of an act of disclosure as such, with its fundamental illocutionary and referential force. This referential force consists in the fact that the narrative act, through the narrative structures, applied the framework of an ordered fiction to the diversity of human action. Between what could be a logic of narrative possibilities and the empirical diversity of action, narrative fiction interposes its schematism of human action. By mapping out action in this way, the storyteller produces the same reference effect as the poet who, in Aristotle's terms, imitates reality in his mythical reinvention. Or, to use the terminology of model theory mentioned briefly above, we may say that the story is a heuristic process of redescription in which the heurisitc function stems from the narrative structure and redescription has the action itself for referent.

This first step into the practical sphere is still, however, of limited significance. Inasmuch as fiction is restricted to mimetic activity, what is redescribed is an action which is *already there*. Redescription is still just a form of description. A poetics of action calls for something more than a reconstruction with only descriptive value.

Now in addition to its mimetic function, even when applied to action, imagination also has a projective function which is part of the dynamics of action itself.

Fiction and the capacity to act

This function is clearly shown by the phenomenology of *individual* action. No action without imagination, so to speak. And this is true in several ways: from the viewpoint of projects, from that of motivation, and from that of the very capacity to act. In the first instance, the noematic content of the project – what I formerly called the *pragma*, that is, the thing to be done by me – includes a certain schematization of the network of ends and means, which could be termed the schema of the pragma. It is, in fact, in the anticipatory imagining of action that I 'try out' different possible courses of action and that I 'play' – in the literal sense of the word – with practical possibilities. It is here that pragmatic 'play' overlaps with the narrative 'play' mentioned above; the function of the project, turned towards the future, and the function of the narrative, turned towards the past , exchange schemata and frameworks, the project borrowing the story's structuring capacity and the story receiving the project's capacity for looking ahead. Next, the imagination shares something of the motivational process as well. It is the imagination which provides the milieu, the luminous clearing in which we can compare and contrast motives as different as desires and ethical demands, which in turn can range from professional rules to social customs or to strictly personal values. The imagination provides the mediating space of a common 'fantasy' for things as diverse as the force which pushes as if from behind, the attraction which seduces as if from in front, reasons which justify and establish as if from underneath. It is in a form of the imaginary that the common 'dispositional' element is represented practically, marking the difference, on the one hand, between a physically constraining cause and a motive and, on the other hand, between a motive and a logically constraining reason. This form of the practical imaginary has its linguistic equivalent in expressions such as: I could do this or that, if I wanted. Language limits itself here to transporting and expressing in the conditional the sort of neutralizing, of hypothetical transposition which is the condition of figurability, permitting desire to enter the common sphere of motivation. Here, language is second in relation to the imaginary unfolding of motives in what has been termed metaphorically a luminous clearing. Finally, it is in the realm of the imaginary that I try out my capacity to do something, that I take the measure of 'I can'. I ascribe my own capacity to myself – as the agent of my own action – only by picturing it to myself in terms of imaginative variations on the theme of 'I could', or 'I could have done otherwise had I wanted'. Here again, language is a good guide. Extending Austin's brilliant analysis in his famous article on 'Ifs and Cans', we can say that in expressions of the form, 'I could, I could have if . . .', the conditional provides the grammatical projection of imaginative variations on the theme 'I can'. This form of the conditional belongs to the tense logic of the practical imagination. What is essential from a phenomenological standpoint is that I grasp the immediate certainty of this power only through the imaginative variations which mediate this certainty.

There is thus a progression from the simple schematization of my projects, through the figurability of my desires, to the imaginative variations of the 'I can'. This progression points to the idea of imagination as a general function of what is possible in practice. It is this general function which Kant anticipates in the *Critique of Judgement* under the term of the 'free-play' of the imagination.

It remains to be seen, with regard to the freedom of the imagination, what the imagination of freedom might possibly be. A simple phenomenology of individual action, however, is no longer sufficient here. This phenomenology has, of course, outstripped the bounds of the purely mimetic function of the imagination. But it has not gone beyond the limits set by the individual character of human action at this stage of the investigation.

Fiction and intersubjectivity

We shall make a decisive step towards the social imaginary by meditating on the conditions of the possibility of historical experience in general. The imagination is implicated here inasmuch as the historical field of experience itself has an analogical constitution. This point deserves careful elaboration, for it is here that the theory of the imagination transcends not only the literary examples of fiction applied to action but even the phenomenology of volition as a principle of individual action. The starting point is found in the theory of intersubjectivity set out by Husserl in the *Fifth Cartesian Meditation* and in Alfred Schütz's development of this theory. We can speak of an *historical* field of experience because my temporal field is connected to another temporal field by what is termed a relation of 'pairing' (*Paarung*). In accordance with this pairing, one temporal flux can accompany another. What is more, this 'pairing' seems to be only a cross-section of an all-encompassing flux in which each of us has not only contemporaries but predecessors and successors as well. This higher order temporality carries with it its own intelligibility involving categories which are not just extensions of the categories of individual action (project, motivation, ascribing an act to an agent who can do what he does, and so on). The categories of common actions make specific relations between contemporaries, predecessors, and successors possible, and among these is found the transmission of traditions to the extent that this forms a tie which can be broken or renewed.

Now the inner connection belonging to this all-encompassing flux we call history is subordinated not only to these categories of common action (which Max Weber discusses in *Wirtschaft und Gesellschaft*), but to a higher order transcendental principle which plays the same role as the Kantian 'I can' which is held to accompany all my representations. This higher principle is the principle of analogy implied in the initial act of pairing diverse temporal fields, those of our contemporaries, those of our predecessors, and those of our successors. These fields are analogous in the sense that each of us, in principle, can exercise the function of *I* just *as any other* and can ascribe his experience to himself. It is here, as we shall see, that the imagination is involved. But first it must be recalled that the principle of analogy has, unfortunatley, most often been mistakenly interpreted in terms of an argument, in the sense of reasoning by analogy; as if in order to ascribe to another the power of saying 'I', I had to compare his behaviour to mine and to employ an argument using the proportional fourth term based on the purported resemblance between the behaviour of others observed from outside and my own experienced directly. The analogy implied in the coupling is in no way an argument. It is the transcendental principle establishing the other as another self like myself, a self *like* my self. The analogy here involves the direct transfer of the meaning 'I'. *Like* me, my contemporaries, my predecessors, and my successors *can* say 'I'. It is in this way that I am historically related to all the others. It is also in this sense that the principle of analogy between the various temporal fields is to the handing down of traditions what the Kantian 'I think' is to the causal order of experience.

Such is the transcendental condition under which the imagination is a fundamental component in founding the historical field. It is not by accident that Husserl, in the *Fifth Meditation*, bases his notion of analogical apperception on that of imaginative transfer. To say that you think as I do, that you experience pleasure and pain as I do, is to be able to imagine what I should think and experience if I were in your place. This transfer in the imagination of my 'here' to your 'there' is the root of what we call empathy (*Einfühlung*), which can be hate as easily as love. In this sense, the transfer in imagination is to analogical apperception what schematism is to objective experience in Kant. The imagination is the schematism belonging to the constitution of intersubjectivity in analogical apperception. This schematism functions in the same way as the productive imagination in objective experience, namely, as the genesis of new connections. The task of this productive imagination is, in particular to keep alive all sorts of mediations which make up historical ties and, among these, institutions which objectify the social link and increasingly transform the 'us' into 'them', to use Alfred Schütz's expression. This anonymity of mutual relations in a bureaucratic society can go so far as to simulate causal connections on the level of objects. This systematic distortion of communication, this radical reification of the social process, thus tends to abolish the difference between the course of history and the course of things. It is then the task of the productive imagination to fight against this terrifying entropy in human relations. To express this in the idiom of competence and performance, the imagination has as its competence preserving and identifying the *analogy of the ego* in all relations with our contemporaries, our predecessors, and our successors. Its competence therefore lies in preserving and identifying the difference between the course of history and the course of things.

In conclusion, the possibility of an historical experience in general lies in our ability to remain open to the effects of history, to borrow Gadamer's category, *Wirkungsgeschichte*. We are affected by the effects of history, however, only to the extent that we are able to increase our capacity to be affected in this way. The imagination is the secret of this competence.

SOCIAL IMAGINARY

The fourth and final step in the study we have placed at the crossroads of theory and practice may possibly have led us too far too fast. Of course, the capacity, mentioned in our conclusion, which delivers us over in the imagination to the 'effects of history' is indeed the basic condition of historical experience in general. But this condition is buried so deeply and has been so neglected that it constitutes nothing more than an ideal of communication, an idea in the Kantian sense. The truth of our condition is that the analogical tie which makes every man another like myself is accessible to us only through a certain number of *imaginative practices*, such as *ideology* and *utopia*. These imaginative practices are broadly defined as mutually antagonistic and as representative of two different pathologies which completely mask the positive function of each, that is, the contribution made by each in establishing the analogical tie between myself and my fellowman. As a result, the productive imagination mentioned above – and which we considered the schematization of this analogical tie – can be restored to itself only through the *critique* of the antagonistic and semi-pathological figures of the social imagination. Mistaking the unavoidable nature of this detour is what I meant above by going too far too fast. We must therefore consider a twofold ambiguity, that which results from the polarity *between* idelogy and utopia and that resulting from the polarity *within* each of these between its positive and constructive side and its negative and destructive side.

With regard to the first polarity, that between ideology and utopia, we have to admit that since Karl Mannheim's *Ideologie und Utopie* in 1929, it has seldom appeared as the object of study. There is indeed a Marxist and post-Marxist critique of ideologies, forcefully developed by K.O. Apel and Jürgen Habermas in line with the Frankfurt school. But, on the other hand, we find a history and a sociology of utopia only loosely connected to this *Ideologie Kritik*. And yet Karl Mannheim had paved the way by showing the difference between these two phenomena on the basis of a common criterion of *non-*

congruence with respect to historical and social reality. In my opinion, this criterion presupposes that individuals as well as collective entities (groups, classes, nations, etc.) are primarily and without exception related to social reality in a manner other than that of direct participation, in accordance with the key figures of non-coincidence which are precisely those of the social imaginary.

The sketch which follows will be limited to drawing the basic traits of this imaginary which point up the analogical constitution of the social tie. The investigation will not be pointless if it re-establishes at the end of its course the initial ambiguities and contradictions of the meditation on the imagination.

I have attempted, in another study, to discern the levels of meaning which form the phenomenon of ideology. I upheld the thesis that the ideological phenomenon could not be limited to the role of distortion and dissimulation, as a simplified interpretation of Marxism would have it. We could not even understand that ideology is capable of conferring such true effectiveness on an inverted image of reality if we have not first acknowledged the constituting nature of the social imaginary. The latter operates at the most primitive level, as is described by Max Weber at the start of his great work when he characterizes social action as meaningful behaviour which is mutually oriented and socially integrated. It is at this radical level that ideology is constituted. It seems related to the need every group has to give itself an *image* of itself, to 'represent' itself, in the theatrical sense of the word, to put itself on stage, to play itself. Perhaps no social group can exist without this indirect relation to its own being through a representation of itself. As Lévi-Strauss forcefully affirms in his introduction to the work of Mauss, symbolism is not an effect of society but society an effect of symbolism. The nascent pathology of the ideological phenomenon arises from its very function of reinforcing and repeating the social tie in situations that occur after the fact. Simplification, schematization, stereotyping and ritualization arise out of the ever-widening distance between actual practice and the interpretations through which the group becomes aware of its own existence and practice. The condition of the production of social messages seems indeed to be a certain kind of non-transparency of our cultural codes.

In the same analysis, I try to show that the function of dissmulation clearly surpasses that of integration when ideological representations are monitored by the system of authority in a given society. Every authority, in fact, seeks to make itself legitimate. Now it seems that if every claim to legitimacy is linked with people's belief in this legitimacy, the relation between the authority's claim and the belief which answers to this is basically unsymmetrical. The claim coming from the authority always contains more than the belief which is accorded this authority. It is here that ideology mobilizes its forces to fill the gap between the demand from above and the belief from below.

I think that the Marxist concept of ideology, with its metaphor of 'turning the real on its head' in an illusionary image, can be set against this double background. For how indeed could illusions, fantasies, or phantasmagoria have any historical significance if ideology did not have a mediating function in the most basic social tie, if ideology were not contemporaneous with the symbolic constitution of social ties themselves? In truth, we cannot speak of a real activity which would be pre-ideological or non-ideological. We could not even understand how an inverted representation of reality could service the interests of a ruling class if the relation between domination and ideology were not more primitive than the analysis based on social classes and were not capable of even outliving the class structure. All that Marx contributes which is new and unquestionably valid stands out against this initial background of the symbolic constitution of social ties in general and of the relation of authority in particular. His own contribution concerns the legitimizing function of ideology with respect to the relations of domination stemming from the division into classes and the class struggle.

Finally, however, it is the polarity between ideology and utopia which makes both its founding role and its specific pathology intelligible. The difficulty inherent in the simultaneous study of utopia and ideology lies in the fact that utopia, unlike ideology, forms a definite literary genre. Utopia knows itself as utopia. It clearly calls out its name. Then, too, its literary status, at least since Thomas More, allows us to approach its existence by way of its writings. The history of utopia is staked out with the names of its inventors, in direct contrast to the anonymity of ideologies.

As soon as one tries to define utopia in terms of its *content*, one is surprised to find that in spite of the continuity of certain themes – the status of the family, the consumption and the appropriation of goods, the organization of political life and of religion – it is not difficult to class diametrically opposed projects under each of these terms. This paradox will lead us later to an interpretation in terms of imagination. But we can already at this point begin to suspect that if utopia is the imaginary project of another society, of another reality, this 'constituting imagination', as Desroche calls it, can justify the most conflicting choices. Another family, another sexuality can mean monachism or sexual community. Another type of consumption can mean asceticism or conspicuous consumption. Another relation to property can mean direct appropriation in the absence of law or detailed artificial planning. Another relation to the government of the people can mean employee-run enterprises or submission to a virtuous and disciplined bureaucracy. Another relation to religion can mean radical atheism or festivity.

The crucial point in the analysis consists in tying all these thematic variations to the more fundamental ambiguities inherent in the *function* of utopia. These functional variations parallel those of ideology. The layers of meaning to be found here must be set out in both cases with the same sense of complexity and paradox. Just as we had to resist the temptation to interpret ideology in terms of dissimulation and distortion alone, we must also resist the temptation to construct the concept of utopia on the sole basis of its quasi-pathological expressions.

The central idea should be that of *nowhere* implied by the word itself and by Thomas More's description. For it is beginning with this strange spatial extraterrestrialness – this non-place in the literal sense of the word – that we can take a fresh look at our reality, in relation to which nothing can henceforth be taken for granted. The field of the possible now extends out beyond the real. It is this field which is staked out by the 'other' ways of living mentioned above. The question, then, is knowing whether the imagination could have a 'constituting' role in this leap outside. Utopia is the mode in which we radically rethink what family, consumption, government, religion, and so on are. From 'nowhere' springs the most formidable questioning of what is. Utopia therefore appears in its primitive core as the exact counterpart of our first concept of ideology as the function of social integration. Utopia, in counterpoint, is the function of social subversion.

In saying this, we are ready to pursue the parallelism one step further, following the second concept of ideology as the instrument for legitimizing a given system of authority. What is in fact at stake in utopia is precisely the 'given' found in all systems of authority, namely, the excess of the demand for legitimacy in relation to the belief held by members of the community. Just as ideologies tend to bridge this gap or to hide it, utopias, one might say, reveal the unstated surplus value attaching to authority and unmask the pretension inherent in all systems of legitimation. This is why all utopias, at one time or another, offer 'other' ways of exercising power in the family, in economic, political, or religious life. This 'other' way can mean, as we have seen, things as diametrically opposed as a more rational or more ethical authority or the complete absence of power if it is true that power as such is ultimately considered radically and inalterably evil. That the question of power is the central question of every utopia is confirmed not only by the description of the literary-type social and political fantasies but also by the different attempts to 'realize' utopia. This basically takes the form of microsocieties, whether passing or permanent, ranging from monastery to kibbutz or hippy commune. These attempts do not attest solely to the seriousness of the utopian spirit, to its capacity for instituting new modes of life; but also to its basic aptitude to come to grips with the paradoxes of power.

The pathological traits of utopia result from this *mad* dream. Just as the positive concept of ideology contained the seed of its negative counterpart, so, too, the pathology specific to utopia can already be glimpsed in its most positive aspects. It is in this way that the third concept of ideology corresponds to a third concept of utopia.

Because utopia stems from a leap into somewhere else, into nowhere, it develops the unsettling features which are easily discerned in the literary expressions of utopia: a tendency to hold reality in the throes of a dream, a fixation on perfectionist designs, etc. Certain authors have not hesitated to compare the logic developed by utopia to that characteristic of schizophrenia: the logic of all or nothing, standing outside the workings of time; a preference for schematizing space; a disdain for intermediary degrees and a total lack of interest in the first step to be taken to move towards the ideal; blindness to the contradictions inherent in action – either that these make certain evils inescapable in the pursuit of certain desired goals or that they point up the incompatibility of equally desirable goals. To this clinical tableau of flight into dreams and into literature, we can also add the regressive features of the nostalgia for a lost paradise hidden under the guise of futurism.

The time has come to account for this twofold dichotomy in terms of imagination, first, the dichotomy between the poles of ideology and utopia and, second, that within each of the terms between the poles of their ambiguous variations.

We must first try, it seems to me, to think of ideology and utopia together in terms of their most positive, constructive and, if we may say so, healthy aspects. Starting from the concept of non-congruence in Mannheim, it is possible to construct both the integrative function of ideology and the subversive function of utopia. At first glance, these two phenomena are simply the inverse of one another. At a closer look, they dialetically imply one another. The most 'conservative' ideology, by which I mean that which exhausts itself in repeating the social tie and reinforcing it, is an ideology only through the gap implied in what we could call, in memory of Freud, the 'consideration of figurability' inherent in the social image. Conversely, the utopian imagination seems merely excentric. This is only an appearance. In a poem entitled 'A Step Outside the Human', the poet Paul Celan refers to utopia in these terms: 'Inside a sphere directed towards the human, but excentric.' We see the paradox here. It has two sides. On the one hand, there is no movement towards what is human which is not first excentric; on the other, elsewhere leads here.

This criss-crossing of utopia and ideology appears as the play of two fundamental directions of the social imagination. The first tends towards integration, repetition, reflection. The second, because it is excentric, tends towards wandering. But neither exists without the other. The most repetitive, the most reduplicative ideology – to the extent that it mediates immediate social ties – the ethical, social substance Hegel would say – introduces a gap, a distance, and consequently something which is potentially excentric. On the other hand, the most errant form of utopia to the extent that it moves 'inside a sphere directed towards the human' remains a hopeless attempt to show what man basically is in the clarity of utopia.

This is why the tension between utopia and ideology is insuperable. It is often even impossible to decide whether this or that mode of thinking is ideological or utopian. The line can be drawn only after the fact and then on the basis of the success of the enterprise – a criterion which, in turn, can be questioned inasmuch as it rests on the supposition that only what was successful was just. But, what of aborted attempts? Will they not return one day, and will they not then obtain the success history has refused them in the past?

This phenomenology of the social imagination gives us the key to the second aspect of the problem, namely, that each term of the pair involves its own specific pathology. If imagination is a process rather than a state, it becomes comprehensible that there is a specific dysfunction corresponding to each direction of the process of imagination.

Ideology's dysfunction is distortion and dissimulation. We showed above that these pathological figures constitute the foremost dysfunction grafted onto the integrative function of the imagination. A primitive distortion, a primordial dissimulation are quite inconceivable. It is in the symbolic constitution of the social tie that the dialectic of hiding and showing originates. The reflective function of ideology can be understood only on the basis of this ambiguous dialectic which already possesses all the features of non-congruence. It follows from this that the tie denounced by Marxism linking the process of dissimulation to the interests of the ruling class is only one aspect of this phenomenon. Any 'superstructure' whatsoever can function ideologically: science and technology just as well as religion and philosophical idealism.

The dysfunction characteristic of utopia is no less understandable on the basis of the pathology of the imagination. Utopia tends towards schizophrenia in the same way that ideology tends towards dissimulation and distortion. The pathology is rooted in the excentric function of utopia. It develops in caricature the ambiguity of the phenomenon which oscillates between fantasy and creativity, flight and return. 'Nowhere' may or *may not* give us a new orientation with respect to the 'here and now'. But who knows whether this or that errant mode of existence is not a prophecy concerning man to come? Who knows even whether a certain degree of individual pathology is not the condition for social change, inasmuch as this pathology brings to light the sclerosis of worn out institutions? To express this in a more paradoxial fashion, who knows whether the disease is not at the same time the remedy?

These troubling remarks at least have the advantage of directing our gaze towards an irreducible feature of the social imaginary, namely, that we reach the social imaginary only through the figures of false consciousness. We can take possession of the creative power of the imagination only through a critical relationship to these two figures of false consciousness. It is as if, in order to cure the madness of utopia, it were necessary to call upon the 'healthy' function of ideology and as if the critique of ideology could only be made by a consciousness capable of looking at itself from 'nowhere'.

It is in this *work* on the social imaginary that the contradictions, which a simple phenomenology of the individual imagination has to leave in their state of contradiction, can be mediated.

NOTE

1 A French version of this article, written in honour of Mgr Henri Van Camp, first appeared in *Savoir, faire espérer: les limites de la raison*, (Publications des Facultés Universitaires Saint Louis, Bruxelles, 1976).

Chapter 7

Radical imagination and the social instituting imaginary

Cornelius Castoriadis

I

I have chosen to speak about imagination and the social instituting imaginary not only because these are central themes in my work, but also for two much less contingent reasons. First, because imagination – the radical imagination of the singular human being, that is the psyche or soul – though discovered and discussed twenty-three centuries ago by Aristotle, never won its proper place, which is central in the philosophy of the subject. Second, because the social imaginary, the radical instituting imaginary, has been totally ignored throughout the whole history of philosophical, sociological, and political, thought.

Given the limitations of space and time, I shall not enter into the history of the subject, which includes the vacillations of Aristotle in the treatise *De Anima*, the Stoics and Damascius, a long development in Britain going from Hobbes to Coleridge, the rediscovery of imagination by Kant in the first edition of the *Critique of Pure Reason* and the reduction of its role in the second edition, the rediscovery of the Kantian discovery and retreat by Heidegger in the 1928 *Kantbuch*, the subsequent total silence of Heidegger on the subject, the hesitations of Merleau-Ponty in *The Visible and the Invisible* as to what is 'reason' and what is 'imaginary',[1] not to speak about Freud, who talks throughout his work about what is in fact imagination, and accomplishes the feat of never mentioning the term.

I shall limit myself to two remarks about the Aristotelian discovery and, later, to a brief discussion of some problems raised by Kant's treatment of the subject in the first edition of the First *Critique*.

It has not been noticed, as far as I am aware, that the Aristotelian *phantasia*, in the treatise *De Anima*, covers two completely different ideas. Most of the treatment corresponds to what I have called *second* (secondary) imagination, imitative, reproductive or combinatory imagination – and has provided the substance of what, for centuries and up to now, passes for imagination. But in the middle of Book Three, Aristotle introduces, without warning, a totally different *phantasia*, without which there can be no thought and which possibly precedes any thought. This I have called *prime* (primary) imagination; it corresponds, roughly, to my radical imagination.[2]

It is, at the same time, characteristic that Aristotle does not establish any relation whatsoever between *phantasia* and *poiesis*. *Poiesis*, for him, is *techne*, and *techne* 'imitates' nature, even in the loftiest case, the case of *techne poietike*.

This ballet, this hide-and-seek game, should of course be explained, or rather understood. The main factor seems to me to be that philosophy from the start has been a search for the truth (*aletheia*) as opposed to mere opinion (*doxa*), and truth was immediately correlated with *logos, nous, ratio*, Reason, *Verstand* and *Vernunft*. *Doxa* was linked with sense impressions, or imagination, or both, and left at best to the 'sophists' and sceptics. Truth about the world and about being was to be found along the ways of *logos*, of Reason, without the question being raised: how can a world, and being, exist for a human subject in the first place? And how is it that these human subjects possess *logos*, language? (In Aristotle *logos* is an extremely polysemous term; but in his dictum, *anthropos esti zoon logon echon*, humans are living beings possessing *logos, logos*, I believe, refers centrally to language; the translation *animal rationale* is Seneca's in the first century AD.) Animals are certainly much more 'logical' or 'rational' than humans: they never do something wrongly or in vain. And human reason, as I shall try to sketch, entails radical imagination, but also would be nothing without language. It would, of course, be preposterous to argue that language is a 'product' of reason. But then where does language come from? It is significant that the dispute about the 'natural' or 'conventional/instituted' character of language was already very heated in Greece in the fifth century BC, with Democritus supplying already unsurpassable arguments for the 'conventional/instituted' character of language; that Plato's *Cratylus* is inconclusive, though it obviously makes fun of the idea of a 'natural' character of the words; and that Aristotle defines the word as *phone semantike kata suntheken*, a 'voice' (or 'sound') signifying according to a convention, but does not push his reflection further. The Greeks had discovered the *phusis/nomos* (nature/institution-convention) distinction, and had already put it into practice by *changing* their institutions. But their most important philosophies stopped short of using it, obviously – at least in the case of Plato – out of fear of opening the way to 'arbitrariness' and freedom.

This also allows us to understand why the social origin – that is, creation – of language and of all institutions, though explicitly known and practically demonstrated at least in the democratic cities, remained without consequences for philosophy. When tradition and/or religion stopped supplying an indisputable source and formulation for the law and for the meaning of the world, philosophy rushed in to take its place. For this it had to find a *fundamentum inconcussum*, an unshakeable foundation, which was to be Reason. And, according to the already emerging basic ontological categories, this Reason could be found in Things, in Ideas, or in Subjects – that is, Substantive Individuals – but certainly not in the anonymous social collective which could only be a collection of such individuals entering in commerce because of need, of fear or of 'rational calculation'.

Also, almost from the beginning (and already in Parmenides) the philosophical tenet *ex nihilo nihil* – a constitutive axiom of ensemblistic-identitary logic[3] – imposed itself. But imagination, and social instituting imaginary, *create – ex nihilo*. Therefore, what they create must be a non-being, *Unsein* – at best, fictions and illusions. Of course, this is a non-solution, since illusions *are* (e.g. they may have tremendous consequences). But this was covered up by the idea of 'degrees of being' – or of 'intensity of existence' – linked very rapidly with the criteria of *duration* – so that permanence, eternity and finally a-temporality became fundamental characteristics of 'true being' – of *immutability* – so that everything belonging to the Heraclitean flux became disqualified – and of *universality* – opposing what must be for everybody to what just happens to be for somebody. *Mutatis mutandis*, all this remains true today, despite talk about imagination and creativity, both of which are rapidly becoming advertising slogans.

II

Before going further, a preliminary explanation of the use of the terms imagination, imaginary and radical may be helpful.

I talk about imagination because of the two connotations of the word: the connection with images in the most general sense, that is, *forms* (*Bilder-Einbildung*, etc.); and the connection with the idea of invention or, better and properly speaking, with *creation*.

The term *radical* I use, first, to oppose what I am talking about to the 'secondary' imagination which is either reproductive or simply combinatory (and usually both); and, second, to emphasize the idea that this imagination is *before* the distinction between 'real' and 'fictitious'. To put it bluntly: it is because radical imagination exists that 'reality' exists *for us* – exists *tout court* – and exists *as* it exists.

Both considerations apply as well to the radical instituting social imaginary. It is radical because it creates *ex nihilo* (not *in nihilo*, nor *cum nihilo*). It does not create 'images' in the visual sense (though it does as well: totem poles, emblems, flags, etc.), but it creates forms which can be images in a general sense (linguists speak about the acoustic image of a word), but centrally are significations and institutions (each of those being impossible without the other).

So, to put it briefly, in both cases we talk about an *a-causal vis formandi*. A-causal does not mean 'unconditioned' or absolute, *ab-solutus*, separated, detached, without relations. All actual and factual relations are *not* causal. The seat of this *vis formandi* as radical imagination is the singular human being, more specifically its psyche. The seat of this *vis* as instituting social imaginary is the anonymous collective and, more generally, the social-historical field.

III

I turn now to the radical imagination of the singular human being. One may take two paths in order to elucidate this idea: the philosophical and the psychoanalytical.

On the philosophical path, we may well start with an *Auseinandersetzung* with Kant. In the *Critique of Pure Reason* (section 24, B151) a proper definition is given: '*Einbildungskraft ist das Vermögen einen Gegenstand auch ohne dessen Gegenwart in der Anschauung vorzustellen*' – 'Imagination is the power (the capacity, the faculty) to represent in the intuition an object even without its presence . . .' One may note that Parmenides was already saying as much, if not more: 'Consider how the absent (things) are with certainty present to thought (*noo*).' And Socrates was going much further when he asserted that imagination is the power to represent that which *is not*. Kant goes on to add: 'As all our intuitions are sensuous, imagination therefore belongs to the sensibility.' Of course, just the reverse is true as I shall try to show presently.

We shall see that Kant certainly intends much more than what is entailed by the above definition: the conception of 'transcendental imagination', the paragraphs on the Schematism and even the substance of the chapters on space and time go far beyond this definition. But the latter is useful in order to oppose to it what I consider to be the proper definition: *Einbildungskraft ist das Vermögen Vorstellungen hervorzubringen, ob diese einen äusseren Anlass haben oder nicht*. Imagination is the power (the capacity, the faculty) to make appear representations ('ideas' is the old English term, e.g. in Locke), whether with or without an external incitement. In other words: imagination is the power to make be that which 'realiter' *is not* (I will revert later to the term 'realiter').

(i) We take first the case of an external incitement (or excitation!). Fichte, who in the first version of the *Wissenschaftslehte* gives much greater weight to the imagination than Kant, speaks of *Anstoß* (shock). In this he is, I think, correct. But Kant speaks about the senses opposing the 'receptivity of impressions' to the 'spontaneity of concepts'. Imagination obviously should go with spontaneity; but curiously, it is left out of this opposition. (And, if it is taken to belong to 'sensibility', as in the citation above, then it should be passive – an idea difficult to make sense of.) But what about this 'receptivity of the impressions'? What about *Sinnlichkeit* – sensibility or sensoriality?

In truth, there is no 'receptivity' or passivity of the 'impressions'. To begin with, there are no such things as 'impressions'. 'Impressions' are a philosophical or psychological artefact. There are, in *some* cases, *perceptions* – that is, representations of 'external' and more or less 'independent' objects. (*Some* cases only: there is an exorbitant privilege of perception in the whole of inherited philosophy, up to and including Husserl, Heidegger and Merleau-Ponty.) These possess certainly a 'sensorial' component. But this component is *itself* a creation of the imagination. The 'senses' make emerge, out of an X, something which 'physically' or 'really' *is not* (if one equates 'reality' with the 'reality' of physics): colours, sounds, smells, etc. In 'physical' nature there are no colours, sounds or smells: there are only electromagnetic waves, air waves, kinds of molecules, etc. The sensible *quale* (the famous 'secondary qualities') is a pure *creation* of the 'senses', that is, of imagination in its most elementary manifestation, giving a form and a specific form to something which, 'in itself', has no relation with *that* form.

These are, of course, Eddington's 'two tables'. *This* table – the one I touch, I see, I lean on, etc. – contains an indefinite plurality of 'elements' created by the singular imagination *and* the social imaginary. The other 'table' – in fact, no 'table' at all – is a scientific construct, *such as* science makes it *today*. (And this does not make it any less imaginary in the sense of the word I am intending.)

As the meaningfulness (at least, the philosophical meaningfulness) of this distinction has been recently disputed, especially from phenomenological quarters advocating the 'first person stance',[4] a digression seems useful.

There is, of course, no real distinction between 'primary' and 'secondary' qualities – number, figure, size as opposed to colour, sound, taste, touch, smell, pain or pleasure. They are all creations of the living body, that is, of the embodied psyche in humans, creations more or less permanent or transient, more or less generic or singular. These creations are often conditioned by an 'external' X – *not* 'caused' by it. Light waves are not coloured, and they do not cause the colour *qua* colour. They induce, *under certain conditions*, the subject to create an 'image' which, in many cases – and, so to speak, by definition in all the cases we can *speak about* – is generically *and* socially *shared*.

This does not mean (the 'idealistic' or 'Cartesian' fallacy) that these images are 'confused ideas' 'in the mind'. They are not 'confused' or 'more or less confused', nor are they 'in the mind'. They are just what they are: images, not in the sense of 'ikons' or 'imitations', but *Vorstellungen*, representations or, better, *presentations*: presentations of something about which nothing can be said except by means of another presentation, about which the discourse will be eternally open, but which is certainly neither 'identical' nor even 'isomorphic' to them. (Analysis of, for example, the 'constancy of colour' on a surface shows this clearly.) They are original ways of 'reacting' (and this only in *some* cases: a composer getting a musical idea is not 'reacting' to anything, at any rate *not* at *this* level and certainly nothing 'external'). This 'reaction' is not an 'idea in the mind': it is a total state of the subject ('body' and 'soul').

But neither does this mean (the phenomenological fallacy) that the 'first person' or 'intentional' stance presents to, or for, me 'the things as they are'. This is the curious realistic delusion of phenomenology, paradoxically coexisting with fatal solipsistic consequences: how do I know that something exists for the next person, or, indeed, that a next person exists at all if I am confined to my 'first person stance'? From the strict phenomenological point of view I have *no access* to the experience of 'other persons'; they and their 'experiences' exist just as *phenomena for me*. The simple *naming* of the problem in Husserl's *Cartesian Meditations* (or in Merleau-Ponty's *Phenomenology of Perception*) is no solution.

The 'first person stance' is bluntly contradictory, even if we leave aside the 'other person'. It tells me, for example, that to move an object, or to move myself, I need *force*. But if I am in a car and the driver breaks abruptly, I am projected through the windscreen without deploying any force. The 'privilege' or 'authenticity' of the 'first person stance' looks philosophically very funny if this stance leads, as lead it must, to contradictions or incoherences in the very 'experience' it keeps celebrating. Husserl's 'The Earth, as *Urarche*, does not move' forces me, for instance, to dismiss as absurd or illusory phenomena of equally compelling immediacy (e.g. Foucault's pendulum, or the yearly parallax of the fixed stars).

Neither does the escape of the later Husserl towards the 'life-world' (*Lebenswelt*) redeem phenomenology. Certainly, the immediate 'first person stance' presents things as they 'appear' in the life-world. But this only means that it presents them as they have been shaped by the generic biological (species) imagination *and* the social imaginary I am sharing with my fellow human *socii*. Now philosophy starts when we begin trying to *break the closure* of this life-world in both its biological and social-historical dimensions. Of course, we can never break it to such a degree as to be able to fly outside any closure, to have a 'view from nowhere'. But break it we do, and there is no point in pretending that we do not know that there is no 'red' except for, in and through a living body – or, for that matter, that there are no nymphs in the springs and gods in the rivers, which were a perfectly legitimate part of the life-world of the ancient Greeks.

Red, or the red object, is not a 'confused idea in my mind' and neither is it a reality 'down there' (Sartre). My, and our, creation of a world entails *also* the creation of an 'exterior' *where* object, colour, etc., present themselves as different and distant from me – me being always and irrevocably *here* – as it entails *also* the creation of a double temporal horizon ('backward' and 'forward') within which I am the permanently moving *now*.

To be sure, all this presupposes that I, somehow or other, 'know' first hand what it is like to see red – but also, that I know first hand what it is like to live in a society where the most important things are social imaginary significations – for example, nymphs. It is true that nobody and nothing can make us '. . . stop living "in" or "through" the experience, to treat it itself as an object, or, what is the same thing, as an experience which could as well have been someone else's'.[5] And, equally true, to continue quoting Taylor, I cannot 'experience my toothache as a mere idea in the mind, caused by decay in the tooth, sending signals up the nerves to the brain'. But neither am I obliged to stick with this 'experience' and ignore other ways of access to the phenomenal fact of toothache, such as they lead me, for example, to take an aspirin or rush to my dentist.

Behind the phenomenological, or 'first person', stance stands the attempt to present 'my own' experience as the only authentic or, at any rate, privileged one – the only one giving access to '*die Sache selbst*'. But in fact this 'experience' is not just 'my own' but shares in a biological and social genericity, otherwise we could never even talk, however 'inadequately', about it; it is not an 'experience', but an imaginary creation; it does not give access to the 'thing itself', but only *encounters* an X, and this only in some cases and only partly. It has no absolute philosophical privilege. It is only an eternally recurring starting and (provisionally) ending point. 'Home is where we start from', wrote, I think, T.S. Eliot. Our 'personal' experience is our personal home – and this home would not be a home, but a solitary cave, if it was not in a village or a town. For it is the collectivity which teaches us how to build homes and how to live in them. We cannot live without a home but neither can we remain hermetically enclosed in 'our' home.

And when one moves, as the last Husserl and the first Heidegger, from the egological, strictly phenomenological point of view (the *je meiniges*, *je eigenes* of *Sein und Zeit*) to the 'life-world', one has just exchanged the egocentric for an ethno- or socio-centric point of view: solipsism on a larger scale. For to know, as we must, that our *Lebenswelt* is but one among an indefinite number of others, is to recognize that there is a multiplicity of 'first person' collective 'experiences' among which there is, at first glance, no privileged one; at second glance, the only 'privileged' one – philosophically and, I would add, politically – is the one which made itself capable of *recognizing* and *accepting* this very multiplicity of human worlds, thereby breaking as far as possible the closure of its own world.

IV

As already stated, we never deal with 'impressions'. We deal with perceptions, that is, a class of representations (*Vorstellungen*). And it is impossible to compose a perceptual representation (or any representation) by sheer juxtaposition of 'sense data'. A *Vorstellung*, however vague or bizarre, possesses a unity and a formidable organization; it is never a sheer amorphous multiplicity, a pure *Mannigfaltigkeit*. There is therefore a tremendous amount of 'logical' work contained in the representation, entailing some of Kant's categories, some of his (wrongly named and placed) *Reflexionsbegriffen* and some others, notably topological schemes (e.g. neighbourhood/

separation or continuity/discreteness) on which I cannot dwell here.

The last considerations are certainly true of any living being – any being-for-itself – but in this case, the 'logical' functions are, in general, simpler and, at any rate, unadulterated by the other functions of imagination in humans. Categories are intrinsic, immanent to the perception. A dog chases *a* (= *one*) rabbit, and usually catches it. A catch surely void of transcendental validity, since the unity of the rabbit caught has not been established through mediations of transcendental schemes from the dog's unity of transcendental aperception. Kant is bound to a Cartesian conception of '*animaux machines*'. True, the Third *Critique* sketches another view, but only 'reflectively' and only as part of a heavy teleological metaphysics. Let us, incidentally, outline my status under the Kantian regime: from the determining point of view, I am a (somatical and psychical) machine; from the reflective point of view I am a mechanistically un-understandable but teleologically understandable being; from the transcendental point of view, I simply *am* not – *Ich gelte*; from the ethical point of view, I *ought* to be what in fact (from the determining point of view) I could *never* be: an agent acting 'outside' any psychological motives. To say, in these circumstances, that I am made out of 'crooked wood' is certainly the understatement of the millennium.

To revert to our main argument: radical imagination (as source of the perceptual *quale* and of logical forms) is what makes it possible for any being-for-itself (including humans) to *create for* itself an own world (*eine Eigen-welt*) 'within' which it also posits itself. The ultimately indescribable X 'out there' becomes something definite and specific *for* a particular being, through the functioning of its sensory and logical imagination, which 'filters', 'forms' and 'organizes' the external 'shocks'. It is clear that no being-for-itself could 'organize' something out of the world, if this world were not intrinsically organiz*able* – which means that it cannot be simply 'chaotic'. But this is another dimension of the question – the properly ontological dimension – which cannot be discussed here.

(ii) But we do not have to do only with representations provoked by external 'shocks'. In relative (and often, absolute) independence from these, we do have an 'inside'. Here we part company with animals, etc. – not because they do not have an 'inside', but because we cannot say anything meaningful about it ('how it feels to be a bat'). This 'inside' is a perpetual, truly heraclitean, flux of representations *cum* affects *cum* intentions, in fact indissociable. (On this indissociation neither Kant, nor Fichte, nor for that matter most of the inherited philosophy, has much to say. At best, all this would be relegated to 'empirical psychology', etc.). I shall not insist upon this aspect: the whole psychoanalytical path has it as its main concern. Suffice it to say that here representations (and affects, and intentions or desires) emerge in an 'absolutely spontaneous' way, and even more: we have affects and intentions (desires, drives) which are creations of this a-causal *vis formandi* in their sheer being, their mode of being and their being-thus (*Sosein*). And, for all we know, this stream of representations *cum* affects *cum* desires is absolutely singular for each singular human being. It may be said that our sensory imagination and its logical components are, for all of us, 'identical' (though essentially similar would be a better term). But, to the extent that its products are decisively co-created by the 'inside', even this sensory imagination is, in the end, singular (*de gustibus et coloribus . . .*).

If, in its first aspect ('perceptual', geared to the 'outside'), the radical imagination creates a 'generic' own world for the singular human being, a world sufficiently shared with the other members of the human species, in its second, fully psychical, aspect, it creates a singular own world. The importance of this could not be exaggerated. It is this 'inside' which conditions and makes possible, first, a 'distanciation' relatively to the world considered as simply 'given', and, second, an active and acting *Einstellung*, position and disposition, towards the world. Representation, affect and intention are at the same time principles of the formation of the own world – even *materialiter spectati* – and principles of distanciation from it and action upon it.

(iii) A few words on a subject alluded to above: Kant's 'transcendental imagination'. Without in the least minimizing the importance of Kant's discovery, one must point to its limits. First, Kant's imagination is subject, throughout, to the requirements of 'true knowledge'. Second – and for this very reason – it is eternally 'the same'. If Kant's transcendental imagination started to *imagine* anything, the world, as constructed by Kant, would instantly collapse. For this very reason Kant cannot or will not see the creative function of the imagination in the cognitive (scientific or philosophical) domain. This is why the existence of a *history* of science must remain in the Kantian framework an enigma or, at best, a sheer cumulation of *inductions*.

Two additional remarks are here in order. The strongest – and truest – point in Kant's conception of the imagination is, of course, the schematism mediating between the categories and the 'sensory data'. Introducing it, Kant says: 'There is a power, hidden in the depths of human soul . . .', which is the source of the transcendental schemata. But one wonders, what business have 'the human soul' and its 'depths' here? The human soul belongs in the domain of the 'empirical psychology', where causality reigns supreme, etc. It has nothing to do with the 'transcendental' dimension, which is supposed to ensure the possibility of *a priori* synthetic knowledge.

The imagination appears also in the *Critique of Judgement*, but is only mentioned, not used. A creative power is recognized, but is not called creative (*schaffen*, not *schöpfen*; the latter word appears only once and in an indifferent context). This is the power of the genius – but the genius works like nature (*als Natur*). We enjoy in the work of art 'the free play of imagination in conformity with the laws of understanding', but the worth of the work of art lies in that it presents in the intuition the Ideas of

Reason. (I confess that I am unable to see the Ideas of Reason presented in *Antigone* or in *King Lear*.)

(iv) I already mentioned the 'logical' organization contained even in the simplest representation, perceptual or not. That this is so should not surprise us. Everything that is must contain an ensemblistic-identitary ('logical', in the largest sense possible) dimension; otherwise it would be *absolutely* indeterminate, and (at least for us) non-existent. *A posteriori*, this is confirmed by the grasp logical categories have on whatever there is (e.g. 'the unreasonable effectiveness of mathematics', to quote Wigner). This, of course, by no means entails that 'what there is' is exhaustively determined by or reducible to 'logic' (not even when we consider 'physical' reality).

This is the 'objective' (or 'in itself') side of the question. The 'for itself' side emerges with life. Living beings would not be there, if they had not developed, as a constituent of the own world they create, a (however rudimentary) logical apparatus fit to cope, somehow or other, with the intrinsic ensemblistic-identitary dimension of the world. There are Kantian categories obviously embedded in the behaviour of dogs, not imposed on this behaviour by the scientific observer.

For all we know, these categories are not 'conscious' in animals (though obviously self-awareness is there), and even less reflected upon. For this to happen, two further conditions are required, which only obtain in the human domain. The first pertains to the radical imagination of the human psyche and its 'pathological' development expressed in its defunctionalization. I have dealt with this aspect somewhat extensively in other texts,[6] so I shall be very brief. Defunctionalization makes possible, first, the detachment of the representation from the object of the biological 'need', therefore the cathexis of biologically irrelevant objects (Gods, King, Country etc.); and, second, the (biologically equally irrelevant) possibility for the activities of the psyche to become objects for themselves, and the labile *quid pro quo*, which is the prerequisite of symbolism.

The second, equally important, condition is the creation by the radical social imaginary of institutions, and, of course, first and foremost, of language. Neither life as such nor the singular psyche as such can produce institutions and language. Understanding and reason are socially instituted, though, of course, this institution leans on intrinsic possibilities and drives of the human psyche.

A last point must be made in this respect. The (Kantian) distinction between categories, 'transcendental' schemes and 'empirical' representations cannot, of course, be taken as a distinction *in re* (neither is taken as such by Kant himself). But one can be more precise. Any representation (I am abstracting here from affects and intentions) contains *qualia* and organization of these *qualia*; this organization, in turn, consists in generic figures and traits and in categorical schemes. In other words, genericity and categoricality are intrinsic and immanent to the representation. To become categories and schemes, they have to be *named* and *reflected upon*. And this – that is, abstract thought as such – is a relatively recent historical creation, not a biological trait of the 'human species', though all members of this species can share in this creation once it is there. But abstract thought itself has always to lean on some figure or image, be it, minimally, the image of the words through which it is carried on.

V

I shall be much shorter on the psychoanalytical path, with which I have dealt at length elsewhere.[7]

This path was opened, as we know, through the immense discoveries of Freud. But as I noted in the beginning, Freud never thematizes imagination as such. One has to use unsystematized, though seminal, indications in his work, to draw rigorous and radical consequences from these and also to go beyond them in order to reach the reality of radical imagination. Among these indications, the main ones are the 'magical omnipotence of thought' (better called the *effective* omnipotence of thought, since we are dealing here with unconscious thought, where, in the first approximation, thinking makes it so purely and simply), and the (practically equivalent) assertion that there is no distinction, in the unconscious, between a strongly cathected representation and an actual 'perception', that is, that there are not in the unconscious 'indices of reality'. Wherefrom we can draw almost immediately a cardinal principle: for humans, representation pleasure prevails as a rule over organ pleasure, from which it also results that both representation and pleasure are *de*-functionalized in humans. Another equally decisive consequence follows: projective schemes and processes have precedence over introjective ones, which should come as no surprise for any non-empiricist philosopher, and in which we just rediscover the very essence of any being for itself: creation of an own world precedes by necessity any 'lesson' events in this world could supply. One particular remark on this: there is, nevertheless, in humans, certainly the specific strength and importance of the *introjective* processes and schemes, which can be understood if we realize that the human psyche cannot live outside a world of meaning and, when its own, initial, monadic meaning is, in the course of socialization, disrupted, as it must be, the resulting catastrophe has to be repaired by the internalization of the meaning supplied by the cathected persons of its environment. This is what is sometimes mistaken as an intrinsic disposition (*Anlage*) of the psyche towards socialization, and which is nothing more than a leaning on of the socialization process, made possible by the vital need of the psyche for meaning and the fact that society itself is nothing but the institution of meanings (social imaginary significations). Socialization is the process whereby the psyche is forced to (never fully) abandon its pristine solipsistic meaning for the shared meanings provided by society. Introjection goes

always much further than animal *mimesis*, because it is always re-interpretation of that which is introjected, and this re-interpretation can only
take place on the basis of the existing own schemes. 'Below' the
Freudian unconscious, we have to postulate a psychic monad, initially
closed upon itself and, up to the end, constantly endeavouring to enclose in
itself whatever is 'presented' to it. *Ich bin die Brust* (I am the bosom),
wrote Freud in one of his last Notes in 1938.

Here again a digression seems useful. Paradoxically, inevitably, and
despite his intentions and his formation, Freud remains a dualist. Soul and
body, psyche and soma, remain for him essentially distinct – despite his
elaboration of the hysterical symptoms, etc. (we could add today what we
know about psychosomatic illnesses). There can be no question of elimin-
ating or 'solving' the time-honoured enigmas of this relation; let us just
remember the amazing antinomies with which the most elementary evidence
confronts us. The psyche is strongly dependent on the soma; even short of
piercing your head with a bullet, I can make you talk nonsense with the help
of some additional glasses of bourbon. The soma is strongly dependent on
the psyche: even without mentioning hysterical symptoms or psychosomatic
illnesses, I decided to write this text, therefore I am banging on my
typewriter. The soma is strongly independent from the psyche: I have no
control over the innumerable organic processes going on all the time within
my body, some of which prepare my death. The psyche is strongly
independent from the soma: even under the most horrible tortures, there are
people who will not give their comrades to the police. This strange
relationship definitely requires from us new modes of thinking. These should
certainly start from something different than a reduction of one of the two
entities to the other, or an irreversible and irreparable separation of soul
and body.

Here are some indications along this line. We should posit 'behind' or
'below' the Freudian unconscious (or the Id) a non-conscious which is
the living body *qua* human animated body in continuity with the psyche.
There is no frontier between this living, animated body and the originary
psychical monad. The monad is neither repressed, nor repressible: it is
unsayable. Nor do we 'repress' the life of the body. We vaguely 'feel'
it, without knowing why and how – the beats of the heart, the movements
of the bowels, probably already, very long ago, our movements within the
amniotic liquid. There is a presence of the living body to itself,
inextricably mixed with what we normally consider as the 'movements of
the soul' proper. And there is the obvious and understandable substantive
homogeneity between the singular person's psyche and soma. Socrates's
dead body is no longer Socrates. Kant's soul could not inhabit Ava
Gardner's body, nor the reverse. Human physiology is already soul-like; auto-
immune disorders, where the *body's* 'defence mechanisms' turn against the
body they are supposed to protect, can hardly be understood as the result of

an external 'influence' of the soul of the body. (This example shows, incidentally, the non-functional, non-'logical' character of the human imagination.) It is in this light that we should consider the idea of a sensory, and more generally bodily, imagination.

These are tentative, embryonic thoughts. But there is a solid conclusion we reach on the psychoanalytic path: that the imagination of the singular human being is defunctionalized. Hegel has said that man is a sick animal. In truth, man is a mad animal, totally unfit for life, a species which would have disappeared as soon as it emerged, if it had not proven itself capable, at the collective level, of another creation: society in the strict sense, that is, institutions embodying social imaginary significations. This creation we cannot help but impute to the creative capacity of anonymous human collectives, that is to the radical instituting imaginary.

VI

To elucidate the idea of the instituting social imaginary we can again follow the two paths: the philosophical and the psychoanalytical.

Along the philosophical path, the discussion need not be long. Philosophy itself, and thought in general, cannot exist without language or, at least, without strong links with language. But any individual or 'contractual' primordial production of language is logically (not only historically) an absurdity. Language can only be a spontaneous creation of a human collective. And the same is true of all primordial institutions, without which there is no social life, therefore also no human beings.

From the psychoanalytic point of view, we never encounter singular psychosomatic humans in the 'pure' state; we only encounter socialized individuals. The psychical nucleus manifests itself very rarely, and only indirectly. In itself it forms the perpetually unattainable limit of psychoanalytic work. Ego, Super-Ego, Ego-Ideal are unthinkable except as the products (at most, the co-products) of a socialization process. Socialized individuals are walking and talking fragments of a given society; and they are *total* fragments: that is they embody, in part actually, in part potentially, the essential core of the institutions and the significations of their society. There is no opposition between individual and society: the individual is a social creation, both as such and in its each time given social-historical form. The true polarity is between society and the psyche (the psyche-soma, in the sense indicated above). These are both irreducible to each other and effectively inseparable. The society as such cannot produce souls, the idea is meaningless; and an assembly of non-socialized souls would not produce a society, but a hyper-boschian nightmare. An assembly of *individuals* can, of course, produce a society (e.g. the *Mayflower* pilgrims), because these individuals are already *socialized* (otherwise they would not exist, even biologically).

The question of society (and, indissolubly, of history) is, of course, an abysmal subject, and I shall not try to summarize inadequately here what I have written at length elsewhere.[8] I shall only outline a few points.

(i)   Society is creation, and creation of itself: self-creation. It is the emergence of a new ontological form – *eidos* – and of a new mode and level of being. It is a quasi-totality held together by institutions (language, norms, family forms, tools and production modes, etc.) and by the significations these institutions embody (totems, taboos, gods, God, *polis*, commodities, wealth, fatherland, etc.). Both of these represent ontological creations. We do not encounter anywhere else institutions as a mode of relation holding together the components of a totality; and we can 'explain' – causally produce or rationally deduce – neither the form institution as such, nor the fact of the institution, nor the particular primary institutions of a given society. And we do not encounter anywhere else signification, that is, the mode of being of an effective and 'acting' ideality, the immanent imperceivable; nor can we 'explain' the emergence of primary significations (e.g. the Hebrew God, the Greek *polis*, etc.).

I talk about self-creation, *not* 'self-organization'. In the case of society we do not have an assembly of already existing elements, the combination of which could possibly produce new or additional qualities of the whole; the quasi- (or rather pseudo-) 'elements' of society are created by society itself. Athens cannot exist without Athenians (*not* humans in general!) – but Athenians are created only in and by Athens. Thus society is always self-institution – but for almost the whole of human history this fact of the self-institution has been veiled by the very institutions of society itself.

(ii)   Society as such is self-creation; and each particular society is a specific creation, the emergence of another *eidos* within the generic *eidos* of society.

(iii) Society is always historical in the wide, but proper sense of the word: it is always undergoing a process of self-alteration. This process can be, and almost always has been, so slow as to be imperceptible; in our small social-historical province it happens to have been, over the last 4,000 years, rather rapid and violent. The question: 'When does a self-altering society stop being "the same" and become another?' is a concrete historical question for which standard logic has no answer (are the Romes of the early Republic, of Marius and Sylla, of the Antonins, etc., 'the same'?).

(iv) Inasfar as they are neither causally producible nor rationally deducible, the institutions and social imaginary significations of each society are free creations of the anonymous collective concerned. They are creations *ex nihilo* – but not *in nihilo*, nor *cum nihilo*. This means, in particular, that they are creations *under constraints*. To mention the most important among these constraints:

(a) There are 'external' constraints – especially those imposed by the first natural stratum, including the biological constitution of the human being. These are essentially trivial (which does not mean unimportant): the society is, each time, conditioned by its 'natural' habitat – it is not 'caused' by it. Inasfar as the first natural stratum exhibits, to a decisive degree, an ensemblistic-identitary dimension – two stones and two stones make four stones, a bull and a cow will always produce calves and not chickens, etc. – the social institution has to recreate this dimension in its 'representation' of the world, and of itself, that is, in the creation of its *Eigenwelt*. This dimension is also, of course, present in language; it corresponds to language as *code*, that is, as a quasi-univocal instrument of making/doing, reckoning and elementary reasoning. The code aspect of language (the cat is on the mat) is opposed to but also inextricably entangled with its poietic aspect carrying the imaginary significations proper (God is one person in three). To these 'external' constraints responds the *functionality* of institutions, especially relative to the production of material life and to sexual reproduction.

(b) There are 'internal' constraints, relative to the 'raw material' out of which society creates itself, that is, the psyche. The psyche has to be socialized and for this it has to abandon more or less its own world, its objects of investment, what is for it meaning, and to cathect socially created and valorized objects, orientations, actions, roles etc.; it has to abandon its own time and insert itself into a public time and a public world ('natural' as well as 'human'). When we consider the unbelievable variety of types of society known, we are almost led to think that the social institution can make out of the psyche whatever it pleases – make it polygamous, polyandrous, monogamous, fetishistic, pagan, monotheistic, pacific, bellicose, etc. On closer inspection we see that this is indeed true, provided one condition is fulfilled: that the institution supplies the psyche with *meaning* – meaning for its life and meaning for its death. This is accomplished by the social imaginary significations, almost always religious ones, which tie together the meaning of the individual's life and death, the meaning of the existence and of the ways of the particular society, and the meaning of the world as a whole.

(c) There are 'historical' constraints. We cannot fathom the 'origin' of societies, but no societies we can speak of emerge *in vacuo*. There are always, even if in pieces, a past and a tradition. But the relation to this past is itself a part of the institution of society. Thus, primitive or traditional societies attempt to reproduce and repeat almost literally the past. In the other cases, the 'reception' of past and tradition is, partly at least conscious – but this 'reception' is, in fact, re-creation (present-day parlance would call it 're-interpretation'). Athenian tragedy 'receives' Greek mythology, and it re-creates it. The history of Christianity is but the history of continuous 're-interpretations' of the same sacred texts, with amazingly differing outcomes. Classical Greeks are the object of an incessant 're-interpretation' by the Western Europeans since the thirteenth century. This re-creation is, of course, always done according to the imaginary significations of the *present* – but, of course also, what is 're-interpreted' is a given, not an indeterminate, material. Still, it is instructive to compare what the Byzantines, the Arabs and the Western Europeans have done with the same Greek heritage. The Byzantines just kept the manuscripts, adding some scholia here and there. The Arabs used only the scientific and philosophical texts, ignoring the rest (cf. the beautiful short story by Borges on Averroes and Aristotle's *Poetics*). The Western Europeans have been struggling with the remnants of this heritage for eight centuries now, and do not seem to be through with it.

(d) Finally, there are 'intrinsic' constraints – the most interesting of all. I can only deal with two of them.

1. Institutions and social imaginary significations have to be *coherent*. Coherence has to be assessed immanently, that is, relatively to the main characters and 'drives' of the given society, taking into account the conformal behaviour of the socialized individuals, etc. Pyramid building with starving peasants is coherent when referred to the whole organization and social imaginary significations of the Pharaonic or Mayan societies.

   Coherence does not preclude internal divisions, oppositions and strife. Slave-owning or feudal societies are, of course, coherent. Things are different with capitalist society, especially latter-day capitalist society, but in this case this is a historical novation, and belongs to another discussion. Coherence is not, generally, endangered by 'contradictions' between the strictly imaginary and the ensemblistic-identitary dimensions of the institution for, as a rule, the former prevail over the latter. Arithmetic and commerce have not been hampered in Christian societies by the fundamental equation $1 = 3$ implicit in the dogma of the Holy Trinity.

   Here belongs also the imaginary reciprocal entailment of the 'parts' of the institution and of the social imaginary significations. This is the enigmatic unity and substantive parenthood between artefacts, beliefs, political regimes, artistic works and, of course, human types belonging to the same society and the same historical period. Needless to say, any idea of a 'causal' or 'logical' explanation of this unity is meaningless.

2. On the other hand, institutions and social imaginary significations have to be *complete*. This is clearly and absolutely so in *heteronomous* societies, where *closure of meaning* prevails. The term of closure has to be taken here in its strict, mathematical sense. Mathematicians say

that an algebraic field is *closed* if the roots of any polynomial of the field are elements of the field. Likewise, in any closed society, any 'question' which can be formulated at all in the language of this society must find its answer within the magma of the social imaginary significations of the society. This entails, in particular, that questions concerning the *validity* of the social institutions and significations cannot be posed. The exclusion of such questions is ensured by the position of a *transcendent*, extra-social, source of the institutions and significations, that is, religion.

(v) Some additional comments on the term social imaginary *significations* may help to prevent misunderstandings. I have chosen the term significations because it seems to me the least inappropriate to convey what I have in mind. But it should absolutely not be taken in a 'mentalistic' sense. Social imaginary significations create a proper world for the society considered – in fact, they *are* this world; and they shape the psyche of individuals. They create thus a 'representation' of the world, including the society itself and its place in this world; but this is far from being an intellectual construct. It goes together with the creation of a *drive* for the society considered (so to speak, a global intention) and of a specific *Stimmung* or mood (so to speak, of an affect, or a cluster of affects, permeating the whole of the social life). For example, the Christian *faith* is a specific and pure historical creation entailing particular 'aims' (to be loved by God, saved, etc.) and most particular and peculiar *affects*, which would have been totally un-understandable (and nonsensical – *moria* says very rightly Saint Paul) for any classical Greek or Roman (and, for that matter, any Chinese or Japanese). And this is understandable, if one realizes that society is a being for itself.

VII

How is it possible that *we* are capable of talking in this way (correctly or not, that is another matter) about societies in general, putting ourselves, as it were, at an equal distance to all of them (be it an illusion, this is also another matter)?

Almost all societies we know have instituted themselves in and through the closure of meaning. They are heteronomous; they cannot put into question their own institution and they produce conformal and heteronomous indi viduals for whom the putting into question of the existing law is not just forbidden but mentally inconceivable and psychically unbearable. These individuals are 'conscious', but not self-reflexive subjectivities.

This state of affairs was broken for the first time in ancient Greece, and this breaking has been repeated after fifteen centuries, with much greater difficulty but also in an incomparably large scale, in Western Europe. In both cases the institutions and the ultimate beliefs of the tribe have been explicitly called into question, and, to a large extent, modified. Partially open societies have emerged, together with self-reflexive individuals. The main carriers of this new historical creation were politics as collective emancipatory movement and philosophy as self-reflecting, uninhibitedly critical thought. Thus emerged what I call the project of collective and individual autonomy.

In both cases the project has not been brought to its completion. One might say that it *could* not be brought to a completion. To this I would answer that neither this statement nor its contradiction can be 'theoretically' demonstrated or established, being understood that the project of autonomy does not aim at establishing Paradise on earth nor at bringing about the end of human history; nor does it purport to ensure universal happiness. The object of politics is not happiness, but freedom; autonomy is freedom understood not in the inherited, metaphysical sense, but as effective, humanly feasible, lucid and reflective position of the rules of individual and collective activity. This is why the social-historical struggles animated by this project have left so many important results, among which are whatever intellectual and political freedom we may be enjoying today. But the philosophically important point is that, even if it finally failed, as in Athens, or if it is in danger of waning, as in the present Western world, its effect has been the creation of a totally new, unheard of, ontological *eidos*: a type of being which, consciously and explicitly, alters the laws of its own existence as it is, however partly, materialized in a self-legislating society and in a new type of human being: the reflective and deliberating subjectivity. And this is what allows us to take some distance from our own society, to talk about society and history in general, and to accept rational criticism of what we say in this or any other respect.

NOTES

1 See my text 'Merleau-Ponty und die Last des ontologischen Erbes' in B. Waldenfels and A. Metreaux (eds), *Leibhaftige Vernunft* (München, 1986), pp. 111–143.
2 See 'La découverte de l'imagination' (1975), reprinted in *Domaines de l'homme – Les carrefours du Labyrinthe II* (Paris, Seuil, 1986), pp. 327–363.
3 On the ensemblistic-identitary logic, see chapter 4 in my *The Imaginary Institution of Society* (1975) (English edition, MIT Press and Polity Press, 1987).
4 See, e.g., Charles Taylor, *Sources of the Self* (Cambridge University Press, 1989), pp. 162ff. Richard Rorty has also, from another point of view, attacked this distinction.
5 Taylor on Descartes, op. cit., p. 162.
6 See 'The State of the Subject Today' in my *Philosophy, Politics, Autonomy* (Oxford University Press, 1991); and 'Logic, Imagination, Reflection', *American Imago* 49, 1 (Spring 1992), pp. 3–33.

7 See the texts quoted in note 6, and chapter 6 of *The Imaginary Institution of Society*, op. cit.
8 See my books quoted in notes 3 and 6 above; also see *Crossroads in the Labyrinth* (1978) (English edition, MIT Press and Harvester Press, 1985).

Chapter 8

Reason, imagination, interpretation

Johann P. Arnason

The following remarks should be read as a contribution to the – still unfinished – hermeneutical transformation of the concepts of reason and imagination. I shall tackle this theme from a particular angle, and other strategies could no doubt be justified in terms of the same ultimate purpose. But to pave the way for the present approach, I should start with a general characterization of the hermeneutical turn as such. To shift our notions of reason and imagination in this direction would be to relate them more closely to the constitution and appropriation of meaning, to patterns of world-interpretation, and to the space that is thus opened up for interpretive conflicts. More specifically, the hermeneutical transformation referred to above would entail a revision of dominant preconceptions: if we still tend to think of reason and imagination primarily as abilities or competences – reason as the ability to ground and justify, to find and give reasons, imagination as the ability to envisage and fantasize, to grasp and generate images – we may have to learn to think of them as dimensions or elements (in the sense that Bachelard, Merleau-Ponty and Castoriadis have given to the term 'element'), i.e. as aspects on components of culture, more precisely of the cultural articulation of the world. This does not mean that the question of anthropological preconditions – dispositions or potentials – cannot be posed, but it can only be formulated from within a cultural horizon, and a clearer awareness of the complexity of its presuppositions should help to avoid an oversimplifying answer.

The following argument can, roughly speaking, be divided into four steps. I will first try to show that the relationship – the parallels, contrasts and complementarities – between the concepts of reason and imagination can only be understood if we place them in a broader cultural context. More precisely: they should be seen as key aspects of the development of modern Western culture, involved in its world-constitutive as well as its self-interpretative dialectic. I shall then – secondly – suggest that the interpretive functions and contents should be more explicitly incorporated into the concepts; in other words, a culturalist reformulation of the received notions of reason and imagination would be appropriate. This in turn leads, thirdly, to a reconsideration of some major conceptual shifts that have already taken place or are in progress, i.e. the moves from reason to rationality and from the imagination to the imaginary, and their significance for the culturalist approach. Finally, I shall add a few tentative remarks on the philosophy of Maurice Merleau-Ponty as a possible starting point for further discussion.

But let us start with a preliminary question: Why should we link the concepts of reason and imagination in this way, put them on equal footing and try to specify structural or developmental parallels between them? A quick look at their careers within the philosophical tradition – and more particularly its modern phase – would seem to lead in the opposite direction: what is most striking is the asymmetry, if not incommensurability, of the two concepts. We need not agree with Habermas when he claims that reason is *the* theme of philosophical thought – explicitly in the case of modern thought, somewhat less so in earlier phases – but we must at least accept that it is one of the most prominent and permanent themes. And there is no reason to disagree with Castoriadis when he singles out the imagination as one of the most obviously and consistently marginalized philosophical themes – linked, it is true, to other similarly or even more occluded ones, such as the ontology of the social-historical. There is, then, a massive contrast between a sustained and systematic elaboration of the concept of reason, closely associated with some of the most basic and least contested presuppositions of the Western philosophical tradition, and the much more intermittent insights into the problematic of the imagination; the latter are mostly followed by retreats rather than by conceptual consolidation. The retreats are perhaps easier to understand if we add that when the imagination is allowed back in, it tends to take over and to become, if not co-extensive with consciousness, subjectivity or culture, then at least dominant within their respective realms.

The answer to this objection – and the starting point of the present line of argument – is that the philosophical asymmetry of the two concepts should not obscure the cultural complementarity of the underlying notions (or socio-cultural significations, if we follow Castoriadis). They are, to put it briefly, at the centre of the two formative currents of modern Western culture: Enlightenment and Romanticism. I am obviously using these terms in a very broad sense, i.e. one that is not limited to a particular epoch; rather, we should think of these two cultural forces as capable of mutations and metamorphoses that often overshadow the underlying continuity, and as capable of conflicting and partially converging with each other. The story of these transformations, fusions, mutual appropriations and re-polarizations has yet to be explored in detail (some very interesting points are to be found in the recent work of Charles Taylor). I cannot discuss it here; suffice it to say that the available evidence is strong enough to suggest that this cultural configuration (rather than an irresistible logic or an uncompleted project of the Enlightenment alone) should be placed at the centre of a theory of cultural modernity. And it should be noted that it is still with us – in more ways than one: much of what passes for postmodern thought is a confused and debased echo of the Romantic tradition.

If we want to claim that the idea of the imagination is as central to Romanticism as the idea of reason is to the Enlightenment, a possible misunderstanding should be avoided. This does not mean that the two currents can be defined in terms of a shared understanding or an uncontroversial model of reason or imagination, or that their modernity consists in a clean break with traditional understandings of the two notions. Rather, there is on both sides a structured field of alternative definitions and conflicting interpretations which can also involve reactivations of the traditional background. Inasmuch as reason and imagination are involved in the ongoing self-interpretation of modernity, they become sources and figures of human autonomy. But they also become battlegrounds between rival conceptions of it; and they can, especially in their more openly one-sided and vulnerable versions, become targets of traditionalist criticism. From this latter point of view the modern ideas of reason and imagination can appear as ontologically impoverished, i.e. as suffering from the loss of contact with – or insight into – a transcendent order or dimension.

If the ideas of reason and imagination – and their role in modern culture – should thus be discussed in terms of a 'structured disagreement' within each side as well as between them, it is relatively easy to measure out the common ground on the side of reason. In other words: there are some well-established conceptual distinctions that have served as starting points for the most significant controversies. There is, first and foremost, the crucial distinction between substantive and procedural reason. As the most forceful advocates of the Enlightenment, from Kant to Habermas, have insisted, a more adequate and therefore more modern understanding of reason is achieved through the shift from a substantive to a procedural conception, i.e. from an idea of reason as embodied in a world order to a project of reason as accomplished in subjective or intersubjective performance. This leaves some space for uncertainty and dissent: there is, at least, the permanent task of defending the principles of procedural reason against the temptation to return to a substantive foundation, and against the suspicion that the unity of reason is no longer safe when it has been reduced to formal rules and their contents have been left to contingency. But, more importantly, the affirmation of procedural reason is inseparable from the division between theoretical and practical reason and from the questions which this dichotomy raises: How can we define theoretical reason in terms of procedures without collapsing it into purely formal techniques? How can we conceptualize practical reason without reducing it to an application of theory? How can we resist the pull towards a fusion of theoretical and practical reason on the basis of an impoverished but also expansionist common denominator, that of calculating and instrumental reason? Finally, there is the recurrent attempt to reaffirm the unity of reason on a stronger basis without returning to traditional models of order, or at least, to move in this direction from within the problematic of procedural reason rather than by opting out of it. This variant – totalizing reason – should not be confused with the more straightforward and therefore less significant restoration of substantive reason; if the Kantian notion of judgement can be regarded as its most seminal formulation, the Hegelian system became its most ambitious and influential version, and its later manifestations can mostly be traced back to that source.

These forms or figures of reason do not, of course, exhaust its trajectory in modern thought and modern culture. I shall return to the story later, but let us first consider the question of whether a similar typology can be constructed on the side of the imagination. It can be taken for granted that this will be more difficult: it is part and parcel of the cultural distribution of meaning between the two currents that I have been talking about that one of them lends itself more easily to philosophical elaboration and conceptual determination than the other. In the case of the imagination, then, we cannot expect the same level of articulation or the same degree of consensus about it as in the case of reason. An inventory of the interpretations or models of the imagination would thus have to be constructed out of a much more fragmentary material than the typology of reason. There have, it seems, been few attempts to do something of this kind. One of the most interesting can be found in an essay by Paul Ricoeur, which I now want to discuss and use as a stepping-stone towards a somewhat different approach.[1]

Ricoeur begins by noting what he calls 'the relative eclipse of the problem of imagination in contemporary philosophy' and adds that this state of things is largely due to the complexity of the phenomenon and the failure of the philosophical tradition to bring its various aspects together, rather than constructing rival theories that emphasize one aspect at the expense of others. These theories can, according to Ricoeur, be classified in terms of two key distinctions. There is, first, the difference between the productive and the reproductive imagination. Those who take the first view are primarily concerned with fictions, i.e. images which bring to mind not absent things but non-existent things; they range from dreams to works of art. By contrast, theories of the reproductive imagination regard the image as a trace of perception and thus as 'a lesser presence', rather than a radical absence. The second conceptual distinction sounds less familiar. As Ricoeur puts it:

the distinguishing factor is whether or not the subject of imagination is capable of assuming a critical awareness of the difference between the imaginary and the real. At one end of the axis – that defined by a complete lack of critical awareness – the image is confused with the real, taken for the real. Here we see the power of lies and errors decried by Pascal; it is also *mutatis mutandis* Spinoza's imaginatio, infected with belief as long as a contrary belief has not dislodged it from its primary position. At the other end of the axis, where critical distance is fully conscious of itself, imagination serves instead as the instrument of the critique of reality. Husserlian transcendental reduction of existence is the fullest illustration of this.[2]

Ricoeur describes these two modalities of the imagination – singled out by rival theories – as fascinated consciousness and critical consciousness.

It seems to me that both distinctions call for some critical comments; let us begin with the first. The contrast between the productive and the reproductive imagination obviously refers to a polarization within modern thought; in fact, Ricoeur mentions Sartre and Hume as representative examples. This argument obscures the more radical difference between traditional and modern conceptions of the imagination. If we follow Richard Kearney's work on the changing status of the imagination in Western culture, it seems clear that despite all the massive differences between Greek and Judaic traditions, their views of the imagination and its place in the order of things are remarkably similar: it appears as fundamentally imitative but potentially deviant, and in the latter capacity it is a source of errors and dangers.[3] By contrast, modern thought can accept that the imagination is essentially and authentically creative. On this view, we might try to understand modern theories of the reproductive imagination as the result of a tension between the cultural recognition of creativity and the lack of adequate conceptual resources to translate this change into a new philosophical paradigm. The Aristotelian concept of the imagination as an echo or after-effect of perception has proved extremely resilient and capable of reasserting itself in different cultural contexts. There is, of course, as Castoriadis has shown, another side to Aristotle – on this matter as on most others – but it has been much more marginal to the philosophical tradition.[4]

We should, then, start with the contrast between the imitative and the creative imagination, and Ricoeur's distinction between the productive and the reproductive imagination seems to be more derivative: it could perhaps be taken as a brief description of the predicament of a philosophical culture that oscillates between the attempt to theorize the cultural vision of the creative imagination and the urge to retreat from its more radical implications. But there are some further controversies inherent in the notion of the creative imagination, and Ricoeur's second distinction should be set against this background. Briefly, it would seem that fascinated consciousness and critical consciousness are not as sharply opposed as he wants to suggest (it is true that he implicitly admits this when he talks about an axis rather than a stark contrast). If we follow the development of the phenomenological approach to the imagination from Husserl to Sartre, detachment and absorption – critical distance and fascinated involvement – appear as two sides of the same coin. The imaginative act that sustains a critical distance from reality is also exposed to the permanent possibility of an uncritical identification with the imaginary realm. As Sartre puts it, to create images is to put reality at a distance; but then it is also to pave the way towards the imaginary life as a form of non-being.[5] The two aspects, taken together, represent the creative imagination in a negative mode; let us call it the *detached* imagination, in the double sense of an act of detachment and the constitution of a detached region or dimension. And the opposite – i.e. positive – mode of the creative imagination has been most convincingly theorized in the work of Castoriadis: it is the *constitutive* imagination, in its capacity as the source of ontological innovation, more particularly as the core component of the social-historical world.

I have tried to reformulate Ricoeur's typology, with more explicit reference to the difference between traditional and modern perspectives, and to conflicts and tensions within the modern context. But to complete this picture, there is one more figure of the imagination that must be added to the list. The *symbolic* imagination involves the most ambitious claim to an alternative – and essentially non-conceptual, hence trans-rational – mode of knowledge; the image as symbol aims at an indirect representation of something that cannot be directly apprehended. From a broader cultural perspective, we could perhaps say that the symbolic imagination is to Romanticism what totalizing reason is to the Enlightenment; but then this analogy also serves to underline the limits to further comparison.[6]

What I have said so far is perhaps enough to indicate that parallels and affinities between reason and imagination, their forms and figures in modern culture, are worth exploring. There are other ways of pulling the two problematics together; as a digression, let me briefly sketch one of them, before I move on to the next step of the argument. There are points of contact and mutually revealing encounters between the Enlightenment and Romanticism, and they can also be regarded as bridges between the trajectories of reason and imagination in modern culture. There can be no doubt that Kant's work is a particularly significant case in point. His philosophy was, as has often been shown – for example, in a seminal essay by H.A. Korff – located on the crossroads between Enlightenment and Romanticism.[7] Not, however, in the sense of a balanced or equidistant relationship to both; rather, he arrived at the most representative formulations of the most fundamental intentions of the former, and at the same time he took a decisive part in opening up the cultural space within which the latter could develop. This double-edged character of Kant's work is, of course, closely linked to the role and status of the imagination in his philosophical project. This is a very complex topic, and I shall limit my discussion to one aspect of it: the changes that took place in Kant's conception of the imagination between the first and the second edition of the *Critique of Pure Reason* and the relevance of Kant's open questions to later theories of the imagination. It is in the first edition of the *Critique* that Kant comes closest to admitting something like a primacy of the imagination, or – in other words – looking for imaginary roots of reason. It is here that he talks about 'a synthesis of the imagination antecedently to all experience', a 'pure transcendental synthesis as conditioning the very possibility of all experience', and a little later he repeats this point in even more forceful terms: 'the necessary unity of the pure (productive) synthesis of the imagination is, prior to apperception, the ground of the possibility of all knowledge, especially of experience'.[8] In the second edition, Kant retreats from this perspective and relegates imagination to a more subaltern and intermediary role between intellect and intuition. But the retreat is accompanied by some additional insights: if the claims made about the imagination in the first version are more radical, some points included in the revised version are more specific. It is in the second edition that Kant defines the imagination as the 'ability to represent an object in intuition without it being present'[9] and he also distinguishes what he calls the 'figurative' synthesis of the imagination from its intellectual counterpart. In the present context, further details need not be discussed; I'd merely like to suggest – as an aside to my main argument – that both the radical perspective of the first edition and the more moderate approach of the second have to a very large extent determined the agenda of later theories of the imagination (it should be noted that here I am talking about specific theories, rather than figures or paradigms, as before: the figures are latent and general patterns of interpretation that can be theorized in a more or less explicit and also more or less selective way). As for responses to the subsequently revoked challenge of the first edition, Heidegger's interpretation of Kant is perhaps the most widely known.[10] In a footnote to the book, he describes his approach to the problem of the imagination in Kant as the opposite of that which prevailed in post-Kantian German idealism. He does not elaborate on the character of this contrast, but the main point is fairly obvious. Heidegger uses the half-developed Kantian notion of the imagination to radicalize the notion of human finiteness, whereas the line of thought that led through Fichte to Schelling aimed at transcending finitude. What I'd like to suggest is that similarly contrasting alternatives can be linked to the point which Kant makes in the second edition. The definition of the imagination as the ability to 'represent without presence' conceals a set of far-reaching questions, and it can be developed in very different directions. If I am not mistaken, the alternatives in this case are most clearly represented by Sartre's and Castoriadis's approaches to the imagination: on the one hand, there is the emphasis on what Sartre calls 'the essential negativity of the imaginary object' and, more fundamentally, the imagination as the key manifestation of the essential negativity of consciousness; on the other hand, the use and re-fashioning of the concept of representation to grasp the positive and positing character of the imagination as *creatio ex nihilo* (it should be added that this allows Castoriadis to take up again the questions tentatively posed in the first edition of the *Critique*). Finally, the puzzling and underdeveloped notion of the figurative synthesis could be seen as a common point of reference for two very different lines of thought: there are, on the one hand, the persistent attempts to reduce imagination to perception, and more particularly to visual perception, or at least to treat it as a derivative variant of the latter; the notion of 'figure' is collapsed into that of image, and the origins of the image are to be sought in perception. On the other hand, the very idea of a mental image has come under fire from the advocates of the 'linguistic turn', and, above and beyond that, there have been some attempts to use the linguistic turn as a starting point for a more positive re-interpretation of the imagination. The most important case in point is, I think, Paul Ricoeur's theory of the imagination. His main thesis – which he has so far illustrated mainly by detailed analyses of metaphor and narrative – is, briefly, that instead of understanding the imagination in terms of the image and the latter as 'a scene . . . played out on the stage of a mental "theatre" for the benefit of an internal "spectator"',[11] we should learn to think of it as an aspect of semantic innovation. 'Imagining', says Ricoeur, 'is first and foremost restructuring semantic fields', and in that sense he can even claim that 'we only see images in so far as we first hear them'.[12] The figurative synthesis is, in this view, a configuration of semantic contents; but it is true that what Ricoeur calls the 'quasi-sensorial aspects of images' cannot be ignored, and that the linguistic version of the productive imagination cannot simply leave the realm of perception behind.

But let me return to my main line of argument. What I have said up to now falls far short of the hermeneutical or culturalist transformation envisaged at the beginning; I have merely suggested, as a preparatory step, that we should – first – locate the modern relationship between reason and imagination within a broader context of cultural interpretation and self-interpretation, and that – second – the reference to this background makes more sense of the parallels and affinities which we can observe when we look at the changing forms and fortunes of the two ideas. Over and above this, the hermeneutical transformation would consist in incorporating the cultural context into the concepts, in moving from the observation that ideas of reason and imagination function as patterns of cultural interpretation towards the ideas of interpretive reason and interpretive imagination, and – at the same time and inseparably – towards a broader perspective which would allow us to see both of them as different but complementary, interconnected and mutually indispensable aspects of cultural interpretation – the cultural infrastructures of interpretation, as it were. As I indicated before, it seems to me that this transformation is going on in contemporary thought – certainly not uncontested, and not always easily recognizable – but it is far from complete. The following discussion will suggest some steps that seem to me to lead further in this direction.

But such steps cannot be taken in a vacuum; and the first thing to do is therefore to relate the projected transformation to the changes that have taken place and that have run their course at least far enough for a provisional evaluation. There has been a shift of interest and analytical focus from reason to rationality, and – although much less generally and less conclusively –

from imagination to the imaginary. And there is no doubt that this change is to a large extent in line with the culturalist transformation that I have been referring to. The conceptual shift is, in both cases, such that we can more easily relate the phenomena in question to a context rather than a subject, and to culture rather than consciousness. It also serves to broaden the frame of reference and the field of application. We can talk about the modern or the capitalist imaginary, the Islamic or the communist imaginary without running the risk of constructing meta-actors or macro-subjects, and we can talk about – or at least raise the question of – the rationality of traditions and world-views, the rationality of magic or the rationality of systems, without imposing a preconceived and normative identity on all those disparate horizons. But it is obviously true that the interest in rationality and the imaginary does not always take a culturalist turn; it can also be associated with the search for transcultural constants, be it on the level of a built-in telos of language or the elementary structures of the unconscious. Moreover, the traditional asymmetry between the concepts of reason and imagination seems to reassert itself in the new context: the problematic of rationality already has a relatively long history, it has been explored from various angles and it has its classics (or at least one of them), but it has also given rise to rival theories. By contrast, the thematization of the imaginary is a much more recent development within a much more restricted context, and the conceptualizing process is still in an earlier phase. We should therefore begin with rationality, and a closer look at its problems may give us some guidelines for the discussion of the imaginary.

There is no general agreement on the relationship of the contemporary concern with rationality to the traditional interest in reason. At one end of the spectrum, Jürgen Habermas seems to take for granted a basic continuity: if reason was, as he sees it, *the* theme of the philosophical tradition, the theory of rationality is – or should be – central to philosophy in its post-metaphysical phase, i.e. in its capacity as an auxiliary of and a temporary substitute for science. Rationality, then, would seem to be simply the secularized, modernized and self-reflexive version of reason; and if we use Habermas's formulation about 'the unity of reason in the plurality of its voices' for our own purposes, we might say that the concept – with its differentiations – helps to go further in recognizing plurality without losing sight of unity. At the other end of the spectrum we could probably place Niklas Luhmann; his essay on European rationality, included in this volume, contains a forceful farewell: 'Never again reason!' (Nie wieder Vernunft!) I take it that he means that a post-metaphysical theory of rationality excludes the kind of unified normative authority that was inseparably associated with the traditional idea of reason. If we try to give a more systematic account of the problem, we could begin by distinguishing three perspectives on – and, correspondingly, three possible interpretations of – the relationship between reason and rationality. They differ in emphasis and direction, but this does not mean that all versions of them are in all circumstances mutually exclusive; there is some overlap, it is difficult to strike the proper balance between them, and it is worth noting that they co-exist – not without tensions and difficulties – within the most seminal work in this area, that of Max Weber. Weber's work is to the theory of rationality what the whole epoch of German idealism – from Kant to Hegel – was to the philosophy of reason.

Let us describe the three perspectives as radicalization, fragmentation and relativization. From the first point of view – that of radicalization – the theory of rationality is seen as continuing and enhancing the trends that were already evident in the modern development of the idea of reason. Thus Weber's interest in processes of rationalization, rather than simply patterns of rationality, appears as a logical continuation of the turn from substantive to procedural reason; and the diversification of rationality, the acceptance of an open-ended plurality of models and processes, would be a new phase of the differentiation of reason that had begun in early modern thought. Thus one might see the early modern idea of theoretical reason as a special case within a broader spectrum of interpretive rationalities, some of whom were analysed by Weber; and similarly, the modern idea of practical reason could be treated as a special case within the more comprehensive category of rational conduct of life. But there would still be a link to a unifying concept of rationality. It cannot be said that Weber abandoned the search for a common denominator; but the closest he got to defining it was the claim that there are two elementary forms of rationality, the logical and the teleological – the coherent use of concepts and the consistent pursuit of goals – and that they are indissolubly linked. He does not specify what links them, but the words he uses suggest that it might be the intention to master reality – which, of course, is already a narrowing down of the concept, a lapse incompatible with Weber's uses of it elsewhere.

The second perspective – fragmentation – is the abandonment of the search for a common denominator that would counterbalance the pluralization of rationality. There are, on this view, at best affinities and family resemblances that can justify the use of the concept of rationality for comparative purposes. In terms of the Habermasian formulation I quoted before, the plurality of voices has now become a Babel, and the unity of reason is no longer audible. It can hardly be denied that Weber was, for much of the time, resigned to this perspective, but, in contrast to some later commentators, I do not think he was ever completely happy with it. At the very end, in the introduction to his collected essays on the sociology of religion, he would clearly like to argue that the Occidental complex of rationalizing processes adds up to something that has 'universal value and significance', i.e. can claim superiority on the basis of some overarching criteria, but it is equally clear that he wanted to put this assumption to the test. As we know, that project was never completed.

The third perspective – that of relativization – could perhaps be described as a more positive counterpart to the second one. If rationality is irredeemably and uncontrollably contextual, if the criteria and directions of rationalization can therefore only be defined with reference to their concrete socio-cultural backgrounds and surroundings, there is a case for linking the notions of rationality and rationalization more closely to that of culture; they would then have to do with the explication – and explicability – of cultural patterns, the clarification of their internal logic, the exploration of their built-in possibilities, the excavation of their latent presuppositions, and so on. We can speak of a relativization, in the sense of making the concept of rationality more explicitly relative to the concept of culture, but this does not mean that we must arrive at radically relativistic conclusions. Whether we slide into cultural relativism or not depends upon the underlying concept of culture, and more specifically on how it balances closure and opening in relation to other cultures and to the world that constitutes their shared horizon.

This last perspective is also present in Weber's work, perhaps most clearly in what I would regard as his most seminal text, known in English as 'Religious Rejections of the World and their Directions'.[13] It seems to me that post-Weberian discussions of rationality have remained within the framework demarcated by the three perspectives, and that the debate between them is still open.

The shift from reason to rationality thus turns out to be a very complex and controversial process. Could anything similar be said about the move from the imagination to the imaginary? As I said before, this shift is a much more recent and limited development than the one from reason to rationality. It has mainly taken place within French and francophone thought. The notion of the imaginary, as distinct from the imagination, emerges in Sartre's early work on this subject: the imaginary appears as the noematic correlate of the imagination, but its analysis serves primarily the purpose of bringing into focus the radical negativity of the imagination and therefore of consciousness as such. I do not want to discuss this conception further; I only mention it in order to contrast it with the very different and much more complex reformulation of the problem which we find in the work of Castoriadis. Here we might say that the imaginary becomes a context rather than a correlate and therefore an object of analysis in its own right and for its own sake, rather than as a detour towards a better understanding of its subjective source. To quote from the concluding section of *The Imaginary Institution of Society*:

The radical imaginary emerges as otherness and as the perpetual origination of otherness, which figures and figures itself, exists in figuring and in figuring itself, the creation of images which are what they are and as they are as figurations or presentifications of significations or meanings. The radical imaginary exists as the social-historical and as psyche/soma. As social-historical, it is an open stream of the anonymous collective; as psyche/soma, it is representative/affective/intentional flux. That which in the social-historical is positing, creating, bringing-into-being, we call social imaginary in the primary sense of the term, or instituting society.

That which in the psyche/soma is positing, creating, bringing-into-being for the psyche/soma, we call radical imagination.[14]

In a sense, we can still think of the radical imagination as the source of the imaginary, but it is a source that is always already transformed by its products, and we may, as I shall try to show, need a more radical conception of that transformation.

But let us look more closely at the shift from the imagination to the imaginary as exemplified by Castoriadis's work, and look at it, to begin with, from the point of departure, i.e. the concept of the imagination. We can read Castoriadis's work as the most important attempt so far to theorize the cultural theme of the creative imagination, a theme that has been around for some time, but not been translated into adequate concepts. The change in question should therefore, in the first instance, be regarded as the elimination of interpretive barriers, or as the destruction of basic assumptions that have blocked the understanding of the imagination; but if we follow its implications further, it can also be seen as a self-transcending of the imagination, to a point where it becomes more appropriate to talk about the imaginary.

There are three main aspects of this change. The first one we can describe, in Castoriadis's own words, as the *defunctionalization* of the imagination.[15] On the level of the psyche, this means that the activity of the imagination is not programmed by organic needs or drives; on the social level, it means that it is not confined within a system of social needs to be satisfied or social problems to be solved; in both respects, this defunctionalized imagination is the source of an open-ended diversity of meaning and divergence of orientation, in other words of the plurality of culture by which it is in turn channelled and circumscribed. The parallel with our three perspectives on rationality should be obvious: there is a recognition of cultural diversity and the different directions which it gives to the imagination, but also an attempt to retain a common denominator – the radical imagination – although every definition of it must remain problematic.

The second aspect is, I think, best described as *deconditioning*. By this term I mean that it is not just the impact of external determinants that is reduced; above and beyond this, the links to external referents are loosened. Hence the tendency of the imaginary to coalesce into a closed world of its own, exemplified on the infra-social level by the monadic tendencies of the psyche and on the social level in the closure of meaning to which – according to Castoriadis – each and every society tends, although – historically speaking – a few of them have proved capable of creating antidotes and counterweights. We should perhaps add that this point also relates to institutional complexes within societies. The parallel to be drawn here concerns the second perspective on rationality, that of fragmentation. The point at issue is the splintering of the social-historical imaginary into separate worlds, closed cultural universes.

The third aspect could be called the *destructuring* of the imagination; it concerns its internal determinations, and it is perhaps here that the shift from the imagination to the imaginary is most important. Neither the representative/affective/intentional flux of the psyche nor the open-ended and self-altering network of linguistic and cultural significations in society can be reduced to determinate structures; more precisely, we have to do here with a mode of being which resists description in the terms of traditional ontology, and for which Castoriadis suggests the concept of magma. His definition of a magma is, briefly, that it is that from which we can extract structural patterns and logical organizations, but which can never be absorbed by these structures and organizations. But I do not want to discuss the ontological question in this context. For our present purposes, the parallel with the third perspective on rationality – the one I described as relativization – is more relevant. The destructuring and destructured aspect of the imaginary is what ultimately undermines closure and makes total identity impossible, makes a culture capable of questioning itself, of confronting other cultures as well as the world in its capacity of – to quote Castoriadis – an interminable enigma and an inexhaustible source of otherness.

I have sketched some implications of Castoriadis's work on the imaginary; I should add that the third perspective seems so far overshadowed by a combination of the first and the second, and this is obviously linked to what seems to me to be an excessive reliance on psychoanalysis.

It has, I hope, become clear that there are some points of contact between the problematics of rationality and the imaginary; and that the most fundamental link between them is the relationship to – or more precisely embeddedness in – culture. The next step should therefore be to develop a frame of reference within which these connections could be made more explicit and systematic. As I suggested at the beginning, the later work of Merleau-Ponty would – especially if it is read as an incipient culturalist transformation of his paradigm of perception, and as an incomplete rediscovery of the previously neutralized or minimized problematics of reason and imagination – seem to be a particularly promising starting point for such a project. A detailed discussion is beyond the scope of this paper, but some signposts can be noted.

Merleau-Ponty's original project can be reconstructed as a combination of two perspectives that turned out to be less compatible than he had assumed. On the one hand, the primacy of perception is the starting point for a re-centring of phenomenology and a revision of basic concepts of the philosophical tradition; on the other hand, this 'rehabilitation of the sensual' (an expression used by Merleau-Ponty to describe both his own project and a tendency which he observed in the later work of Husserl) is closely linked to a conception of philosophy as 'relearning to look at the world'[16] and an understanding of subjectivity as open to the world rather than constitutive of it. It is the rediscovery of perception as an original and privileged access to the world that will – as Merleau-Ponty puts it in an early programmatic statement – enable us 'to recast certain psychological and philosophical notions currently in use'.[17] As the introduction to *Phenomenology of Perception* shows, this was meant to apply to some of the most basic philosophical concepts. In particular, rationality is to be redefined: 'To say that there exists rationality is to say that perspectives blend, perceptions confirm each other, a meaning emerges.'[18] From this point of view, it is possible to understand 'our communication with the world as a primary embodiment of rationality'.[19] There is no explicit reference to the imagination in this context, but a critical review of Sartre's first work on this subject shows that Merleau-Ponty was well aware of the implications of his own approach: a rethinking of perception would inevitably lead to a new understanding of the imagination.[20]

Merleau-Ponty's introductory remarks on rationality are preceded by some comments on the concept of civilization – it can, for our present purposes, be taken as synonymous with the concept of culture – and the new meaning that the phenomenology of perception lends to it. The main point is the interpretation of a specific civilization, as a 'certain way of patterning the world'.[21] The differences between *Phenomenology of Perception* and Merleau-Ponty's later work (especially *The Visible and the Invisible*) can be analysed from many angles, but in the present context the signs of growing tension between the culturalist perspective and the exclusive focus on perception are particularly interesting, and the most revealing statements are to be found in the 'working notes' at the end of *The Visible and the Invisible*. Merleau-Ponty's main concern is still with what he calls 'modulation of the being in the world',[22] but he has now moved beyond the framework of a phenomenology of perception. Rather than taking perception as a model of the cultural articulation of the world, the emphasis is on 'this informing of perception by culture, this descent of the invisible into the visible'.[23] To recognize the autonomy of culture – and the transcendental function of the interpenetration of nature and culture – is to accept that 'perception itself is polymorphic and that if it becomes Euclidean, this is because it allows itself to be oriented by the system'.[24] The last formulation can be read as an allusion to a rationalizing process that takes place within a cultural context.

There is no extensive discussion of rationality or the imaginary in *The Visible and the Invisible*, but some of the 'working notes' reveal a growing interest in both themes and suggest ways of linking them to an interpretation of culture that is striving – albeit not without reservations and reversals – to relativize the paradigm of perception. For Merleau-Ponty, the question of rationality is inseparable from that of language; more generally speaking, 'the problem of the relations between rationality and symbolic function is posed: the exceeding of the signified by the signifier essential to "reason".'[25] But the exceeding of the signifier is matched, on the other side, by the exceeding of the world, 'the totality which is not a synthesis', the 'whole where each "part" when one takes it for itself, suddenly opens unlimited dimensions, becomes a *total part*'.[26] It is this double surplus of meaning that is subsumed under more or less stable and comprehensive patterns; Merleau-Ponty describes them as institutions, but he also uses the Husserlian notion of *Normierung*, as well as new terms of his own: he wants to 'replace the notions of concept, idea, mind, representation with the notions of dimensions, articulation, level, hinges, pivots, configuration. . .'.[27] The main point is, for our present purposes, that these patterns can be seen as frameworks and guidelines for the plural constitution of rationality within cultural horizons, and Merleau-Ponty makes it clear that the development of scientific rationality – the activity which 'renders explicit the structures, the *pivots*, certain traits of the inner framework of the world'[28] is part of the picture. The emphasis on cultural presuppositions does not entail a radical relativism.

But the articulations and configurations in question also have an imaginary component. Although Merleau-Ponty remains convinced that the distinction between figure and ground is more fundamental than any other, he now tries to give it a broader meaning than it had in *Phenomenology of Perception*. The patterns of perception are co-determined by imagination: if the senses are, in relation to the world, 'apparatuses to form concretions of the inexhaustible, to form existent significations', their content is by the same token 'a precipitation or crystallization of the imaginary, of the existentials, of the symbolic matrices. . .'.[29] Merleau-Ponty's interest in the figurative constitution of meaning is a counterweight to his growing interest in language and prevents him from taking an unconditional linguistic turn: the ongoing appropriation of extra-linguistic significations is, as he sees it, essential to language, and it involves the imaginary as an 'element', i.e. as co-constitutive of the cultural world, rather than – as Sartre misguidedly argued – a separate region.[30]

The 'working notes' – especially the suggestions quoted above – constitute a programme that Merleau-Ponty did not live to carry out, but it would have opened up a new phase in the development of his main theme: the idea of philosophy as a rediscovery and articulation of the opening to the world that is constitutive of the human condition. This problematic has been explored by later authors (Castoriadis, Charles Taylor, Marc Richir *et al.*), but mostly in a selective way, and a return to *The Visible and the Invisible* can still help to balance their different perspectives.

NOTES

1 Paul Ricoeur, 'Imagination in Discourse and Action', originally published in Anna-Teresa (ed.), *Analecta Husserliana*, vol. VII: *The Human Being in Action* (Tymieniecka, Dordrecht, 1978), pp. 3–22; also included in this volume.
2 Ibid., p. 5.
3 Richard Kearney, *The Wake of Imagination* (London, 1988).
4 Cf. Cornelius Castoriadis, 'La découverte de l'imagination', *Domaines de l'homme* (Paris 1986), pp. 327–363.
5 Cf. Jean-Paul Sartre, *L'imaginaire – Psychologie phénoménologique de*

l'imagination (Paris, 1940); particularly the last section, 'La vie imaginaire', pp. 159–226.

6   It should be noted that I am trying to construct a typology, rather than a genealogy: the reference is to the place of the symbolic imagination within the cultural complex of Romanticism, not to its role in the transition from Enlightenment to Romanticism. The latter problematic – and the more specific questions it raises – is beyond the scope of this paper. For a forceful contemporary but traditionalist defence of the symbolic imagination, cf. Gilbert Durand, *L'imagination symbolique*, 3rd rev. edn (Paris, 1976).

7   H.A. Korff, 'Das Wesen der Romantik', *Zeitschrift für Deutschkunde* 43 (1929), pp. 545–561; reprinted in H. Prang (ed.), *Begriffsbestimmung der Romantik* (Darmstadt, 1968), pp. 195–215.

8   Immanuel Kant, *Critique of Pure Reason*, trans. Norman Kemp Smith (London, 1978), p. 133 (A101).

9   Ibid., p. 143 (A118).

10   Ricoeur, op. cit., p. 6.

11   Ibid., pp. 8, 9.

12   Cf. the introduction to Jürgen Habermas, *Theory of Communicative Action*, vol. 1 (Boston, 1984); cf. also his essay 'Die Einheit der Vernunft in der Vielfalt ihrer Stimmen', *Nachmetaphysisches Denken* (Frankfurt, 1988), pp. 153–186.

13   Max Weber, 'Religious Rejections of the World and Their Directions' in H. Gerth and C. Wright Mills (eds), *From Max Weber*, pp. 323–359.

14   Cornelius Castoriadis, *The Imaginary Institution of Society* (Cambridge, 1987), p. 369.

15   Cf. *The Imaginary Institution . . .*, chapter 6, pp. 273–339; also Castoriadis's essay 'The State of the Subject Today', *Thesis Eleven* no. 24, pp. 5–43.

16   Maurice Merleau-Ponty, *Phenomenology of Perception* (London, 1962), p. XX.

17   Maurice Merleau-Ponty, *Texts and Dialogues*, ed. Hugh J. Silverman and James Barry Jr (London, 1992), p. 75 (the text in question is a research proposal written in 1933).

18   Merleau-Ponty, *Phenomenology . . .*, p. XIX.

19   Ibid., p. XXI.

20   Merleau-Ponty, *Texts. . .*, pp. 108–114: 'On Sartre's *Imagination*' (published in 1936).

21   Merleau-Ponty, *Texts. . .*, p. XVIII

22   Maurice Merleau-Ponty, *The Visible and the Invisible* (Evanston, 1968), p. 194.

23   Ibid., p. 212.

24   Ibid., p. 212.

25   Ibid., p. 168.

26   Ibid., p. 218.

27   Ibid., p. 224.

28   Ibid., p. 226.

29   Ibid., p. 192.

30   Cf. the critique of Sartre, ibid., p. 266.

Epilogue
Sublime theories: reason and imagination in modernity

David Roberts

The present paper takes up the thematization of reason and imagination in the contributions to this volume from a specific perspective. The contemporary renewal of interest in the sublime, most notably in Lyotard, has refocused attention on Kant's theory of the sublime. The gap which the Kantian analysis of the experience of the sublime opens up not only between reason and imagination but also between reason and imagination and their other – nature, being, the world – poses the question of the limits of reason and imagination in a double form; as the theory of the sublime on the one hand and what I shall call sublime theory on the other. If Kant's *Critique of Pure Reason* finds its complement in his analytic of the sublime, contemporary theories of the sublime point in turn to the enquiries into the limits of the world constituting capacity of reason and the imagination such as we find in the writings of Luhmann and Castoriadis. I would like to suggest that the split between reason and imagination, which Markus sees as the constitutive feature of modern culture, also raises the question of the underlying split between mind and being which defines modernity for good and evil as an inescapable process of self-creation. At the heart of the quarrel between reason and imagination is the project of a self-creating modernity.

Let me recall, with the aid of Robert Legros,[1] what is at stake in this modern quarrel – modern in that both Enlightenment and Romanticism mark the break with the closure of the pre-modern world, the end of what Niklas Luhmann calls the continuum of rationality but which may also be understood as the continuum of nature. This break called forth the opposed responses of Enlightenment and Romanticism. If man can no longer be defined by reference either to the model of ideal nature or to the sensibilities of immediate nature, then the humanity of man becomes the question of the nature of his socialization, or as Legros calls it, his naturalization. For the Enlightenment, naturalization signified alienation or dehumanization, since man becomes human and regains his birthright of freedom only by breaking out of enclosure in any particular society or tradition. Man is the maker of his own humanity and the supreme norm is individual autonomy, whose preservation demands the eternal vigilance of reason, which must scrutinize all 'natural' conventions and replace them by self-critical norms. Essential humanity thereby emancipates itself from all particularism to emerge as the project of universal autonomy, made possible by man's right to think and judge for himself. The humanization, i.e. the denaturalization of man, is the task of reason.

What by contrast is the task of imagination? It is to undo the Enlightenment's radicalization of the dualism of Western thought which has reached its apogee in the metaphysics of a self-constituting subjectivity. Romanticism in this sense defines itself in terms of its critique of the Enlightenment, indeed it already articulates the dialectic of Enlightenment formulated by Horkheimer and Adorno, whose concept of mimesis is a muted natural-theological echo of the romantic imagination. The modernity of Romanticism lies for Legros in its definition of man's humanity. If man is nothing by nature then he is indeed nothing outside of a particular human culture. If alienation is given not by the acceptance of naturalization but by its rejection, then the central paradox of Romanticism resides in the attempt to think the universal and the particular together. Tradition, in the widest sense of embeddedness in history, nature, culture and society, is the second nature of our naturalization, which is primary in relation to human nature. The epitome of this second nature, which is both transcendent and immanent, is natural language. Man accedes to his universal humanity through learning his own particular mother tongue, entering thereby into the world of (a particular) culture with its already given matrix of meanings, what Legros calls in phenomenological terms the *mise en forme et en sens du monde*. This entry is to be conceived as *incarnation* as opposed to the radical *abstraction* from the given, inherent in the idea of the transparent subject of will and consciousness of the Enlightenment (but which, as Rousseau's *Confessions* already shows, always escapes itself).

From this opposition of radical abstraction (individualization) and historical incarnation (particularization) flows the romantic critique of a modernity which seeks to ground itself in the conception of man as subject. On the one hand, the failure to recognize that man is the product of history leads to the revolutionary and terroristic illusion that we can extract ourselves from history and reconstruct society as a political experiment. On the other, the subject's separation from nature – the illusion that the subject can define himself as external observer of the world, outside of the context of human experience – makes nature the object of scientific experiment and reduces the sensible to objective matter, devoid of meaning. Or rather, meaning results from an abstraction, since if man is subject and centre, the meaning of the world is defined only in relation to men's ends. This reduction of meaning to a function of interest goes together with the interest in function which progressively transforms reason into rationality and its modes of rationalization. Moreover, we may note that the combination of abstraction and interest consigns all particular concrete interests to the realm of the ideological. Rationalism's division of the world into the rational and the irrational is accompanied by the shadow of ideological suspicion, the ever-present reminder of the danger of the (paranoic) closure of reason.

For the Romantics the very project of autonomy with its radicalization of dualism signals the closure which separates man from nature and history. They oppose to autonomy an imaginative openness which draws its strength from the acknowledgement that nature and history transcend the subject. If individualization brings with it an emphasis on the primacy of cognition and the will, particularization makes sensibility the essential faculty of man, that is, sensibility to the historically given, infused by the spirit of tradition. This spiritual sensibility comprehends our relation to nature and to history as incarnation; the sensible and the intelligible, the visible and the invisible are one (Novalis). Sensibility is thus related to the imagination as sensation is to reason. Nature speaks to us not by means of external impressions (sensations) but through the inner impressions (images) of the imagination. Creation is to be understood not as the giving of form to natural material but as the giving of expression to spiritualized nature. The image expresses the 'mystery of incarnation' (Legros, 115); its organ is the imagination, traversed by the creative power of the unconscious (Schelling), its medium is the genius, medium precisely because his creativity transcends autonomous subjectivity. The genius is defined not so much by autonomy as by originality, in the original meaning of the word. He is the voice of nature who gives, in Kant's famous formulation, the rules to art. And this means that originality no less than the autonomy of reason signals the break with the 'natural' order of the imitation of nature, even if the intention is contrary to that of the autonomous subject. That is to say, the work of art is conceived not as the object of the subject but as a presence which opens onto the infinite. Just as religion is characterized by Schleiermacher as the intuition of the infinite in the finite, so for Schelling the romantic work of art undertakes the 'imagining' (Einbildung) which joins the finite to the infinite.

In this sense Romantic religion, philosophy of nature and art may be thought of as sublime theories. The very stress on the primacy of the creative imagination is both the acknowledgement of and the protest against the Enlightenment's disenchantment of the world. The sublime is born from the concealment of God. As Marcel Gauchet puts it: when the gods withdraw from the world, then the world itself starts to appear as other, to reveal an imaginary depth which becomes meaningful in itself. The imaginary apprehension of the real, no longer channelled, coded and contained by a religious comprehension of the order of things, is now released in its own right to explore the mysteries of the sensible world, and to find expression in the aesthetic experience of otherness. Modern art is the continuation of the sacred by other means. But if the sacred – or the sublime – is predicated on the paradox of the presence of absence,[2] Romanticism's legacy – its conception of art as the representation of the unrepresentable, as the expression of the invisible at the heart of the visible (Legros, 114) – points in opposite directions. The mystery of incarnation returns on the one hand in Merleau-Ponty's flesh of the world, the chiasm of being and consciousness realized in the co-constitution of the image which is both seen and sees itself and whose privileged medium is the painter's eye. On the other hand, the presentation of the unpresentable defines for Lyotard the impossible and inescapable dynamic of modern art, which is modern insofar as it is romantic. When Lyotard speaks of the withdrawal of the real in the modern world, which calls forth the abstractions of the avant garde, he echoes, even if he does not share their nostalgia, the laments of Romanticism. At the heart of the modern is the irruption of the sublime, the unbridgeable chasm between our capacity to imagine and our capacity to think the world. The crucial figure here is Kant, since his analysis of the sublime opens up the radical incommensurability of idea and image.

Kant's analysis of the sublime, which foregrounds the whole problematic of the relation of reason and imagination, places him at the turning point between the Enlightenment and Romanticism. For Markus he is both the summation and the deconstruction of the Enlightenment concept of culture, which subjected the received understanding of culture as the 'symbolic dimension' of social behaviour to an ever more radical critique, which delegitimated the normative claims of tradition and replaced the principle of imitation with that of rational innovation. The idea of perfectibility appealed to the creativity of time in the progressive realization of the genuine, freely-posited nature of man, embodied in the objectivations of high culture, characterized by Kant in terms of the division of labour between the sciences and the arts, the understanding and the imagination. This construction of the dichotomous unity of culture, in which aesthetic experience is called upon to mediate between pure and practical reason, is self-negating: 'The premises of the Weberian conclusion concerning the irreconcilable conflict between the great cultural value spheres were already, even if unintentionally, laid down by Kant'. Moreover, the very process of the transformation of reason into partial, competing rationalities is complemented by the inability of practical reason (unlike science or art) to institutionalize itself as a direct cultural power in place of positive religion. The aesthetic sentiment of the (moral) sublime can fill the gap only negatively by foregrounding the chasm between the imagination and reason's idea of totality. Kant's construction and deconstruction of the Enlightenment concept of culture is encapsulated as it were in his analysis of the sublime.

Arnason's hermeneutic reading of reason and imagination in modernity assumes Markus's two concepts of culture – the anthropological and the high cultural – but not in order to stress their incompatibility, but rather the primacy of the symbolic order, the *mise en forme et en sens du monde*, in relation to high culture. Reason and imagination thereby appear not only as the two formative currents central to the self-interpretation of cultural modernity, but also as the schemata of world-constitution, the cultural infrastructures of interpretation, which both underpin and call into question the dichotomies of high culture and at least indicate the possibility of a more deeply configured *rapprochement*. It is against this culturalist perspective that Arnason traces the trajectories of reason and imagination since Kant, i.e. the fragmentation of substantive reason into separate and competing paradigms of reason and then into contextual spheres of rationality and the equally important but as yet barely thematized transformation of the imagination into the imaginary. It is clear that Arnason's culturalist reformulation of the imagination has strong connections with the tradition of Romanticism even if they are not spelled out. Kant's construction and deconstruction of high culture stands at the crossroads of these trajectories. If Weber remains the key figure for the typology and problematic of rationality, then not least because he ratifies in a double sense the cultural implications of the post-Kantian differentiation of reason: the very process by which rationality destroys the symbolic unity of culture reveals at the same time the embeddedness of its autonomous logics in occluded imaginary significations.

Weber's sociology of culture thus opens up, on the one hand, to Castoriadis's theory of the creative imagination which seeks to redress the inadequacies of Kant's treatment of the imagination. On the other hand, Weber's pluralization of rationality points the way to the debates of the 1980s on modernism and postmodernism, which, if we follow Lyotard's influential presentation, replay Kant's construction and deconstruction of the unity of culture, exemplified by the hiatus which separates the aesthetic experience of the beautiful and the sublime. Habermas's project of Enlightenment appeals once more to aesthetic experience 'to bridge the gap between cognitive, ethical, and political discourses, thus opening the way to a unity of experience', which will overcome the splintering of culture.[3] The aesthetic experience of beauty – the harmony, the agreement of reason and imagination – serves as the model for a unity of experience in the life-world, which will counterbalance and reconnect the separated discourses (language games) of modernity. In Lyotard's terms, Habermas represents a resolutely anti-sublime position. For Habermas the mimetic powers of the imagination are integral to an expanded concept of communicative reason and their task is profane not sublime illumination.

Lyotard's version of aesthetic education by contrast is predicated not on the beautiful harmony of the faculties but on the negativity of the experience of the sublime. 'If it is true that modernity takes place in the withdrawal of the real and according to the sublime relation between the presentable and the conceivable, it is possible, within this relation, to distinguish two modes . . .'[4], which he terms the modern and the postmodern, to be understood as the construction and deconstruction respectively of the grand narratives of modernity. The modern sublime expresses the nostalgia for presence, the postmodern (the other face of the modern) has abandoned this nostalgia to engage in the sublime game of searching for 'new presentations, not in order to enjoy them but in order to impart a stronger sense of the unpresentable'. In this permanent process of invention (*creatio ex nihilo* also in the secondary sense of coming after Nietzschean nihilism) we recognize Lyotard's postmodern version of the genius, who works without rules 'in order to formulate the rules of *what will have been done*'. The rules come after the work, the work comes after nihilism: the work is the event that something happens and, as such, it is the manifestation of the sublime. What aesthetic experience offers for Lyotard is the presence of absence: the knowledge that there is no 'reconciliation between language games (which, under the name of faculties, Kant knew to be separated by a chasm)'[5], and the injunction to wage war on the terror of totalizing reason.

Lyotard's affirmative postmodern version of the sublime, which has broken with the modern nostalgia of presence, may be related to the resurgence of apocalyptic thinking as we approach the millennium. As Martin Jay observes in his paper on the contemporary apocalyptic imagination, in the cultural ruminations of such figures as Jean Baudrillard, Jacques Derrida and Jean-François Lyotard, explicit evocations of apocalyptic imagery and ideas can also be found. These are often linked, and not for the first time, with an aesthetics of the sublime. What distinguishes the postmodern from the modern imaginary, however, is the suspension of the end, the end which never comes but which is nevertheless the 'Figure Foreclosed' (Lyotard) of modernity. Jay argues that the source of the permanently deferred longing for the end, the permanently suspended desire for the other, is the inability to mourn. That which is lost – the origin, the mother, mother nature – is transformed into the eschatological expectation which has already anticipated the end. Origin and goal coalesce in the Saturnine melancholy of postmodernity – Saturn's golden age has turned into the revolution which devoured its children. *Posthistoire* mourns not only the death of God, history and man but also the end of the future.

This closure of *posthistoire* suggests a conclusion of a kind, that of the historical trajectory of the sublime which traces the parabola of modernity's sublime expectations of self-transcendence and their exhaustion. If the postmodern reflection on our (unsurpassable) modernity is to mean something more than post-history, presided over by Benjamin's Angel rather than Hegel's Owl of Minerva, it must go beyond the 'Figure Foreclosed' of the dialectic of Enlightenment and the dialectic of Romanticism, fused and frozen in perpetuity. And this going beyond, I would like to suggest, takes us back to Kant and from the theory of the sublime to sublime theory. Castoriadis's reconceptualization of the imagination and Luhmann's reconstruction of reason, in rethinking Kant's legacy, engage with the crucial question of presentation. My point of entry is Jean-Luc Nancy's analysis of the imagination in Kant.

The schematism of the understanding, which rests on the power of imagination *a priori*, is a hidden art in the depths of the human soul. The imagination is the faculty of presentation which seeks a form which accords with its own free play. Aesthetic judgement is thus the reflexion or self-presentation of the faculty of presentation: aesthetic judgement schematizes the imagination's operation of schematization without concepts, i.e. the unity of presentation given by the schema presents itself to itself as unity. It is accordingly the model for the agreement of the faculties. The hidden art of the soul, which comes to self-presentation in the experience of beauty, is, Nancy argues, the art of reason. In other words: reason uses the synthesizing art of the imagination – the prefiguration of the unity of the manifold under a principle or law – for its own self-production and presentation. Beauty and truth are one. That is to say, beauty finds its completion in philosophy.[6] This beautiful aesthetic of reason, however, does not take into account the sublime, which undoes the free pleasurable feeling of the affinity between the presentable and the conceivable, occasioned by form. The sublime unfolds the contradiction as it were of a presentation without presentation – it thus poses the problem of (re)presentation as such.[7] In the sublime the limited and the unlimited, the formed and the unformed, what Nancy calls the inner and the outer border of presentation, oscillate in infinite play. This can be conceived as the very ground and operation of presentation:

> As ground: 'Unity comes from its limit – let us say from its internal border; but *that* there is unity, absolutely, or again that this trace makes a *whole*, this arises ... from the external border, from the limitless dissolution (*enlèvement*) of the limit.'[8]

> As operation: 'Presentation "itself" is the instantaneous division of the limit, by the limit, between figure and limitation, the one against the other, the one on the other, the one to the other, formed and separated by the same movement, by the same incision, by the same oscillation (*battement*).'[9]

This sublime oscillation at the limit is the very chasm/chiasm of presentation 'itself'. The chasm opens onto the abyss, the chaos from and against which all figures take shape, from which the forms of the imagination arise. Castoriadis's theory of the creative imagination is not a theory of the sublime but a sublime theory of the mysterious interplay of *natura naturans* and *natura naturata*, of the instituting and the instituted. And if we turn from ground to figure then the *chasm* mutates into the *chiasm* of instantaneous division, graspable only as the divided unity of the two sides of the figured, forever joined and severed by the same incision, the drawing of the limit, of the distinction which separates figure and ground. And it is this *operation* of distinction – 'the instantaneous division of the limit' – which is the key to Luhmann's theory of rationality, which is also a sublime theory of what we might call the mystery of distinction.

In approaching Castoriadis and Luhmann through the Kantian theory of the sublime I am suggesting that their theoretical projects can be regarded as

...me theories. By this I mean a self-limiting theory which is aware that it cannot encompass and exhaust the transcendence of the world and knows the limits of conceptualization and systematization. With Castoriadis, the inexhaustibility of the magma and our necessarily fragmentary knowledge of the social-historical indicates the limits of explanation. With Luhmann, the decentring of reason and its differentiation into system rationalities makes the world as such inaccessible, that is accessible only within the closure, the limits of each system. This is not of course to deny the very different focus of their work. Indeed they may be considered the most prominent contemporary representatives of the transformation of imagination into the imaginary and of reason into rationality, identified by Arnason as major conceptual shifts within modern culture.

Although Castoriadis scarcely acknowledges the Romantics' thematization of the creative imagination, his concept of the social-historical clearly stands in the tradition of the Romantic understanding of the humanization of man as neither the accomplishment of nature nor of self-sufficient reason. If the Enlightenment project of human autonomy is the goal of man's humanization, it is such precisely as a self-projected goal which cannot be deduced from the inherent intelligibility and rationality of the human world.[10] The humanization of man is the product of socialization, the entry through language into a given cultural world of what Castoriadis calls social imaginary significations. The social-historical in each of its multiple historical realizations is the institution of this imaginary as a world of meaning which is not reducible to rationality. The instituted social imaginary entails the transcendence of language, culture and tradition in relation to the socialized individual.

As incarnated meaning, the mode of being of the social-historical is the radical imaginary in its interplay and tension of instituting and instituted significations. Each society is thus to be thought of as the institution which arises as form from the magma of imaginary significations, the ground of the social-historical. Each institution is thus a creation *ex nihilo*, a self-creation of humanity, whose amazing variety and diversity of incarnated meanings cannot be subsumed under the teleology of the world spirit or reason. However, the very irreducible multiplicity of the social-historical with its incommensurable gamut of values, which opens onto the Weberian perspective of the warring gods, confronts us with the question of values and this choice is in a certain sense necessary, since the very possibility of reflective choice – the questioning of the institution – already supposes the autonomy of reflexion.[11] Autonomy transforms the humanization of man (the truth of Romanticism) into the praxis of the self-institution and self-governance of the collective of autonomous human subjects (the idea of Enlightenment). Autonomy *qua* value/goal marks the break with the closure of man's humanization, it represents a new stage in the ontology of the social-historical which corresponds to Gauchet's distinction between heteronomy – the definition of the social-historical in terms of the transcendent other – and autonomy, whose transcendent other consists of the open horizons of the future.

It is thus necessary to divide the levels/regions of living being posited by Castoriadis into the given – living being, psyche, social individual and society – and the possible – the autonomous human subject and society.[12] This division allows us to distinguish between the self-finality, inherent in the ontogeny of living being from the simple cell to the institution of society, and autonomy as project and value, while at the same time insisting on the central role which the imagination plays in the discontinuous leaps of creation, which is creation *ex* but not *cum nihilo* in that it is dependent upon but not determined by the preceding level. The imagination is always creative but from the perspective of autonomy its creativity remains within the closure of self-finality.

This functional or operational closure is that of the autopoiesis of living being, i.e. the closure whereby the self (the for-itself) of living being creates a world of its own with a highly selective openness to the environment. This creation is the work of imagination, whose 'hidden art' (Kant) is to transmute external shocks – the Kantian X – into images. X 'becomes something only by *being formed* (in-formed) by the for-itself that forms it: the cell, immune system, dog, human being, etc., in question'[13]. This transmutation of the X into a presentation – which is precisely *not* representation – expresses the cognitive function of the imagination which combines sensorial image and logical relation (organization).

> The living being therefore possesses an 'elementary' imagination which contains an 'elementary' logic. By means of the imagination and this logic, it creates, each time, its world. And the property characteristic of this world is that it exists, each time, in closure. Nothing can enter it – save to destroy it – except in accordance with the laws and forms of the 'subjective' structure, of the in-itself in each case, in order to be transformed in accordance with these forms and these laws.[14]

The functional closure of the originary imagination is broken by the co-emergence of the human psyche and the social-historical, which transforms the autopoiesis of living being into the world of human self-creation. Between autopoiesis and institution, nature and culture lies a new creation *ex nihilo*, made possible by the defunctionalization of the psyche in relation to its biological substratum (the breakdown of instinctual regulation), given by the replacement of organ pleasure by representational pleasure. To this autonomization of the imagination corresponds (in a circular relation of cause and effect) language's power of substitution, which makes it *the* model as it were of the work of sublimation, without which society would not be possible. Castoriadis's distinction between the human psyche and the social individual is the basis of his two forms of imagination – the radical imagination of the singular psyche and the social instituting imaginary of the anonymous collectivity. The spontaneous flow of representations (within the monadic closure of the psyche) constitutes the magmatic reservoir from which imaginary significations are collectively generated. Society and history are thus a process of permanent creation given by the permanent tension between the instituting and the instituted. The crucial dimension in this process lies in the imagination's radical capacity not only to present to itself objects in their absence (Kant), but to posit imaginary objects. This imaginative power is for Castoriadis the absolute condition of autonomous reflexion, which replaces the self-reference intrinsic to self-finality by self-reflexion, the capacity to posit the self as object of interrogation. We may thus conceive of reason as the creation of the radical imagination.

Although Castoriadis's synthesis of Romanticism and Enlightenment is clearly modern – his ontogeny of living being and of the social-historical incorporates basic elements of contemporary theories of the self-organization of matter and the autopoiesis of life – his theory of the creative imagination also stands in the tradition of *natura naturans* going back to Greek philosophy. There are thus for example close affinities to Paracelsus's concept of the imagination.[15] *Creatio ex nihilo* is the privilege of God, to it corresponds, however, the ceaseless creativity of the vital forces of nature and its equivalent in man, the ceaseless productivity of the imagination. Just as God created the world by imagining it, so the imagination in man is the creative force *par excellence*, which mediates between thought and being, the invisible and the visible: the image is embodied desire, will, thought. Since man is made both in the image of God and of nature, the magic power of the imagination rests on the correspondence between the microcosm and the macrocosm. What separates Castoriadis from this tradition of theological metaphysics and philosophy of nature, with its assumption of a continuum between thought and being, is on the one hand the Kantian X, the abyss between *natura naturans* and *natura naturata* from which his theory of the imagination as *creatio ex nihilo* arises, and on the other hand the gulf beween nature and culture or the social-historical.

Just as the Kantian X leads to Castoriadis's reconceptualization of the imagination, so we can observe its comparable role in Luhmann's reconceptualization of European reason. The thing-in-itself represents the inescapable conclusion of the dissolution of the rationality continuum of European thought since the Greeks. The Cartesian dualism of thought and extension sundered the continuum which united observer and world in the assumption of the convergence of thought and being, action and nature. The one world splits into the dual ontologies of subject and object. It led to the elevation of man to the subject of the world at the same time as this emancipated rationality splits apart into the partial rationalities of differentiated functional systems. Kant's Enlightenment concept of the unity of culture stands in the historical context of the emergence of the functional differentiation of modernity which has deconstructed his and all subsequent attempts to think this unity. The typologies of rationality (Weber, Habermas) are all that remain of the wreck of reason. One is tempted to call Luhmann's deconstruction of European rationality 'shipwreck with observers' (Blumenberg) – a not inappropriate (sublime) metaphor for his own theory. Nevertheless, Luhmann's emphatically anti-Hegelian version of the 'rationality of the real' proposes the (real-descriptive) convergence of thought and social being, logic and history in his social systems theory.

The convergence, which Luhmann proposes, however, is one which unfolds the paradox, which remained latent within the unity of the old European rationality continuum, emerged into the open with the dualism of subject and object, and yet remains occluded as long as the blind spot of rationality – the observer – remains unobserved. What is this paradox? It is quite simply this: the unity of the world disappears with the observer. Or to point the paradox even more sharply: observation makes both the world and the observer invisible. Observation is the operation of drawing a distinction. It tells us that in the beginning was difference – the difference which we have to think not only logically but also historically, since difference is the condition of differentiation, i.e. of the evolutionary construction of complexity. The Hegelian odyssey of the world spirit from undivided unity to the final differentiated totality of complete self-comprehension, which reveals the identity of logic and history, returns with Luhmann as the paradox of George Spencer Brown's calculus of form, which begins and ends with distinctions, taking us in the process from uncomprehended to comprehended difference, from the invisible to the visible observer, from the latent to the manifest re-entry of the form in the form. The re-entry of form constitutes, for Luhmann, the key to the problem of European rationality. It transfers our attention from what is distinguished to how it is distinguished and by whom. Who divides the world into thought and being? The answer of course is thought. All distinctions involve the re-entry of the distinction in the distinction. Thus the distinction between thought and being, drawn by thought, means that thought is defined by the difference thought/being – or what amounts to the same thing, being is only available to thought as the thought of being. The (invisible) re-entry of the distinction in the distinction is the corollary of the (invisible) break in symmetry between the two sides of the distinction, the break which becomes visible with the dissolution of the rationality continuum into the duality of subject and object, whose problematic can only be *fully* comprehended and deconstructed, Luhmann argues, when this asymmetrical duality is grasped as the unity of the two sides of distinction. Grasping the unity of the distinction cannot undo the break in symmetry between observer and observed but it does allow us to observe that the unity of the distinction is invisible to the observer (the observer is the distinction) and is accessible only to a second observer. What is needed is a new logic based on the observation of observation, i.e. second-order cybernetics which observes the use of distinctions by observing systems.

In observing systems, logic and evolution, theory and history converge. The starting point of social systems theory is the unity of the distinction systems/environment; 'Thus it does not describe certain objects, called systems, but orients its observation of the world to a certain (and no other) distinction – that between system and environment.' The theory – itself an observing system in an environment – can then observe the re-entry of the distinction in the distinction: systems observe by means of the distinction between system and environment, self- and external reference. This re-entry of the form in the form, which effects the break in symmetry is, as we have noted, the condition of evolution. It describes the real-logical condition of the ontogeny of living being from the minimum of selfhood of the single cell to the level of the autonomous reflexion of the social-historical. Castoriadis's theory of the imagination and Luhmann's theory of rationality are both theories of autopoiesis. System and environment are equally given, all systems exist in an environment but the environment is accessible only within the system. All 'information' is the product of the observing system and is information for the system, i.e. the system excludes itself *operatively* from the environment (its operative or functional closure) and includes itself (participates) through *observation*, based on the distinction between self- and external reference. The rationality, which from the standpoint of the observer reflects the unity of the difference between system and environment, is identified (from the inside as it were) as the world-creating capacity of the imagination. To Luhmann's second-order rationality corresponds Castoriadis's self-questioning reflexion. Second-order observation confines itself, however, to the rationality of the instituted: it is the operational modus of functional systems (science, market economy, politics, law, art, etc.). They are the executors of the rationality of modern society. By contrast, reflexion for Castoriadis is integral to the project of autonomy, which opposes to the rationality of the real the instituting power of the imaginary.

Nevertheless, for all the distance between functional rationality and creative imagination, the logical symmetry break of re-entry and the evolutionary leap of *creatio ex nihilo* depart from the same autopoietic premiss: the world of living social being, the world of visible objects and of invisible meanings, is not representation but presentation (whether we call it construction or creation). The world as such, the substratum of all environments, the medium of all forms, is forever inaccessibly other – abyss, ground, magma for Castoriadis, the world divided by distinction for Luhmann, the distinction which is the mark of the paradox of form which re-enters (and creates) all forms of the world. The paradox of form lies in the (forever present/absent) unity of distinction, in which we recognize at the heart of Luhmann's imaginative appropriation of Spencer Brown's calculus of form the chasm/chiasm of the theory of the sublime. It accords art a privileged place in his theory, since art becomes *the* form of the reflexion of form. If the reflexion of form is the meta-theory of systems theory, then Luhmann's construal of modern art as world art[16] reveals his theory of form as an analytic of the sublime. Conversely Castoriadis's concept of political autonomy could be thought of as a generalization of artistic creativity in conjunction with a permanent self-interrogating praxis which sets its own limits.

The reflexion of form, for Luhmann, presupposes the undivided identity of Form and World. The World divided by a distinction gives the two sides of Form. On the one side are all the forms of the world, on the other side is the 'other' of rationality, the 'unmarked state' – God, world, chance, chaos, the unlimited.[17] Reason cannot cancel the division (never again reason!), rationality cannot bridge the gap once the illusion of reference has been replaced by the self-referential distinction between self- and external reference. This distinction is *the* form of rationality, constituted by the re-entry of the form in the form and the corresponding recession of second- and third-order observation. As Luhmann puts it: re-entry symbolizes the paradox of the world (the difference World/world). Or alternatively: the paradox of form, which necessarily excludes the other side (the difference Form/form), is the paradox of 'the representation of the world in the mode of unobservability' – or, to recall Lyotard's formula for the sublime, 'the presentation of the unpresentable'.

Luhmann suggests that the freedom of imagination fills the space opened up by the self-limitation of rationality, the space once filled by religion. The privileged form of the freedom of the imagination is art. It would be wrong, however, to think of art simply as the other of rationality. On the contrary, as Nancy demonstrates, the 'hidden art' of the imagination, which presents itself to itself in aesthetic judgement (and here we must remember that the artist works through self-observation, that the work is the aesthetic judgement in *statu nascendi*), is the art of reason's self-presentation. Let us say rather that modern art, which works in the mode of the sublime, constitutes in its freedom the imaginary form of rationality, by presenting the imaginary space of the reflexion of form. The task of modern art, *qua* presentation of presentation, is to probe to the limit and make visible the hidden paradoxes of form. But equally, of course, *qua* presentation of the faculty of presentation, art manifests the imagination's hidden power of *creatio ex nihilo*. Luhmann and Castoriadis depart from autopoiesis and meet at the limit of presentation 'itself' – the 'instantaneous division of the limit' (Nancy) between the formed and the unformed, the observable and the unobservable, the instituted and the instituting.

This 'instantaneous division of the limit' points to both sides of divided form (the imaginary space of art). The paradox of form activates what Castoriadis refers to as the two paradoxes of ensidic logic: self-reference and infinity. Self-reference tells us that the imaginary is accessible only within the forms of rationality. The reflexion of this closure is the re-entry of form within the form, which aesthetic theory has thematized since Fichte and Friedrich Schlegel as romantic irony. Infinity tells us that sublime art undertakes the impossible attempt to present the unity of the two sides of form, the sublime oscillation of the limited and the unlimited. The corollary of closure is openness. For both Castoriadis and Luhmann what Lyotard calls the withdrawal of reality in modernity opens the horizon of possible worlds, whether we call it the freedom of creation or of contingency.

And here we might conclude. The thematization of the world-creating powers of rationality and of the imaginary in Luhmann and Castoriadis draws the consequences of Kant's first Copernican revolution, which based reason and imagination in the subject. For Kant, however, the first revolution implied a second: the assumption of the working out of nature's purpose in history, developed in his late writings on politics, society and history. Such a teleology – the application of the practical, i.e. moral principles of possible experience to the question of man's self-realization and self-determination – serves to uphold the prospect of a convergence of the two realms of the sensible and the supersensible, of history and philosophy, of nature and freedom. Nature's purpose, however, is none other than man's capability of realizing his full potential through the exercise of his freedom of will and of his reason. The normative idea of history is rooted in an anthropology which is both pragmatic and practical. Rundell can thus suggest at the end of his closely argued examination of the *Critique of Pure Reason* and the *Critique of Judgement* that we need to look beyond the transcendental conditions of knowledge and the regulative principle of teleology to the hidden anthropological contextualization of reason and the imagination in Kant's *Critiques*. This perspective is further developed in the work of Agnes Heller. Heller appeals to the transcendent moral gesture which existentially centres life. In so doing Heller challenges Habermas's tripartite division of reason as a reductive reading of Kant.

As with Weber, Habermas's division of reason decentres ethics. It is one sphere of decentred modern culture. Habermas follows Kant in making communicative action a procedural rationality, in which the forms of agreement about knowledge and norms precede and produce their content, just as for instance the categorical imperative constitutes its maxims. But to read Kant thus is to level the absolute difference between knowledge and ethics. Knowledge indeed becomes decentred in Kant but not morality. In moral action the individual is related practically not theoretically to transcendence (freedom). Moral action can of course become the subject-matter of moral discourse but practical reason cannot be reduced to theoretical reason, that is, to a sphere of decentred knowledge. The source of morals is prior to discourse. This means that the transcendent character of morality cannot appear in questions such as: 'Why is it good to be good?' Such questions belong to the discourse of morals and do not cross the threshold between knowledge and action. Rather the question we should ask is: 'What should I do?' This transcendent question cannot be rationalized; on the contrary, in Heller's words, it grants rationality. The centre, the freedom of the moral will, is the transcendent condition of moral action, since moral action – 'What should I do?' – already presumes the resolve to act morally, to take responsibility. There is no escape from this circularity, which Heller insists has always been the case. As moderns, however, we need to be aware of the transcendent character of our initial moral gesture since it defines the universal value of freedom as the centre of our decentred world.

NOTES

1 Robert Legros, *L'idée d'humanité. Introduction à la phénomenologie* (Paris, Grasset, 1990). In the following I summarize salient features of Legros's comparison of the Enlightenment and Romanticism.
2 Marcel Gauchet, *Le désenchantement du monde. Une histoire politique de la religion* (Paris, Gallimard, 1985), p. 297.
3 Jean-François Lyotard, *The Postmodern Condition: A Report on Knowledge* (Manchester, Manchester University Press, 1984), p. 72.
4 Ibid., p. 79.
5 Ibid., p. 81.
6 Jean-Luc Nancy, 'L'offrande sublime', *Poesie*, vol. 30 (1986), pp. 81–83
7 Ibid., pp. 87–88
8 Ibid., p. 89
9 Ibid., p. 92
10 Cf. Cornelius Castoriadis, 'Individual, Society, Rationality, History', *Thesis Eleven* 25 (1990), pp. 59–90.
11 Cf. Castoriadis, Ibid., pp. 84ff.
12 Castoriadis, 'The State of the Subject Today', *Thesis Eleven* 24 (1989), pp. 10–12.
13 Ibid., p. 13.
14 Castoriadis, 'Logic, Imagination, Reflection', unpublished ms.
15 Here I follow Alexandre Koyré's exposition in *Mystiques spirituels, alchemistes du XVIe siècle allemand* (Paris, Gallimard, 1971), pp. 75–131.
16 Niklas Luhmann, 'Weltkunst' in Luhmann, Frederik Bunsen and Dirk Baecker, *Unbeobachtbare Welt. Über Kunst und Architektur* (Bielefeld, Verlag Cordula Haux, 1990), pp. 7–45.
17 See David Roberts, 'The Paradox of Form: Literature and Self-Reference', *Poetics* 21 (1992), pp. 75–91 and Dirk Baecker, 'Die Kunst der Unterscheidungen' in Ars Electronica (ed.), *Im Netz der Systeme* (Berlin, Merve Verlag, 1990), pp. 7–39.

Name index

Subject index

building control